KATE

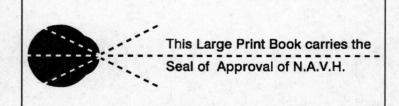

This Large Print Book carries the
Seal of Approval of N.A.V.H.

KATE

THE FUTURE QUEEN

KATIE NICHOLL

THORNDIKE PRESS

A part of Gale, Cengage Learning

GALE
CENGAGE Learning®

Detroit • New York • San Francisco • New Haven, Conn • Waterville, Maine • London

GALE
CENGAGE Learning®

LIBRARY OF CONGRESS CATALOGING-IN-PUBLICATION DATA

Nicholl, Katie.
    Kate : the future queen / by Katie Nicholl. — Large print edition.
       pages cm. — (Thorndike Press large print biography)
    Originally published : New York, NY : Weinstein Books, 2013.
    Includes bibliographical references.
    ISBN-13: 978-1-4104-6429-3 (hardcover)
    ISBN-10: 1-4104-6429-6 (hardcover)
    1. Catherine, Duchess of Cambridge, 1982– 2. Princesses—Great Britain—
Biography. 3. William, Prince, Duke of Cambridge, 1982– —Relations with
women. I. Title.
DA591.A45W55713 2013
941.085092—dc23
    [B]   2013036726

Published in 2013 by arrangement with Weinstein Books, a member of
Perseus Books Group, LLC

FOR MATILDA ROSE,
the most important chapter of my life,

AND CHRIS,
for always loving and believing in me

CONTENTS

PREFACE

When Catherine Elizabeth Middleton married Prince William, the future King of the United Kingdom, a new chapter of royal history was written. Kate, as she is best known, was the first "commoner" to marry into the royal family since the seventeenth century. Since her arrival, she has revitalized the British monarchy, whose members in turn have enjoyed a resurgence of popularity they feared might never occur following the death of Diana, the Princess of Wales, in 1997.

Now we have Kate. On July 22, 2013, at 4:24 P.M., she delivered a son, Prince George Alexander Louis of Cambridge, an heir and future King. She has, both metaphorically and literally, breathed new life into the British monarchy, producing the first Prince of Cambridge for over a century, and securing the lineage of the House of Windsor. Great Britain now has three generations of heirs awaiting the throne for the first time since Queen Victoria's reign, 150 years ago.

Royal constitution dictates that King Charles and possibly Queen Camilla will reign before King William V and Queen Catherine, but it is most likely that it will be Kate and William who will continue to drive and revitalize the monarchy over the coming years.

While Diana reignited the royal family, she also rocked the royal institution to its core. Kate, however, has taken to her role seamlessly, embracing the royal rule book. She is adored by the Queen and has won the admiration of the rest of the family. Now the world will wait to see how she and William raise their firstborn. Those close to the couple believe it will be with a hands-on approach, with as little stuffiness as possible. Although this child will always be His Royal Highness, destined to rule and be raised in palaces, Kate, along with her close-knit loving family, will enrich this future monarch's life considerably.

For the very first time, the direct heir to the throne has middle- and working-class blood coursing through his veins. With his mother's ancestry rooted in the mines of Durham and the textile mills of Leeds, this is a prince descended from coal miners as well as kings and queens. Kate is a middle-class girl, one of the people. She is truly a "people's princess." Certainly, since her and William's fairy-tale romance and now the birth of their first baby, Kate has enchanted her future subjects. She is that iconic British girl from the Home Counties who got her prince and is now the mother of the future King.

This is the story of a young woman who now calls Kensington Palace home and is reshaping the future of the world's most famous royal family. This is the story of *Kate: The Future Queen.*

CHAPTER 1
ONCE UPON A TIME

As she listened to the silence across the white snow-carpeted fields outside her window, Carole Middleton began to feel uneasy. On the radio, the Met Office was issuing a severe weather warning, and she knew that one more heavy snowfall would mean that her village would be cut off. Inside, the log fire offered warmth and some comfort, but Carole, who had been in the first stages of labor since the early hours, decided she had waited long enough to make the call.

Her husband, Michael, a flight dispatcher with British Airways, was working shifts at the airport, a forty-minute drive away, and had asked Carole to call him as soon as the contractions started. Not knowing how they would feel and aware that first babies can take their time to arrive, Carole had held off speaking to him until she was sure that the pains were not false alarms. She had

13

called the local GP, who put her mind at rest by reassuring her that he would send an air ambulance if Michael wasn't back in time to drive her to the labor ward. Carole wasn't quite sure if he was joking.

Carole's friend and neighbor, a woman who was known to everyone in the village as George Brown, who was also due to give birth that same week, remembered the morning well, "It was a bitterly cold winter, there was lots of snow and we were both worried we would not make it to the Royal Berkshire Hospital because the snow was so heavy. Carole was really very concerned, but the doctor said he would get a helicopter to land in the field if need be."

In the event, Carole and Michael did get through the snow and to the hospital in time, and their baby, Catherine Elizabeth Middleton — known today as Kate — was born on January 9, 1982. The birth went smoothly; Carole delivered her firstborn naturally, recovered well, and was home within several days, with her precious newborn daughter.

"I saw Carole a week later," recalled Mrs. Brown. "She had had an easy and natural birth, which didn't surprise me. Carole was fit and competent from the word go. She seemed to take to motherhood amazingly well, and when I went round to see her, she was happily breastfeeding and seemed to know exactly what she was doing. Catherine was a lovely little baby, cherubic and chubby cheeked and so good. I remember she didn't cry much at all. I think that was probably because Carole was so relaxed."

She had always wanted to be a mother and shortly after she found out she was pregnant, Carole, a flight attendant for British Airways, decided to leave her job. Although she loved her career, she knew that globetrotting, working shifts, and spending days and nights abroad were not conducive to raising a family. So it was with some sadness that she gave up work, as she had dreamed of being a flight attendant since she was a schoolgirl. A university education had not been an option for her because there was simply not enough money, and no one in her family had ever gone on to further their education. After leaving school at sixteen and working for a while in the clothing store C & A, Carole enrolled in a training program with British Airways. It was 1974 and air travel was still a novelty — the majority of the British public had never even been on a plane — and being a flight attendant was seen as prestigious and glamorous. Working for a high-profile airline such as British Airways was a feather in Carole's cap. Slim and pretty, she cut an elegant figure in her tailored blue jacket and skirt, red cravat, and smart pillbox hat, a uniform that she wore with great pride.

Carole was excited about the prospect of jetting around the world. Coming as she did from a modest background, family holidays were always spent in Britain on the south coast or walking in the countryside, and so the prospect of a job flying to exotic corners of the globe was wonderfully tantalizing. Her younger brother, Gary Goldsmith, recalled how she would practice flight announcements to perfect her technique. "I remember her training," he told the *Mail on Sunday.* "She used to practice doing her announcements on a tape recorder, much to my amusement."

When Carole qualified, her parents, Ron and Dorothy Goldsmith, were "over the moon," according to Gary. At school she had worked hard to pass her exams and now she was truly making something of her life. According to Jean Harrison, Dorothy's cousin, "When Carole became an air hostess, Ron and Dorothy were thrilled. It was a big job. I worked for British Airways at the same time Carole was there, but I was on the computer side. It was a big, exciting business to work for and a very respectable role."

The only daughter of Ron Goldsmith, a painter and decorator from Southall, and Dorothy Harrison, a shopkeeper from Hetton-le-Hole, a Durham coal-mining town, Carole came from humble roots. She had her parents to thank for the fact that she was given a decent education and a loving family home. Their upbringing had not been nearly as comfortable as hers.

Dorothy — Kate's maternal grandmother — was born into abject poverty. She was the daughter of Thomas Harrison and Elizabeth Temple. Thomas grew up in northeast England, close to the historic town of Durham, where his father and several generations before him had been coal miners. One of six siblings, Thomas was just fourteen years old when his father, John Harrison, was killed during World War I, a few weeks before armistice. The loss of her husband and the brutality of coal mining impelled Thomas's mother, Jane, to try to carve out a different path for her son, and she apprenticed him to her carpenter father, determined that at least one of her children would learn a trade.

It turned out that she was tremendously forward thinking, for during the Depression of the late 1920s, as the demand for coal decreased, the industrial areas of the northeast were badly hit and mining no longer offered the job security it had for so many previous generations in Thomas's family. Fortunately, there was a construction boom after the war, and tradesmen were in great demand. Thomas was therefore able to put his carpentry skills to use and spent the interwar years working in different parts of the northeast. It was while living in Easington Lane, a village near his mother, that he met Elizabeth Temple, the daughter of a farmworker. She already had a daughter, Ruth — scandalously born out of wedlock — a sweet child who Thomas took to at once.

Kate's great-grandparents, Thomas and Elizabeth, married in 1934 and moved back to his home village of Hetton-le-Hole. A year later Elizabeth gave birth to her second daughter, Dorothy, and life passed by uneventfully until the outbreak of World War II, when Thomas was called up to fight. Unlike his father, Thomas survived the war, and on his return, fearing that there wouldn't be enough work in the north of the country, he moved his family down to Southall on the outskirts of London, where he hoped to find enough employment to support his family.

Life postwar was tougher than Thomas had ever experienced. He found it hard to make ends meet and was forced to live in a dilapidated house in Bankside at the edge of the Grand Union Canal. Elizabeth contributed as much as she could, raising chickens and growing vegetables on a small farm nearby, but Ruth and Dorothy often had to go without. Despite their poverty, the two parents worked extremely hard, and Dorothy came to admire them and appreciate the values they instilled in her. As she grew into adolescence, she turned out to be a feisty girl with a steely determination to achieve. She dressed well and went out to earn money as soon as she was able, finding work as a sales assistant in local shops. It was while working in a branch of Dorothy Perkins that the teenage Dorothy met a young man named Ronald Goldsmith at the wedding of a mutual friend and fell head over heels in love.

Jean Harrison recalled, "Dorothy had met Ron when she was just sixteen. She used me as an excuse to go to a dance so that she could meet him again and they started courting. Ron was a very nice and easygoing person. He would always say hello and stop for a chat whenever I saw him."

At the time, Ronald Goldsmith — Kate's maternal grandfather — was working for his brother-in-law's haulage company, though his real love lay on the more creative side, in painting, baking, and making things. Ron was a kind, gentle man, liked by all who knew him, and, much like Dorothy, he had come up the hard way. His father, Stephen Charles — known as Charlie — worked as a construction laborer and, later, in a factory. Although he had managed to survive World War I, he died in 1938 of acute bronchitis at only fifty-three, leaving Ron's mother, Edith, with their six children. Fortunately, by this time four of the children were of working age, but Ron and his sister Joyce were still youngsters and needed a roof over their heads. Edith was penniless, so when Charlie died she had no choice but to move to a condemned apartment on Dudley Street, Southall. She took a job working on the production line in the local Tickler factory, which manufactured jams and jellies, but the wages never lifted her above the poverty line. Her older children helped look after Ron and Joyce, but even so, life was relentlessly harsh and food had to be stretched and shared in order to feed the ever-expanding family of brothers and sisters-in-law. When the going got really tough, the ever-resourceful, razor-sharp Edith resorted to pawning various items in order to raise money to feed her younger children. Ron was very close to his mother, and the whole family stayed within a few streets of each other throughout World War II, which was a great support through the hard times.

At seventeen, just after the war had ended, Ron got his call-up for national service and was sent to Aqaba in Jordan, where he worked as a baker, a skill that stayed with him for life. He returned a year later and went to work for his brother-in-law's haulage company. After a few years spent courting Dorothy, he proposed, and they were married on August 8, 1953, at the Holy Trinity Church in Southall. The wedding of Kate's grandparents was traditional and simple. The bride wore an Elizabethan-style lace gown with a taffeta underskirt and an embroidered veil pinned to her hair with orange blossoms. According to Jean Harrison, who attended the ceremony, "They were married when Dorothy was eighteen. She was very young, but she knew Ron was the man she wanted and that was that. The wedding was lovely and they held the reception at the Hambrough Tavern, which was the pub at the top of the road."

To begin with, the couple moved into Edith's tiny apartment on Dudley Road, a stone's throw from the busy Uxbridge Road, but it wasn't long before Dorothy — or "Lady Dorothy" as Edith and her family referred to her — called on her quiet ambition and moved them out to a nearby council house.

Over the next few years, with a lot of careful saving and some help from Ron's extended family, Dorothy and Ron were able to afford a deposit on a house of their own and moved to a small house on Arlington Road, to the north of Southall. By this time, they were proud parents of a daughter, Carole, and while Ron worked hard — taking evening classes to hone his skills — Dorothy took part-time jobs that she could work around motherhood. "We used to go and see Ron and Dorothy a lot when Carole was a baby," recalled Jean Harrison. "Dorothy was a very good mother, and very proud of her baby. She stopped working when Carole was born, but she went back to work once she could. She got a job at a jeweler on Hounslow High Street. I lived nearby, so I would often pop in to see her. She didn't work full time, but she wanted to get back to work. Money was sparse in the early years and she and Ron weren't well off. Dorothy liked nice things, she always did as a little girl."

Dorothy spent hours walking Carole around in a Silver Cross baby carriage — the same upscale brand used by the royal family — which she and Ron had been saving for ever since she got pregnant. It took some years before another baby graced the prized carriage, for it was not until eleven years later that Dorothy and Ron were blessed with another child. They had been trying for a baby for some time and were overjoyed when Gary arrived. "There was a big age difference between Carole and Gary," said Jean Harrison. "It's quite possible Dorothy miscarried, but things like that weren't talked about in those days. Ron and Dorothy were very old-fashioned people." With their family now complete, the Goldsmiths were happily married and earning decent money, and they invested everything in their children.

By the late 1960s, Ron and Dorothy had saved enough money to move to a larger house on Kingsbridge Road in Norwood Green — a newly built semidetached house with three bedrooms. At this point Ron decided to leave the haulage firm and set up as a builder. He had always loved working with his hands and he was talented, having once made a violin for Dorothy from scratch. Dorothy supported his career change; she believed he had the vision and ability to make a success of going it alone.

It was a vision that his children had also inherited. Carole was a hard worker, and like both of her parents, she was determined to do well in life. It was at British Airways that she met Michael Middleton, a handsome flight dispatcher who had one of the best paid and most important management jobs at the airport — the same rank as captain, though confined to the ground. At Heathrow, Michael was responsible for coordinating British Airways arrivals and departures, managing flight schedules, and occasionally handling passenger- and cargo-related matters. In his navy uniform and red cap, the well-spoken and always immaculately turned out Michael was considered quite a catch among the coterie of air hostesses. But it was Carole who caught his eye. Eventually he plucked up the courage to ask her on a date, and within a matter of months, they were in a serious relationship. Carole, who had never had a long-term boyfriend before, found Michael charming, thoughtful, and fun. Jean Harrison recalled that it was love at first sight, just as it had been for Ron and Dorothy: "Perhaps it is something in the Harrison bloodline. Dorothy's mother, Elizabeth, who we called Auntie Lily, had a long marriage and lots of children, Dorothy fell in love and married her sweetheart, and so did Carole."

Carole's job often took her overseas, so in order to make the most of the time she was in the country, she and Michael decided to move in together. They rented an apartment in Slough, a sprawling industrial town twenty-two miles from Central London and conveniently close to Heathrow Airport. They lived there quite happily for several years, and before long they were engaged to be married. "I remember Carole coming in and showing off her ring," recalled one of her oldest friends, Martin Fiddler, who runs the Bladebone Butchery in the village of Chapel Row in Berkshire. "Carole, like many of the airport industry, was living nearby and my wife, Sue, and I got to know her well as she often dropped in. She was always smiling and happy and there was just something lovely and fresh about her; she used to leave a scent of perfume in the shop. She was always chatty, bubbly, and lots of fun. She was delighted to be engaged, and I remember one day she brought Mike in and introduced him. She was a stunning lady and they were a great couple, a really good mixture."

Michael and Carole were married the following year on June 21, 1980, at the Parish Chapel of St. James the Less in the village of Dorney in Buckinghamshire — two years to the day before Prince William was born. Ron and Dorothy contributed to the wedding, but the amount they gave was a fraction of the total cost, because the Middletons were in a different league. Kate's father, Michael, was comfortably middle class and well off, having had a very different start in life than his bride. His family had the security that money can afford, and like his father and his grandfather, he was fortunate enough to have gone to a private school, receiving a good education and the attendant privileges of boarding school.

Michael also had all the benefits of being part of a close family — Peter, his father, and Anthony, his uncle, had married twin sisters and had four children each — and the eight cousins lived on neighboring streets in the well-to-do Roundhay district in Leeds, where they grew up together. Michael was proud of his father, an airline pilot and flying instructor, and was deeply appreciative of his mother, Valerie, who had spent part of her childhood in Marseilles and had stayed at home to bring up her four sons.

Michael's forebears were wealthy; his mother's father, Frederick Glassborow, worked in a bank, and his paternal grandparents, Olive Lupton and Noel Middleton, were the descendants of two of the most prosperous families in Leeds. Noel — Kate's great-grandfather — came from a line of famous and successful Leeds solicitors and received an inheritance following the death of his father, John Middleton, that was worth the equivalent of close to $4 million. Noel's wife, Olive Lupton — Kate's great-grandmother — descended from a long line of wealthy Yorkshire wool merchants, and her lineage was equally impressive. An Edwardian society beauty, she had a number of illustrious family members through marriage, including the children's writers Arthur Ransome and Beatrix Potter, and she could trace her lineage way back to Sir Thomas Fairfax, an attendant at the Tudor Court and a Parliamentarian general in the English Civil War. It is through Sir Thomas Fairfax that the Middleton family can, in fact, trace their lineage to royalty.

Olive's grandfather, Frank Lupton, a forward-thinking man, had expanded the family cloth business by buying an old mill and a finishing plant, thereby enabling his clothing merchants to own all parts of the production process. Philanthropic by nature, he gave back some of his wealth by helping to clear the slums of Leeds; his contribution was recognized by the town council, which named two streets after him. Frank was able to send his sons to public school, and as a result of his fine education, Olive's father, Francis, attended Cambridge University. Tragically, all three of Olive's brothers were killed in World War I, decimating her family, but it was of some relief that her mother had not lived to know of their senseless deaths. Olive and her sister inherited the family wealth on the death of their father and became enormously wealthy, with a personal fortune that amounted to the equivalent of nearly $15 million today. The trust fund Francis established was set up to ensure the stability of his descendants, and the trustees were instructed to pay the beneficiaries and fund the education of their children. When Olive died, she left behind an estate worth the equivalent of $13 million, to be divided among her four children. That meant Michael's father was a very wealthy man indeed.

According to members of the Harrison family, Dorothy was delighted that Carole had not only fallen in love but was marrying into money. On her wedding day, Carole had arrived at the church with her father in a horse-drawn carriage. She had four bridesmaids and wore a beautiful white gown, and she had asked her brother, Gary, who was fifteen at the time, to be an usher.

Unlike Ron and Dorothy's wedding reception at the local pub in 1953, Carole and Michael celebrated their wedding day in June 1980 in considerably more style with a sit-down luncheon at the exclusive Dorney Court, a Grade 1–listed Tudor manor house near Windsor in Berkshire. Unlike the Hambrough Tavern, which was on a busy main road, Dorney Court was set in the middle of the countryside with beautiful views of the surrounding fields and the River Thames. It was quite a step up from Southall. Guests were asked to wear dresses and lounge suits, and at the champagne reception, canapés were served from silver platters. Carole's brother, Gary, recalled, "It was a real departure for our family, and everything my mother could have wished for. It was natural, informal, and classy, but it wasn't pretentious or ostentatious." The party continued after the reception at Michael's brother Simon's house for homemade chili, drinks, and dancing. Michael's family was close and welcoming — that was one of the things that had immediately drawn Carole to him.

Both Michael and Carole wanted a family of their own, and at twenty-five, Carole felt ready. Shortly before their wedding, they had begun house hunting in the nearby Royal County of Berkshire. Carole loved its picturesque villages — among them Bradfield, a sleepy rural hamlet surrounded by beautiful English countryside and offering a charming central green where there was an annual summer fete and, above all, a friendly community.

According to their friend Dudley Singleton, a real estate agent who has known the couple for more than thirty years, they immediately fell in love with West View, a pretty redbrick semidetached cottage on Cock Lane, a winding country way just a short distance from the village. The house had four bedrooms, a pretty country kitchen with an Aga range, and a sitting room and dining room, each with working fireplaces. It was exactly what they were looking for, and they were delighted when their offer was accepted, according to Mr. Singleton: "They moved to West View to start a family, and Bradfield is a pretty desirable spot to live. Theirs was a modest country cottage and they did some nice things to it. It was a very comfortable home with plenty of character. Carole made it very pretty. She has a lot of style and arranges things very nicely. It was intrinsically pretty, with lovely sash windows and open log fires in the two reception rooms. When they moved in, they didn't have oodles of money, but Carole made it look great. She has a great eye for color and fabrics. She was always a very stylish woman and very traditional."

In the spring of 1981, Carole found out she was pregnant. The baby, due in early January, was to be Ron and Dorothy's first grandchild, and they were, as were Michael's parents, ecstatic. As her pregnancy progressed smoothly, the Middletons enjoyed the summer, joining with the rest of the country in celebrating the marriage of the Prince of Wales and the shy and enchanting Lady Diana Spencer. Carole, who came from a family of "complete royalists," according to her brother, and Michael were among the 750 million people worldwide who watched the wedding on their televisions. Diana, in her beautiful bridal gown with its twenty-five-foot-long train, was the epitome of a fairy-tale princess, and the wedding of the future King of England at St. Paul's Cathedral in Central London was a cause for celebration.

Now that she was expecting a baby, Carole decided it was the right time to leave British Airways. By a stroke of luck, the company was axing jobs at the time and she was offered a $7,000 redundancy package, enough money to put toward her planned loft conversion and kitchen expansion. George Brown remembered that the original kitchen was small, and Carole, who was an accomplished cook and an enthusiastic baker, was grateful for the extra space once the work was done. "Carole made the house a home. She had given up working as an air hostess, but Mike was still working at the airport and I remember by then he had had enough, he didn't like it much."

With a baby on the way, a mortgage to pay off, and only one salary, Michael took his position as the only breadwinner very seriously. Although he came from a wealthy family, the major part of his inheritance was tied up in the family trust fund, which was intended for their future children's education. As soon as Kate was born, they were determined to provide their daughter with the best of everything. They purchased a brand-new Silver Cross baby carriage, just as Carole's mother had years before, and in the spring they started to plan a christening. There were two churches in the village, but both Carole and Michael preferred the more traditional St. Andrew's Church of England in the old part of Bradfield, which overlooked the River Pang. Kate was christened on June 20, 1982, and Carole and Michael proudly posed for pictures outside the church in the summer sunshine, holding Kate, who was dressed in a full-length traditional christening gown. Although they weren't regular churchgoers, it was important to the Middletons that their daughter be baptized, and after the ceremony they hosted a party at West View. They had become friendly with their next-door neighbors David and Kirsty Phillpot. Mrs. Phillpot was the church treasurer and helped them organize the service. "The christening was a big occasion," recalled George Brown. "Carole did all the catering herself, from the sandwiches to the cakes, which she baked, and I remember she had lots of chilled champagne. All the grandparents were there, and it was a very happy occasion." The following day, June 21, Prince William was born, and thousands of people gathered outside Buckingham Palace to wait for the announcement to be displayed at the wrought-iron gates.

Within a year of Kate's birth, Carole was

pregnant again, and on September 6, 1983, Philippa Charlotte Middleton was born at the same hospital as her older sister. The following March, "Pippa," as she was known to the family, was also baptized at the local parish church. With a baby and a toddler to look after, Carole's hands were full. She filled her days taking Kate (who was known as Catherine until her university days) to play sessions at St. Peter's Church Hall in the village while Pippa slept in the same Silver Cross carriage that Kate had used when she was a baby. Carole loved village life, and in her jeans and Wellingtons she fitted right in. She baked cakes for the village summer fete, got involved with the Christmas Nativity plays, and helped out with refreshments at the mother and toddler groups she attended with her daughters. It was completely different from her old life jet-setting around the world, but she loved motherhood and the relaxed pace of village life.

It was, therefore, with a degree of trepidation that in May 1984, four months after Kate's second birthday, the family packed up their belongings to leave for Jordan in the Middle East. Michael had been offered a transfer of two and one-half years to the capital, Amman. The salary was good, and although packing up their home would be an upheaval, the prospect of living somewhere else for a while appealed to both Michael and Carole, who both loved visiting new places. With Kate nearing nursery-school age, Carole and Michael had already started thinking about her education. Bradfield, the Church of England primary school that was next door to their home, seemed the obvious choice, but having spoken to some of the local mothers, Carole had heard excellent things about St. Andrew's Pre-Prep in the nearby village of Pangbourne. It was a fee-paying nursery school with an outstanding prep school attached, and although money was tight for the couple, they knew they had Michael's trust fund to go toward their children's education. Before they left for Jordan, they met with the headmaster, Robert Acheson, so that they could reserve a place for Kate. "I first met them in 1983 before they went abroad," he recalled. "They had inquired about the school and I sent a prospectus out. They explained they were going away but wanted a place for when they returned. They wanted coeducational from the start. They are a lovely family — very solid, and Carole and Michael were the sort of parents we wanted at the school; they were very supportive and trusted us to get on with the job."

Life in Amman could not have been more different from Bradfield. The densely populated city, which is situated over seven hills, is one of the largest in the world. It was an exciting and exotic destination with a long summer season, hot but dry, and the additional attraction of plenty of places to visit, including ancient ruins and the Red Sea. Michael had flown out ahead of Carole and the girls to find a house to rent, and within a few weeks he put a deposit down on a villa in the upscale neighborhood of Um Uthaina in the western part of the city. Compared to their attractive redbrick semi, the two-story building was nothing grand, but there was an excellent nursery school nearby.

The property, fully furnished and air-conditioned, came with a small garden with a swing where Kate and Pippa could play. The neighbors, Intissar and Nicola Nijmeh, remembered the Middleton family as friendly and kind. "They were good people," said Mr. Nijmeh. "I remember once when we were traveling to London and Michael saw us at the airport. He upgraded our tickets to first class."

Michael was based at the airport and was in charge of four airplanes, a TriStar and three Boeing 757s, which flew direct from London to Amman four times a week. Hanna Hashweh, a sales agent for General British Airways who worked alongside Michael in Amman, said that he was popular and quickly earned the respect of his team. "I remember him well. He was distinguished and a man of integrity, and he stood out from all the other managers. He had a sharp personality. Michael used to deal with passengers, and as part of our business we dealt with each other on a daily basis. As a director he was flexible, and the employees liked him."

Because the inbound flights arrived overnight, Michael worked nights. While he caught up on his sleep during the daytime, Carole and the girls would meet some of their new friends and go out for walks in the surrounding countryside. As soon as they had moved in, they bought a patio furniture set with a sun umbrella and an inflatable paddling pool for the small garden. Carole loved to sunbathe and read while the girls had their afternoon naps, and when the afternoon had cooled off, they often enjoyed tea outside together. The weekends were family time. Eager to explore and get to know the country, they visited the tourist attractions, including Petra and

Jerash, to see the famous Roman ruins.

A sociable couple, Michael and Carole wanted to make new friends and decided to join the British Club in the nearby Abdoun neighborhood, where they met fellow expats and other employees at British Airways. An avid sportsman, Michael loved to keep fit and often played tennis. They had soon created a circle of friends, and because they enjoyed entertaining, they hosted regular garden and dinner parties at their home. Carole was known to cook splendid three-course meals, and sometimes there would be up to thirty friends gathered in their dining room. Kate, who was about to turn three, was allowed to stay up until dinner was served, a treat she always enjoyed. Mr. Hashweh was often invited: "They frequently threw dinner parties and invited me and my wife and our employees. We would be around seventeen couples and the food was homemade. Kate was little and she was like a butterfly. We used to see her at dinner parties. She accepted people and she was sociable."

By her third birthday, Kate was enrolled in Assahera, a local nursery school just a short walk from their home and run by a local teacher, Sahera al-Nabulsi. It was brand new, built only two years before, and

was the most expensive nursery for three-
to five-year-olds in the district. Carole
dropped Kate off in the mornings, and Michael would often collect her in the company car in the afternoon. "Her father used
to pick her up in his work uniform, and the
kids used to get excited and run to see him,"
said Mrs. al-Nabulsi.

Kate had a multicultural start to her
preschool life. There were children from all
over the world, and though some of her new
friends were British, she also mixed with
Japanese, Indonesian, and American children and was taught by British and Jordanian teachers in Arabic and English. The
children learned Arabic and listened to pas-
sages from the Koran. "The morning routine included having all the children sitting
in a circle where they would all sing 'Incy
Wincy Spider' both in English and Arabic,"
said Mrs. al-Nabulsi. "We would also read
one short verse from the Koran to improve
their Arabic and tell stories about the
Prophet's companions, like Omar bin Khat-
tab. The idea was to reinforce concepts such
as respect and love. The teachers used to
ask in Arabic, 'who is wearing red today?' so
that children then would recognize the colors."

Each morning at 9:30 A.M., Kate and her

friends would have a traditional Jordanian breakfast of hummus, cheese, and *labneh,* a condensed yogurt similar to spreadable cheese, which was accompanied by olive oil and thyme and served on a fish-shaped plastic plate. "We taught them table manners," said Mrs. al-Nabulsi. "Each of them would take a sandwich and then pass the plate to the other. They also had a snack of apples, carrot sticks, and green peppers as well as crackers, salty sticks, and biscuits, known as Mary Biscuits."

With an emphasis on play, the children were encouraged to use the designated sandbox and areas set aside for painting, and to Kate's delight there was a costume wardrobe. By the time she was four, she had already developed a feel for the stage and enjoyed the plays the nursery staged each term. Kate loved to dress up and took part in a fashion show in which the children dressed in different Arabic costumes that represented the Middle Eastern countries. There was a playhouse with small wooden toy beds, and according to Mrs. al-Nabulsi, another of Kate's favorite games was to pretend to have tea parties. She also loved to paint, and twice a month the nursery arranged visits to the local bird zoo and to the nearby markets, where the children held onto a beaded rope and walked in a line so they didn't get lost. At Christmas, the children were encouraged to dress up and act out scenes from the Nativity, and Mrs. al-Nabulsi dressed as Santa Claus. They also learned about Ramadan and other significant observations in the Islamic calendar.

Living in a different country and becoming part of the local community, getting to know a different way of life, the two and one-half years in Jordan were some of the happiest years of Michael and Carole's lives, but in the summer of 1986, Michael's transfer came to an end. And so, the adventure over, Carole, Michael, Kate, and Pippa returned home.

Chapter 2
Moving Up in the World

Moving back to Bradfield after living in Amman was something of a culture shock for the Middletons. Britain was not in great shape. Prime Minister Margaret Thatcher was running the Conservative Party with an iron fist, having secured a major political victory over Arthur Scargill and his National Union of Mineworkers. While the Middletons had been overseas, the miners' strike had changed not only the political panorama of the country but the physical landscape of the north of England, Wales, and Scotland, all of which suffered terrible social and economic depression when twenty mines closed within a year and took 20,000 jobs with them. These closures had a dramatic impact on working-class Britain, and the Middletons were returning in a time of tumult and despair, especially in the north of England where Carole's great-grandfather, John Harrison, had once made a living working the very mines that were being shut down.

However, at the same time, trouble was also brewing in the already volatile Middle East, in Lebanon. Across the border from Amman, the British TV journalist John McCarthy had been kidnapped in Beirut by Islamic Jihad terrorists that April, so coming home was, in the end, something of a relief for Carole and Michael. Shortly after they got back, Carole was delighted to discover she was pregnant again. With two little girls already, both she and Michael were hoping their third child would be a boy to complete their family.

Kate, who was by now four years and eight months old, had grown into a delightful little girl. She was tall for her age, with curly hair, bleached blonde from her years in the sun. Ever since they had left Jordan, she had counted down the number of sleeps until her first day at school.

The Middletons were fortunate enough to be able to draw on the trust fund that had been set up solely for the education of the family's ongoing generations. Like his father and grandfather, Michael had gotten his high school education at the fee-paying Clifton College, in Bristol, and had thrived there both academically and on the sports field. Carole's schooling had been less privileged. Her parents had not been able to afford to send her to an affluent school. Instead, she attended the local public school, Featherstone High School. Former head teacher Alfred Borg remembered her as "quite bright, but [she] did not stand out academically. That said, she was very well-behaved and beautifully mannered." Although the school was not able to offer the same facilities as Clifton, the young and popular Carole was an avid musician and played cornet with the school brass band, making friendships that would last to this day. Later, her parents managed to scrape together enough money to send Carole on a school trip to Austria with the rest of the band.

Although the Middleton inheritance spanned generations, there was still money left in the pot for Michael and Carole's children's education, and they both recognized that a good education provided the building blocks for success in later life. St. Andrew's Prep filled the bill. It was small, with just three hundred pupils, and had a Christian foundation and ethos. Perhaps more important to the Middletons, it was also a "feeder" school for some of the best independent schools in the country. According to the headmaster, Dr. Acheson, Kate threw herself into daily activities as soon as she arrived. The school's motto, "Altiora Petimus" (We Seek Higher Things), encouraged an emphasis on pastoral care, playing, and making friends. The children enjoyed trips to local farms, going on nature trails, and looking after the school's guinea pigs, Pip and Squeak, nicknames that were then given to Kate, who was known as Squeak, and to Pippa, known as Pip when she later joined the school. Kate loved to climb the trees on the grounds, and her sports instructor, Denise Allford, remembered her "tearing around the place. She was a one-hundred-m.p.h. girl." On sports day, when the children were allowed to wear fancy dress as a special treat, Kate showed off the speed and agility that would years later see her win medals and cups. "Catherine joined us in Reception when she was four. The philosophy at the school was the same throughout: if children aren't happy they won't learn and they won't grow into rounded adults. We treated them as individuals from the start and encouraged them to develop their skills. Catherine was a delight to teach right from the start," said Dr. Acheson. "As a four-year-old she did as she was told and worked hard. I think a lot of that was down to the parents. They worked jolly hard when they got back from Amman. I get a bit fed up when people describe Carole as pushy — she wasn't. Like all good parents she wanted the best for her children."

While in Amman, Carole had mulled over the idea of setting up a small home business. Before leaving, she had helped a number of local mothers throw birthday parties for their children and, while abroad, realized that she had spotted a gap in the market. Shortly after her return, she decided the time was right to launch a mail-order children's party business that would sell everything a host could possibly need, sent straight to the customer. Carole was an expert at throwing themed birthday parties for her own children, and her party bags were locally renowned. Initially, she sold the party bags at St. Peter's Church Hall in the village, where Audrey Needham, chair of the preschool play group, helped get her budding business off the ground. According to Mrs. Needham's widower, Alan Needham, who was then the church warden, "Audrey bought about twenty bags for the children in the preschool one Christmas, and they went down very well. I remember that party bags were big in America then, but not so much in the UK then. It was a clever idea, and Carole was very ahead of her time."

Carole would pack the brightly colored bags with plastic toys, party bubbles, Wiz candy, foam planes, party streamers, and balloons at her kitchen table. The other mothers were relieved not to have the pressure of having to pack their own party bags, and Carole was delighted to be able to help out and make a bit of cash on the side. "I came up with the idea for Party Pieces when I was looking for party paraphernalia for my own children's parties," Carole recalled. "It was impossible to find anything easily in the shops, and trying to find value for party bag presents was a complete nightmare."

It was a case of word of mouth, and Carole's party bags became so sought after that she could no longer continue packing them at the kitchen table. She decided to empty out the shed in the garden and use it as a small office, with Michael helping by installing a heater and an electric light. He was a talented carpenter, often helping around the house and doing small jobs for some of their neighbors. Eager to help his pregnant wife, he spent a weekend extending the shed to accommodate the boxes of stock that Carole was ordering daily. "We are the original UK mail-order party company — starting from a shed in the back garden in 1987," Carole explained years later. "We have come a long way since then, but we are still very much a family business; I am still actively involved and love sourcing and developing new party products."

Party Pieces was an obvious and clever idea that required very little investment, and with her creative flair and entrepreneurial skills, Carole found that her business quickly thrived. By now Kate and Pippa were both attending pre-prep school, so it was the perfect way for Carole to fill her days before the new baby arrived. George Brown recalled, "Carole started Party Pieces in the garden shed. It was before James was born, and I would see her taking boxes down to the post office herself. Then suddenly the business took off and the shed was packed to the ceiling with bits and bobs. She was wonderful when it came to throwing parties, and she was always very clever when it came to making up party bags. I remember Catherine's fifth birthday party, which she did at the house. Carole did everything from start to finish, and everyone got wonderful bags to take home. I think Carole wanted to keep busy. She wasn't good at sitting around and doing nothing."

Certainly now with three young children to look after — a longed-for baby boy, James William Middleton had arrived on April 15, 1987, thus completing the family — resting on her laurels would not be an option. What had started as a small and local project soon snowballed. Carole's brother, Gary, had advised her to put Party Pieces online. According to one family member, "Gary told Carole to stop selling paper party bags from home and get them on the Net. Carole was reluctant and said, 'Mums don't use the Internet.' Eventually she gave in and decided to set up an online company called Party Pieces." The canny move proved to be the making of the Middletons' fortune. Party Pieces became so successful that Michael handed in his notice at British Airways so that he could also get involved, and Carole leased an office space in the nearby village of Yattendon because they needed more room. She got Kate and Pippa to model the goods, which included personalized T-shirts, and posted the pictures on the company's website. "I remember by then Michael had had enough at British Airways and didn't really like his job much, so he gave it up to help Carole out. He was a good man and very competent," said George

Brown. As with starting any business, there were some stumbling blocks at the outset, and at the time, setting up an online business was a relatively new idea. According to Martin Fiddler, "At the start they had problems like everyone else; it was a slow starter but they kept working at it, and it paid off. They were 100 percent in it together. Mike and Carole are a real team."

Three years after she launched the business, Party Pieces started selling its signature party-themed boxes, which contained everything you needed for an at-home birthday party. "Way back in 1990 we launched our first in-house designed boxes," Carole revealed in a rare interview. "They were such a hit with everyone that now we try and make sure we have party boxes to go with every party theme." She admitted that she worked around the clock: "It's great fun but not for the fainthearted," she said. "I still work through to the early hours to hit a deadline and never take our success for granted. Your child's birthday is always a very special occasion so I think everyone tries to do something to celebrate the day even if money is tight. We've always believed that parties do not have to be lavish and expensive occasions and have always selected wonderful traditional and inexpensive games, tableware and activities."

According to Carole's brother, the business was so successful that Carole soon became a millionaire. Gary told the United Kingdom's *Daily Mail* that, "No one seems to have picked up on the fact that both my sister and I were millionaires before we turned thirty." He had made $25 million when he sold his shares in a UK-based IT recruitment business. "She with her Party Pieces business and me with my company." By the end of 1986, Carole was thirty-one and very possibly a millionaire. Because Party Pieces is a private partnership, the accounts are not publicly accessible, but there was no doubt that the Middletons' finances were flourishing. They traded their old estate car in for brand-new Land Rover Discovery and started looking for a bigger house. Dr. Acheson recalled the business doing well within a short period of time after they returned from Jordan: "Things took off for them, but they worked very hard."

It was around this time that Carole suggested to her parents, Ronald and Dorothy, that they move from Norwood Green to Pangbourne. Carole was close to her mother and father, and as they got older, she wanted them to be nearer so they could

51

spend time with their grandchildren. Financially, the Middletons were also in a position to put some money toward a property for them. Through a local estate agent in Bradfield, they found a charming cottage situated on the bank of the River Pang, overlooking the water and a little wooden bridge. It was chocolate-box pretty, and Ron and Dorothy fell in love with the cottage as soon as they saw it. But leaving Southall was a life-changing move for the retired couple, and they had a change of heart at the last minute. "They backed out of the sale and I told them they were mad," said Dudley Singleton, who eventually managed to sell them the property after much persuasion. "They were worried it didn't have a garage and the gardens were small. I told Ron he was silly not to buy the house, and they did say on many occasions afterwards, 'Thank God you persuaded us to buy it.' Dorothy was very strong-willed, just like Carole. She had second thoughts, but it turned out to be the perfect house and they were very happy. They made new friends in Pangbourne, went for long walks, and were often seen together at the local pub. They loved it, and the move and the house was right for them." Dorothy, who had worked as a shop assistant throughout her life, found a part-time job at WH Smith a few doors down in Pangbourne, and Ron spent Saturday afternoons with his grandchildren once they had finished games at school. On Sundays, the whole family would get together for a roast lunch at the local pub.

Even in Pangbourne, Dorothy had made an impression on the locals and was known by her nickname "the duchess": "The one thing I would say about Dorothy is you would never have known she came from a working-class background in the north. She had a good speaking voice and a lovely manner, which is why she was nicknamed the duchess," said Mr. Singleton. "She was always well turned out and very much Carole's mother. She was a strong-minded lady with a lot of natural charm that Carole inherited. Ron was a very nice man, very gentle, a bit like Michael. He didn't have a strong personality like Dorothy." Once a year, Ron and Dorothy, and Michael's parents, Peter and Valerie, who lived in Hampshire, were invited to Kate and Pippa's school for Grandparents' Day, when the children would perform plays and concerts. "They would come into the classrooms, and the children would put on concerts and productions and recite poetry for them. Ron and Dorothy were always there to watch them," recalled Mrs. Allford, who taught girls' sports and, later, was their housemistress. "Dorothy was tall and statuesque — you noticed her. She was always made up. Ronald was very low key; he was such a lovely man, he had a twinkle in his eye, and when I met James, I always saw a bit of Ron in him."

Weekends and holidays were family oriented. Wanting the girls to be kept busy and make local friends, Carole enrolled Kate and Pippa in the first local St. Andrew's Brownie troop in Pangbourne. In their uniform of brown culottes and yellow sashes, the girls made their Brownie Guide Promise to be good and help others. With three fingers raised and a toadstool in her left hand, a demure eight-year-old Kate pledged, "I promise that I will do my best to love my God, to serve the Queen and my country, to help other people and to keep the Brownie Guide Law." Once she became a fully fledged member of the troop, she was determined to collect as many badges as she could. Kate had no problem getting her housekeeping badges; she knew how to brew a pot of tea and boil an egg. June Scutter, the troop leader, known as a "Brown Owl," recalled Kate earning further badges for toy making and performing: "For the

Jester badge, the girls had to get together and make a scene from whatever theme they were doing, and also make up a poem, to read aloud to the others." Then there were the Brownies' adventure-packed excursions to local places such as Hog's Farm, where they could see the animals close up, as well as camping holidays at Macaroni Wood in the Cotswolds, where the girls enjoyed a summer vacation with the rest of the troop. Former Brownie Isobel Eeley, who went on a Brownie trip with the Middleton sisters, remembers the girls loving the long walks and arts and crafts activities. Isobel, a cerebral palsy sufferer, remembered how Kate was kind-natured and took Isobel under her wing, "She helped me if I ever got stuck doing things. I can only use one hand, so she would help me with anything that needed two hands."

Back at school, Kate and Pippa were thriving. Avid musicians, they learned to play the flute and piano. They were such enthusiasts that they took extra piano lessons at home. Daniel Nicholls, who taught them, remembered Kate as a "really delightful person to teach. I don't think anyone would say she was going to be a concert pianist, but she was good at it. She always did everything she was told. I actually taught the whole family except Mike." Along with playing instruments, the girls loved to dance. Kate was especially good at tap and ballet. By the time she was in the prep school, she had made a circle of close friends in her year, among them Chelsie Finlay-Notman, Emily Bevan, who is still one of her best friends today, Zoe de Turbeville, Fiona Beacroft, and Katherine Nipperess.

There was no doubt that Kate was happiest on the playing field. She loved hockey and went on to become one of the best players in the under-thirteen team. Jill Acheson, who was known to the pupils as "Mrs. A," had spotted Kate's ability at all things sporting and recognized her potential to become one of the school's star players. The sports and drama teacher was the first person to hand Kate a hockey stick, noting that she was a natural player.

Denise Allford, who also taught in the pre-prep before moving to the main school as a sports instructor, also recalled both girls' natural agility at sports. "Both Catherine and Pippa stood out at sport because they were so good. We had games every afternoon. In the summer they would play from 4:30 until 5:45 P.M., and in the winter, it was after lunch and then lessons until about

5:30 P.M. It was a long day, and by the end of the week they were shattered, but their work ethic was tremendous." Kate was a member of the top hockey, netball, and tennis teams. The facilities at the school were excellent and included netball, tennis, and football courts, a hockey field, and an outdoor swimming pool. She was a fearsome swimmer, and her fast front crawl and backstroke enabled her to beat many of the school's records.

Kate was so happy at the school that when she was nine years old and about to start Year 5 (fourth grade) in fall of 1991, she told her parents she wanted to be a weekly boarder. "After a while a lot of the pupils decided they wanted to board," recalled Mrs. Allford's husband, Kevin Allford, who was Kate's class tutor from age eleven to thirteen and taught sports, French, and German. Although the eye-watering $4,000 per term was manageable, Carole and Michael knew that having Kate away during the week would mark a change in the family dynamics. The Middletons were an exceptionally close family, and Carole and Mike enjoyed the vibrancy of their children, the stories and noise and laughter. Every weeknight, they would eat a home-cooked supper together around the kitchen table.

Mealtimes were an opportunity to bring the family together, and all three children were expected to help. One would lay the table, another would clear up, and they were not allowed to leave their seats until their plates were clean. "As children, we had to eat absolutely everything," Pippa recalled about family suppers in an article she wrote about her childhood.

According to George Brown, who was often at West View for tea with her daughters, Carole was a formidable cook and could mix up and bake a perfect Victoria Sponge in minutes: "She was what I would call a real homemaker. She was also a great baker and taught the girls to bake. The kitchen was a traditional cottage kitchen and the hub of the house, and Carole was always busy cooking up something." Certainly, the kitchen at West View had happy memories for all three siblings. Birthdays were always a special occasion and often themed. Kate recalled dressing up as a clown in giant dungarees, and playing musical statues, and how on her seventh birthday her mother made "an amazing white rabbit marshmallow cake." One of James's earliest childhood memories is of dressing up in his favorite Red Indian outfit and of the pirate-themed parties his mother used to organize, complete with water bombs and musical chairs. He said, "[I remember] my sister trying to make the cake and forgetting to add the self-raising flour! She ended up using the flat sponge to make a trifle cake instead. Boys don't like trifle when they should have had a pirate cake!"

When it came to holidays, the Middletons rarely went overseas. Weekends were spent walking and picnicking in the surrounding Berkshire countryside, and they would enjoy sailing holidays in Norfolk. Often, they rented a cottage for the school holidays in the Lake District. "The girls would talk about these wonderful holidays they had at the cottage with no water and no electricity," recalled Denise Allford. "They never came back with suntans; they holidayed in the UK most of the time. It was typical of their very grounded life."

By the time James was in pre-prep, Kate and Pippa were boarders, having won their parents over. The girls' boarding house was on the top floor of the newly built science block, and they lived with matron — a kindly woman named Margaret Hamilton. They settled in quickly, proud to be wearing their new uniform — a grey skirt and green sweater with the St. Andrew's tie in the winter and a green-and-white checked dress in the summer. The week worked by routine: Wednesdays and Saturdays were sports match days; hair washing was on Thursday evenings; the school day started at 9:00 A.M. after assembly and ended at 6:00 P.M.; every afternoon at 4:00 P.M. the boarders had tea on the lawns, unless it was raining. This was one of the highlights of Kate's week — the kitchen staff wheeled out trolleys piled high with homemade Marmite and peanut butter sandwiches, buns, and doughnuts. With such intense physical activity during the school week, Kate was burning so many calories that she had lost weight. Carole was concerned enough to pay a visit to the school. "Carole was very worried that Catherine wasn't having enough to eat. She was so thin, her school dress was hanging off her," recalled Mrs. Allford. "Carole came at least once to see Yvonne Blay, the school secretary, to ask her if Kate could be given seconds if they were available because she needed to eat more. Catherine was always tall and slim; she had a fast metabolism and was always tearing around the place. She would often come to see us in the two-bedroom flat we lived in at the school, particularly after our daughter Angharad was born. She and Pippa and their friends Thierry Kelaart and

Joanna Hodge would come for toast and hot chocolate and to play with Angharad in the Wendy House. We tried to feed Catherine up, and the girls were allowed midnight feasts usually on Wednesdays, which were more relaxed because it was match day. They were allowed to change into their home clothes and buy some treats from the Tuc shop, which I organized. Catherine had braces at that time so couldn't have anything too sticky — I remember she loved penny sweets and chocolate."

On Saturdays, Michael and Carole would pick Kate up, and often her friends were invited to stay the night. According to Kate's good friend Fiona Beacroft, they would enjoy Saturday nights watching the TV show *Gladiator* and the movie *Cocktail* with Tom Cruise, which was Kate's favorite film: "We stayed at each other's houses many times. I remember camping in the backyard with Catherine and Pippa many times. The family are lovely people, very sociable and the house was always filled with laughter."

Being a boarder meant that during the week Kate could play sports as much as she wanted after school. Often once supper was over, she would head to the netball court with some friends for a practice game —

taking up her position of goal defense — or to the tennis court for a knock-around with Pippa. But though she was a good all-rounder and fiercely competitive — "putting a lot of pressure on herself," according to Mrs. Allford — Kate did not always emerge triumphant. In Year 8 (seventh grade), when she was thirteen, she lost out on being "head girl," one of the most sought-after positions in her class year, to her friend Chelsie Finlay-Notman. The staff and pupils voted on their first choice, and it was Chelsie who emerged with the honor. Although Kate was successful, she was shy and introverted compared to some of the other pupils; Chelsie was more outgoing. Mrs. Allford remembered that Kate was "disappointed but she never showed it. It was a big deal, but Catherine was having so much success in sports it didn't matter. I think part of her wanted it but she cared about games more. There was always a competition between Chelsie and Catherine. When I was choosing the under-thirteen netball captain, it was between the two of them once again. In the end I made them joint captains."

Kate also had to contend with her sister doing better both in the classroom and on the playing field. While Kate had to put the hours in, Pippa, who was known at St. Andrew's as "Perfect Pip" — a sobriquet that would stick — was a natural at anything she tried. Many older siblings would have been jealous, but Kate was only ever happy for her younger sister. "They had such drive and were very competitive, particularly Pippa, but never against each other, they were very much a team," recalled Mrs. Allford. "Pippa was one of the youngest in her year and very bright and good at everything. I remember she wanted to be a professional sportswoman. She was such a good tennis player, she partnered up with Jim Boyd in the pupil-teacher end-of-term tennis championship. She was more athletic than Catherine, and more of a team games girl. She was the best in the school at rounders. I used to bowl five balls and Pippa would hit every one, and she could place the ball. She was amazing, and she was academically bright."

With their daughters in nearly every play, sports match, and concert, Carole and Michael became a regular fixture at the school. "You looked forward to seeing Mike and Carole," said Mrs. Allford. "They were at the school every Wednesday and Saturday for matches. They would turn up in their Discovery, and Carole was always very well turned out, stylish and slim. You got the impression life wasn't as serious for Mike — he would always make a joke. He brought some balance to the family, I think. Carole was in charge of negotiating the children's education; as parents they were a great team."

Carole enjoyed being involved with the school and joined a staff and parents' netball team that Mrs. Acheson and Mrs. Allford had started. Match nights were on Wednesdays in Newbury, and according to Mrs. Allford, Carole was an impressive goal attack. "She loved it. We used to train on Saturday morning, and Carole would come in early to the school and practice shooting. On a Wednesday night, we'd go to someone's house for a team dinner. Carole didn't keep it up for long because the business started to get busy. She gave up after a season."

At the end of the term, when the teachers wanted to give small presents to their class, Carole would help, and Mrs. Allford recalled her generously bringing leftover Party Pieces stock for the children: "She was very involved. I remember we put a pool table in the boys' quarters and made it into a common room, and Carole called up and said it wasn't fair that the boys had a common room and not the girls. The rules were changed, and we allowed the girls to go and use the common room until the youngest boarders had to go to bed. It was a very British compromise, all down to Carole. I don't remember Catherine or Pippa playing pool, though, but that wasn't the point; for Carole it was all about the principle. She wanted the best for her girls."

Carole and Michael's hands-on parenting paid off, and Kate and Pippa proved to be model pupils. "[Catherine] was a perfectionist and took great care over everything," said Mr. Allford. "She worked hard to keep up in lessons, and endeavor, diligence, and concentration got her through. She was meticulous about everything, and her handwriting was beautiful. Her reports were all first class, and parents' nights were a joy. They were great girls and in the classroom at 8:00 A.M. tidying up before classes. Catherine was tremendous fun. I remember she loved the TV show *Absolutely Fabulous,* and she was a great mimic. She used to do an impression of Joanna Lumley, and would always joke to her friends when she thought the teacher wasn't listening: 'That's absolutely fabulous, darling!' "

Kate was consistently well behaved and got along well with her teachers. When Dr.

and Mrs. Acheson left the school, Kate presented them with a teddy bear that everyone in the family had signed. She had carefully inscribed it with the words that Dr. Acheson had instilled in her: "I'll always keep smiling." "She had the most fabulous smile, and I always told her, whatever happens in life, keep smiling," he recalled.

She was also extremely fond of the Allfords, to whom she gave a framed print of a Picasso painting when she left. She had two other favorites: David Gee, who taught her physical education and math, and Jim Boyd, who headed up the English and drama departments. For a shy girl, Kate was surprisingly extroverted on the stage. The school put on two productions every year, and during her time there, she was in almost every play. It didn't matter whether she had a lead or supporting role; Kate simply relished being part of a team and a production and loved the opportunity to dive into the costume wardrobe. The school had an impressive drama department, with performances staged in the sports hall, known as the New Hall. The teachers and pupils made sets, and rehearsals often took place after class. "Catherine was in most of the school plays I produced, and she was a real joy to direct," said Jim Boyd. "She always remembered her lines, and she was very reliable when it came to rehearsals, which is why she always got good parts. She had a great voice and would often do solos, and she was very confident. If she didn't get a big part, she was never bothered, which was very endearing. She was also up for anything, especially if it involved her dressing up. For one of the parts she played, I had to draw a birthmark on her leg in red lipstick, and she was always happy getting dressed up for something like Comic Relief [the charitable organization]."

One of Kate's greatest achievements was playing the protagonist in *Dick Whittington,* which required her to wear a green bodysuit and green tights. Pippa scurried along the floor as King Rat in the production, along with their brother, James. "They learned their lines while sitting around the kitchen table at home because it was one of the plays we did in the school holidays," explained Mr. Boyd. "Catherine was brilliant as Dick and managed to carry off playing a total buffoon very professionally. She had to be pretty stupid and gormless, and she executed her lines with great comic timing. I remember there was one line she had to say that went, 'I'm such a prat with a stupid cat,' which really made everyone laugh."

All three children loved being in school plays so much that during the summer holidays, they attended Mr. Boyd's drama camp. "[Rehearsals] would take place from 9:00 A.M. until 4:00 P.M. every day. We would always do a pantomime at Christmas and a play in the summer," recalled Mr. Boyd. Kate was given leading roles in *Snow White* and in *Cinderella,* in which she played Prince Charming opposite her best friend, Emily Bevan, who would later become a successful actress. Kate also played a gypsy queen in a play written by Jim Boyd called *Strange Happenings at Spittlebury Manor,* and she had a key role in *Murder in the Red Barn* alongside Barnaby Rodgers, the son of screen legend Anton Rodgers, that rather eerily entailed her falling in love with a boy named William who took her to London. When footage of the play was posted on YouTube years later, it caused a sensation. The grainy home video captured a thirteen-year-old Kate speaking to a soothsayer wearing a scarf and gold hoop earring. "Will he fall in love with me?" inquires Kate when she is told she will meet a rich landowner named William. "Indeed he will," responds the fortune-teller. "And marry me?" asks

Kate. "And marry you," he confirms, after reading her palm. "It is all I ever dreamed of," she confides to the audience, adding to much laughter, "Oh how my heart flutters." Prophetically, a young man named William then proposes to Kate on bended knee.

As one of the school's best singers, Kate was also chosen to narrate a production of *Joseph,* in which she mostly sang. Both she and Pippa were in the school choir, but when it came to singing, Kate was better than Pippa and wore a dark blue ribbon — to indicate her higher rank — over her chorister robes. Both girls attended choir every Sunday night in the school's chapel. Kate would often be chosen to sing with the head chorister, Andrew de Perlaky, who also starred alongside her in *My Fair Lady.* Early in Year 5 (fourth grade), she had been picked to play Eliza Doolittle, which was quite a coup as she was just ten. Now a successful West End stage star known as Andrew Alexander, he recalled how Kate successfully mastered a cockney accent, "We worked a lot together on stage, and I remember she was very good at pulling off a cockney accent." Andrew played the role of Freddie, who falls for Eliza, but she rebuffs him. There was a twist of irony to the tale, for in real life Kate had quietly fallen for

Andrew, the blond-haired blue-eyed chorister with the voice of an angel. He was the best-looking boy in her year, and Kate had gotten to know him well as they were both in the school choir, but sadly for her, Andrew was already "dating" her friend Fiona Beacroft. "It was funny because it was passed on to me, as happens at school, that Catherine liked me. She never told me that herself, she didn't have the confidence," said Mr. Alexander. "One of her friends, Fiona Beacroft, was my girlfriend at the time. She was more of a chatterbox and a bubblier character, but these were very innocent relationships, and very fleeting — sometimes they lasted a matter of days. I do remember we would go off to the woods to play spin the bottle, and we even staged pretend marriages and had a quick kiss, but Catherine was never a part of that. She was on the outskirts and much shier than the other girls."

Pippa was far more likely to get involved in such hijinks, and when it came to the end-of-year school disco dance, she had to bat the boys away. Fellow pupils and teachers recalled how she was the more gregarious and extroverted of the two sisters, and the prettier of the two. Kate was tall for her age, lanky, and still wearing braces, and

Pippa was more popular with boys. "I remember Pippa was more outgoing out of the two of them," said Mr. Alexander. "Catherine was very sweet, but quite shy and retiring, more than most. She wasn't one of the most popular girls in the school. I don't think she had a best friend as such; she had lots of friends. We all got along together and were best friends. No one was left out and there was no bullying. She was friends with everyone and everyone was friends with her."

Although she wasn't especially interested in boys, the arrival of one particular young man had caught her attention. Nearby Ludgrove Prep school would often play matches against St. Andrew's Prep, and there was much excitement when Prince William, a left back on Ludgrove's Colts team, came to St. Andrew's to play a hockey match when he was nine years old. William, like Kate, loved sports and was one of the best hockey and rugby players in his year. Of course, the arrival of the prince generated a flurry of excitement. "I remember when William came to play hockey. The boys wanted to know why so many cars had stopped on the way in because it was unusual," remembered Mr. Allford. "It was William's protection officers and bodyguards, and it caused quite a stir. It went round the school like wildfire." It was the first time Kate had set her eyes on the young prince, but certainly not the last.

CHAPTER 3
A MODEL PUPIL

Like many pupils, Kate bade farewell to the secure and happy environment of St. Andrew's Prep in 1995 with apprehension. Not only was she leaving what had become a second home, but she was on the brink of beginning the next chapter of her life, and she was understandably daunted.

Kate's hard work and diligence in the classroom paid off, and she had gained a place at the prestigious independent all-girls school Downe House. She had visited it with her parents, who considered it the perfect choice. Set within 110 acres of wooded parkland on the outskirts of Newbury in the pretty area of Cold Ash, the school was a convenient ten-minute drive from the Middletons' new home. The family had spent the summer packing up West View, and they were moving to a beautiful detached house in the nearby hamlet of Chapel Row in the village of Bucklebury, which was three miles from Bradfield. Oak Acre was a serious jump up the property ladder and meant a bigger mortgage, but Mike and Carole could well afford it. Party Pieces was bringing in a handsome income, and West View had proved a wise purchase; after buying the property in 1979 for $52,000, they sold it for a substantial profit.

Chapel Row, with its wide tree-lined avenues, is more picturesque and wealthier than Bradfield. Most of the houses cost more than $1 million, and many belong to celebrities and millionaires who want to be in the countryside yet close to the M4 so they can commute to the capital. The village comprises an old part by the River Pang, a large common where the annual summer village fete is held, and Upper Bucklebury, which affords beautiful views of endless green farmland. Compared to West View, Oak Acre, with its five bedrooms, open-plan kitchen, and spacious reception rooms, was like a mansion. Set off a small country lane, the house had purple wisteria climbing up the walls, its own front gate, a gravel driveway, and well-tended front and rear gardens with panoramic views of the countryside. Much to the children's delight, there was also a tennis court.

Pippa's teacher Mrs. Allford recalled that

she could not stop talking about "the big house," and the family hosted a housewarming party as soon as they moved in: "You could tell they came into money when they moved into the new house. Their place in Bradfield was tiny compared to Oak Acre, and they were all so excited, Catherine and Pippa especially because it had a tennis court." According to Mr. Singleton, who oversaw the sale of West View, Oak Acre had great potential: "It was a good stock country house; they bought more land because they had the money and they made it really nice. They bought a good few acres, because it was only sold with about three-quarters of an acre. Carole called in designers to help her do it up. She would go off to London to Sloane Square to get ideas and fabrics. The house had very nice soft furnishings — I remember Carole having a thing for tassels at one time, but it wasn't over the top or pretentious. She had a real vista for Oak Acre and she and Michael did a fair bit of work."

By now Party Pieces had been relocated from a rented warehouse in Yattendon to a more spacious converted barn house in Ashampstead Common, a mile down the road from the Middletons' new home. Carole and Michael employed a staff, although Carole was determined the enterprise should retain the feel of a family business. The new office space had a number of outbuildings spaced around a central courtyard and plenty of room for expansion. Now that the business was online, orders were coming in from all over the country, and the warehouses were stacked to the rafters with boxes of party toys.

The Middletons were no longer solely reliant on Michael's trust fund for the education of their children, and Party Pieces' profits helped with the $45,000-a-year fees at Downe House. The school had a good sports record, but above all else, it was known for being academic and getting its pupils into some of the country's best universities. According to the website, it has "strong educational traditions, a firm Christian foundation and a reputation for excellence that goes back over 100 years." Some of the pupils have been daughters of wealthy aristocrats, including Prince and Princess Michael of Kent's daughter Lady Gabriella Windsor — a notable former alumna who was suspended for being caught with cigarettes.

With its impressive position in sports ranking, Michael and Carole were confident going to the school was the right move for their daughter, but Kate had reservations from the outset. Possibly intimidated by the scale of the school, she opted to be a day girl rather than a boarder. Her parents agreed, but it was to prove a terrible mistake as most of the girls in her year were boarders and many had been there from the age of eleven. When Kate arrived at age thirteen, class friendships had already been formed and she struggled to find her place. Being especially slender and a head taller than her peers, she stood out for the wrong reasons and was teased for being gangly and lanky.

According to former pupil Emma Sayle, who was four classes ahead of Kate, "Part of the problem was that Kate was a day girl. Most of the girls were boarders and all of the bonding and friendship-making happened in dorms. Kate missed out on all of that and because she joined when she was thirteen rather than eleven, she had to try and make friends with girls who had been there for two years and had already formed friendships. . . . It is a very cliquey school and there was a lot of pressure. The girls were all high achievers, and there were lots of girls with eating disorders. Everyone wanted to be the best, the fittest, the prettiest. I think Kate was miserable from the start."

Former pupil Taffeta Gray recalled in an article she wrote for the *Spectator* that Kate was "quiet and square with brown hair. She was a day girl, which is always difficult. In the cliquey atmosphere of a girls' boarding school, to be a day girl makes you an oddity. The day girls tended to keep to themselves, and we boarders looked at them with suspicion." Georgina Rylance, another former pupil, agreed that Kate was at a disadvantage. "I was there from eleven till sixteen and I was four years above Catherine. It does make a difference going from eleven. You have two years of bonding, your first time away all together," she told the *Sunday Times*. "Even some of the most popular girls in my school had a hard time when they came in at thirteen. And of course she was a day pupil. In boarding schools a lot of the bonding takes place late at night, or at the weekends, going to the local sweetshop."

Kate missed out on the nocturnal bonding and banter in the dormitories. She arrived in time for assembly, and then it was straight into lessons. Even by the time she got to class, she found that many of the girls had already paired up with their best friends. Compared to the curriculum at St. Andrew's, the lessons were hard, and she struggled to keep up with her peers academically. Even when it came to sports, where she should have excelled, Kate found she was out of her league. The predominant game at Downe House was lacrosse, which she had never played, and there was no hockey on the curriculum. According to her headmistress, Susan Cameron, who gave an interview to the *Mail on Sunday,* "She was not selected for the school teams during her time with us, which, given that she was very sporty at her last school, was slightly unusual. Kate may have felt slightly out of things because people at that level would have been well into lacrosse, and I think she probably had never played. It strikes me that could have been a crushing disappointment. You pick up a lacrosse stick and think you're good at games, then someone says to you, 'That's not how you pick up a lacrosse stick,' and you feel rather squashed. It's a delicate age."

Disappointed not to be part of a team on the sports field and shy compared to some of her more outgoing classmates, Kate retreated into her shell. She found the all-girl environment alienating and had little in common with many of the wealthy pupils who owned ponies and came from high-society families. Others, like former pupil

Emma Sayle, came from precocious private London schools. There was a hierarchy in place, and according to Emma, you were judged on your class, your background, and how pretty you were. Socially forward girls seemed to have the advantage, as did those who were more developed. Some of the older girls had experimented with alcohol, some had boyfriends, and others were already secretly smoking, but not Kate, who by nature was not transgressive. As her former teacher Mr. Boyd recalled, "Catherine had no interest in boys. She was always very innocent." At Downe House, her naïveté and natural kindness made her a target, and she was picked on. "There was a group in our year called the 'London Trendies,' " said Emma, who became friends with Kate years later when they took part in a charity boat race together. "Kate just wouldn't have fitted in with that sort of thing. She also didn't know anyone, and I think she was very lonely."

Word that Kate was struggling reached her old teachers at St. Andrew's. "We heard quite soon that Catherine wasn't happy at Downe House. It was talked about in the staff room," recalled Mrs. Allford. "It seemed to be more a case of her not fitting in. She was very innocent and ordinary, and the other girls might have been more sophisticated. Catherine had always been sheltered and protected." Mr. Boyd agreed: "I can see why she didn't settle into Downe House; she was an all-rounder and not just a straight-A student."

Although she was desperately unhappy, the headmistress, Miss Cameron, who met with the Middletons several times, played down reports that Kate was badly bullied. "She may well have felt a fish out of water, or unhappily not in the right place. Certainly I have no knowledge of any serious bullying at all. But there's what everyone calls bullying, and there's actual real, miserable bullying where someone has a dreadful time. That certainly didn't happen," she said. "Yes, there would be teasing. It's all part of the normal competition of growing up, of establishing a pecking order. Girls are cliquey by nature and they can be rather cruel. If you're attractive, too, that can be seen as rather a threat. They can sense those who are slightly weaker or who haven't shown their strengths yet, and it's those girls who are likely to end up being picked on or teased. I think it's fair to say she was unsettled and not particularly happy. Maybe in Catherine's case she just kind of went quiet and didn't say anything."

Kate's experience wasn't unique. Some of her friends from St. Andrew's Prep also found the transition of moving to secondary school challenging. "I can totally imagine why Kate had a hard time at Downe House," said Andrew Alexander, who went to Bradfield College. "We'd had such a lovely, innocent time at St. Andrew's Prep, and secondary school was very different. When I went to Bradfield College, I was stunned when I saw people smoking — it was drilled into us not to smoke. It was a shock. St. Andrew's was a complete bubble. Back then Kate wasn't gregarious or assertive, so I can see she might have struggled and didn't fit in. It felt like a rat race compared to the paradise of St. Andrew's."

Not so far away, thirteen-year-old Prince William was also struggling to adjust to his new life at Eton College in Windsor. Whereas his parents — who had separated three years earlier — posed as a happy family outside Manor House, his boarding school, the public appearance, which was captured by no less than three hundred photographers, masked an unhappy truth. The Wales's marriage was over, but their private lives were being relentlessly raked through in the tabloid press. Within William's first term, he had to deal with reports that his mother was having an affair with England's rugby player Will Carling and then a London-based art dealer, Oliver Hoare. He was mortified when Princess Diana gave a now-infamous interview to the BBC's *Panorama,* during which she lifted the lid on her marriage and revealed her husband's affair with his long-term mistress, Camilla Parker Bowles, who was married to Andrew Parker Bowles at the time. "There were three of us in this marriage, so it was a bit crowded," she told interviewer Martin Bashir. To William's horror, she also spoke candidly about her affair with former Life Guards officer James Hewitt, a family friend who had taught William and Harry to horse ride. Despite the college's best efforts to protect the prince, many of his peers watched the program, and for weeks, paparazzi lurked in the shadows of Windsor Castle, waiting to get a shot of William, who would head there at weekends to stay with his grandparents. It was a difficult start for the schoolboy prince.

William managed to settle in and find his feet, but Kate did not. She hated the name-calling and practical jokes, which were part of the school's rite of passage. Her father, Michael, who under duress had been "a fag" (servant to senior pupils) at Clifton

College, remembered how testing school life could be. As a young pupil, Michael had to wait on the older prefects, and he was tasked with shining their shoes, cleaning their studies, and making cocoa, or he risked being punished. He urged his daughter to follow the family mantra and "grin and bear it," but after a second term, it was apparent Downe House was not going to work.

As Pippa and James were still at St. Andrew's and Kate had been so happy there, Michael and Carole paid a visit to the headmaster, Jeremy Snow, for some advice. He suggested that Kate might be happier at Marlborough College in Wiltshire, with its national reputation for sports and academic excellence.

So after visiting Marlborough, the Middletons took their daughter out of Downe House. Leaving halfway through the academic year could have had repercussions on her school reports, but there was no other option, according to Mr. Acheson, "They did the right thing and pulled Catherine out when they realized she was unhappy. It was absolutely the right move. Marlborough was the right choice." Being that it was an hour's drive from home, it was agreed that Kate would be a boarder, which meant

Carole and Michael would only see her for weekends every fourth week.

Set on the edge of a historic market town where it dominates local life, Marlborough College is an impressive collection of original buildings scattered around the beautiful Wiltshire countryside. The school, considered to be one of the most promising coeducational establishments in the country, was founded in 1843 for the sons of Church of England clergymen. The $44,000-a-year college counts the poet Sir John Betjeman; singer Chris de Burgh to whom Kate is distantly related through her father; the Prime Minister's wife, Samantha Cameron; and Princesses Beatrice and Eugenie as notable former alumni. Out of its fourteen boarding houses, it educates a total of 889 pupils from the ages of thirteen to eighteen, about two-thirds of them girls.

It was a warm spring morning in April 1996, the sun shining on what the Middletons hoped was an auspicious new beginning. As Carole and Michael arrived at the school, they were characteristically optimistic and upbeat. Dressed in her new uniform of a dark green kilt, round-necked navy sweater, and blue-and-white striped cotton shirt, Kate knocked — a little tentatively — on the front door of her new home, Elm-

85

hurst, an impressive Victorian house with a modern extension. Her housemistress, Ann Patching — who became something of a surrogate mother during the school year — was there to greet her. Kate said good-bye to her parents and went upstairs to her room, her trunk packed full of notebooks, mementos, and pictures of her family and friends, plus a pretty bedspread Carole had sent along to make her feel at home.

Kate wasn't the only pupil to join halfway through the academic year: Sebastian Robles-Rudd, a boy from Argentina, also arrived on the same day. As a governor of St. Andrew's, the headmaster of Marlborough, Edward Gould, was aware of the circumstances under which Kate had left Downe House, and he took her under his wing, inviting her to join him and his wife for occasional mealtimes so that he could keep an eye on her. According to another pupil, Gemma Williamson, who lived in Mill Mead boarding house a short walk away, Kate arrived a slip of a girl and painfully shy. "Apparently she had been bullied very badly at her previous school and she certainly looked very thin and pale. She had very little confidence," she told the *Daily Mail*.

Kate's residence house tutor, Joan Gall,

recalled how timid she was on arrival and that she suffered from mild eczema, often a result of stress. "When she first arrived, she was very quiet. Coming into a big school like Marlborough was difficult, but she settled quickly," she recalled. Ann Patching, who worked at the school for over a decade and was married to Mitch Patching who taught rugby and French at the college, said that Kate didn't talk about her past experience. "She didn't make a big deal about it. I can't remember if it was her or Carole who mentioned Downe House. It was a concern, but they were determined to move on."

Another pupil, Hannah Gillingham, who was in Kate's boarding house, was assigned to look after her, but Kate made friends quickly and was affectionately known as "Catherine Middlebum." An early riser, she had no problem with the 7:00 A.M. wake-up calls and was always the first at breakfast, where she typically enjoyed fresh croissants. Lessons started at 8:45 A.M. and continued until lunch at 1:00 P.M. Afterward, pupils played sports until 4:00 P.M., when it was time to head back into the classroom until supper at 6:00 P.M. Mealtimes were relaxed and pleasant in the atmosphere of the Victorian dining room, complete with its original arched beams. According to Mrs.

Patching, Kate had a healthy appetite and soon put on the weight she had lost at Downe House. "Catherine loved eating. She loved lasagnas and pasta bakes, good old carb stuff. I used to do a chicken pesto. The girls were great to cook for because they would eat anything. Catherine always stayed very slim but she always had a very healthy appetite."

Students did their homework, or "prep," in the communal dormitories from 7:30 until 9:00 P.M., with house tutors on hand to help. There was then time for some rest and relaxation. Walkmen were the latest thing, and Kate loved to either listen to music or read a novel. Her favorite TV show was *Friends.* According to Miss Gall, she was such a fan of the American sitcom that at one of the end-of-year concerts known as the "House Shout," Kate belted out the theme tune with her friends. Lights-out was at 10:30 P.M. Mrs. Patching had a no-nonsense approach, and any horseplay would mean being assigned an early morning run the next morning.

Unlike at Downe House, Kate's class year was small. There were seventy girls in her house and just fourteen pupils in "The Remove," as her year was known. She lived in a dormitory with three others — the girls didn't get their own rooms until they entered sixth form (the last two years of secondary school) — and in order to prevent them from becoming too cliquey, Mrs. Patching chose the dorm mates and rotated them every term. "It was a way of keeping things fresh," she explained. "Catherine was able to settle in very easily, as soon as she joined. She got involved in school life and loved sport and music."

It wasn't long before Kate's sporting prowess was observed, and she gained a coveted place on the school's hockey and netball teams. Much to her delight, she was made joint captain of the first tennis team with her friend Alice St. John Webster. Miss Gall, who was also head of physical education, recalled that Kate switched positions to goal attack in her netball and "was very good, but her hockey was stronger." She also excelled in high jump and swimming.

Eager to ensure their daughter was happy, Carole and Michael visited Kate regularly. They came to watch interschool matches on Saturdays, and as the spring and summer terms progressed, she began to come out of her shell. During the summer holidays, she was full of stories about her school life, eager to make Pippa, who would be starting in the new academic year, feel excited and part of the school community. The fact that Pippa had won an all-rounder scholarship to Marlborough was a source of pride to the whole Middleton family. "Pippa came into the school as a sports scholar. Catherine was very protective, but I don't think Pippa needed much protecting — she was very successful," recalled Mrs. Patching. "She was in the first hockey team from a young age, while Catherine worked her way up. She settled in easily and Catherine kept an eye from a distance. There could have been jealousy on Catherine's part because Pippa was very talented. She was good at everything and sharper academically, but I don't think Catherine ever resented that. She was always pleased for her sister's success." From her very first day, Pippa exuded a natural confidence, and along with her bubbly exuberance, she made friends easily, attained grade A's effortlessly, and was known, as she had been at St. Andrew's Prep, as "Perfect Pip."

Both siblings continued with their music. Kate sang in school concerts and played the flute and piano. "There was one occasion when Catherine was playing a game and Pippa was in a concert, so Michael and Carole split up so they could both support the girls," recalled Mrs. Patching. "I remember once they played a duet on the piano in one of our house concerts, which we had on a Sunday and Michael and Carole were there for that. I seem to remember a giggle after the first couple of bars; they'd made a mistake and cheekily turned to the audience and said, 'We think we better start again!' "

Both girls were on the First Hockey team with Hannah Gillingham, Alice St. John Webster, and Emilia d'Erlanger, all boarders in Mill Mead House. "The girls all became close and we would have a lot of fun together," said their hockey teacher, Jon Copp. "I used to tease them and challenge them. I remember Emilia was quite a character and cheeky from the start. She put a snowball down my neck in the first term. Alice St. John Webster was a bundle of energy and Hannah Gillingham was one of the school's best hockey players. They gelled as a group and became great friends. We used to have pizza parties at the end of term to celebrate our wins."

The only unhappy spell at Marlborough came when Kate was forced to stop playing hockey. She had discovered a lump on the left-hand side of her head. Evidently concerned, the school called Carole who rushed Kate to their doctor. The lump was considered potentially serious, and Kate was operated on within a few days. Mrs. Patching recalled, "I can remember the incident and her having an operation. I don't recall anything happening on the hockey pitch [field] that had anything to do with the lump," she said after some of the media reported that her scar might have been the result of a sporting accident. "Catherine had the operation during her term time. She was back at school very soon afterwards. As usual, nothing was too much of a big deal for her. You could never accuse Catherine of being a drama queen, but Carole was very worried, as any mother would be."

One former pupil said that the operation "was pretty serious" and alarmed everyone, as it happened shortly after the tragic death of a fellow pupil, Hugo McDermott, from a brain tumor. "Catherine and Pippa were very kind to Hugo's brother Ed who was also at the school when his brother died, and they got involved with some fundraising," recalled a former student. The operation left Kate with a small scar on her hairline that is still visible today, though it mostly stays hidden under her hair. Privately, she and William — who uncannily also bears a scar on his head from being struck by a golf club at age nine — are said to refer to their wounds as their "Harry Potter scars."

It was a brief moment of concern amid an otherwise very happy time. "It was like a big happy family in Elmhurst," said Miss Gall. "We would do things like bake cakes and watch videos." As she made her way through her school days, Kate made friends for life. As well as her hockey friends, she was close to Susanna Housden in her house, and Catriona Lough and Gemma Williamson, who both boarded at Mill Mead House. The girls would catch up in "Court," the principal meeting place by the main school building and the hub of the school. On weekends, they were allowed to take tea at the Polly Tea Rooms in the town center. In the evenings, they would relax in the common room of their house, which had its own TV and a small kitchen — known as a "brew" — where Catherine would make her favorite microwaved Marmite sandwiches. Sometimes the Patchings, whose children, Bethan and Daniel, were in Catherine's year at the school, would host barbecues for the pupils. "The Patchings and Mrs. Gall were totally wonderful, like surrogate parents," recalled former Elmhurst pupil Alex Martin. "We had dorms in the first two years, which gave the house a family feel, but mainly it was all the extras the Patchings arranged — spontaneous barbecues on weekdays in the summer after prep, trips to the cinema on Saturdays, weekends away in the Wye Valley camping and canoeing, an annual house walk and sleep over in a barn. The Patchings would welcome us into their home and were always around for a chat.'

As she gained in confidence and maturity, Kate was seen as one of the school's most promising students, and as such she was given more responsibility than most. She was made a "guardian" for new pupils in the first year — a job that she took seriously. Having experienced what it was like to feel overwhelmed and unhappy in a new school, she was perfectly positioned to help others who might have been homesick and apprehensive. "She would take care of the newcomers. You could see that Catherine wasn't a threatening character, the new girls could talk to her and approach her, they felt comfortable with her," said Mrs. Patching.

Kate studied hard, sitting for various exams for the General Certificate of Secondary Education (GCSE) in the summer term of 1998. Intending to make the most of her freedom afterward, she and her friends took part in a school hockey and rugby trip to Argentina. Returning home,

Kate and her family spent the remainder of the summer in the sun-kissed Caribbean. When she went back to school for the lower sixth in September to study for the first year of her A-levels (the academic track), it was obvious to everyone that sixteen-year-old Kate had undergone something of a metamorphosis. "It happened quite suddenly," Gemma Williamson recalled. "Kate came back after the long summer break an absolute beauty. Although she was sporty, Kate was very feminine, too. She always had a lovely willowy figure, but now she had filled out and the color was back in her cheeks . . . every boy in the school fancied her rotten." With her honed figure, blonde highlights, and attractive dimples, she was suddenly top of the "Fit List," ahead of Alice, Emilia, and Pippa. "We had fit lists that the boys pinned on the walls. Kate was at the top," said a former pupil. Denise Allford also recalled being bowled over by Kate's transformation when she came back to St. Andrew's to collect James, who was about to start at Marlborough. "Carole had taken the girls shopping on the King's Road for the day. Pippa was always a tomboy, but Catherine had lost her braces and looked stunning. She was wearing makeup and looked amazing."

As a sixth former, Kate no longer had to wear a uniform; instead, she was allowed to wear a long black skirt that she could team with a jacket — so long as it was tailored. Even then she favored simple classic designs and had a collection of blouses and sweaters from the high street store Jigsaw. She also had a penchant for gilets (waistcoats), which were fashionable at the time. For the first time she also used makeup — only a hint of blusher and a lick of mascara. Always lithe because of her love of sports, Kate had filled out physically. One entry in the school's yearbook read, "Catherine's perfect looks are renowned . . . but she is often found squinting down her top, screaming, 'They're growing!' "

Although the girls and boys at Marlborough had lessons together, there were strict rules when it came to socializing. Mrs. Patching allowed boys into the boarding house, but any visits had to be cleared by her in advance. Kate never took advantage of Mrs. Patching's liberal attitude, and according to those who knew her well, she wasn't particularly interested in having a serious boyfriend until she got to the sixth form. Being educated with boys for most of her life, Kate was relaxed around them and had plenty of male friends. She got along particularly well with some of the boys in her year: Hugh Macdonald-Brown, Mrs. Patching's son Daniel, Hugh Twort, and Andrew Coventry. She had her first kiss with Woody, the elder brother of her friend Alice St. John Webster. Their innocent relationship involved nothing more than some harmless smooching behind the Mound, a renowned landmark at the heart of the college grounds, where, according to Arthurian legend, Merlin's bones are buried. Woody was in the year ahead of Kate, and they had gotten to know each other through Alice. A boarder in Cotton House and captain of the rugby and tennis teams, Woody was remembered by one former pupil as "popular and kind." With his athletic physique and boyish good looks, he had caught Kate's eye. But the relationship was short-lived, and even when she developed a crush on Willem Marx, a dashing floppy-haired boarder, Gemma Williamson felt that Kate was hanging back: "I got the distinct impression that Kate wanted to save herself for someone special. It was quite an old-fashioned approach, especially at Marlborough, where half of the pupils were already having sex."

Kate was still a virgin, and she did plan to save herself for someone special. At school, it was Pippa who was more popular with boys. "She could hold her own in any social situation. She was bright, pretty, sweet and always tanned," recalled one of their contemporaries. "Even though Kate was older, it was Pippa who got talked about more. She was more light-hearted and up for a party, whereas Kate was reserved and didn't like to drink that much. Pippa was never short of male attention." Pippa dated several boys at the school, including one of Marlborough's best rugby players, but Kate didn't have a serious boyfriend, though according to her dorm mate Jessica Hay, she harbored a crush on the teenage Prince William. "She would joke, 'There's no one quite like William.' She had a picture of him on her wall," Miss Hay told the *Mail on Sunday.* But Kate laughed off the story in her first-ever interview years later: "No, I had the Levi's guy on my wall, not a picture of William." Indeed, when William came to Marlborough for interschool events, Kate was more interested in playing hockey than waiting at the goal line on the hockey field above Wedgewood, where some of the girls congregated to gawp at the prince. Others would gather outside Mill Mead, where the buses parked, so they could chase after the boys as they drove off. But not Kate. "There was a little bit of spying by some of the girls, but Catherine was busy playing hockey," said Mrs. Patching. "Afterwards, she would host a table for the away team. She and William may have bumped into each other then, because the home and away teams all ate in the dining room."

Painfully shy and acutely aware of his unwanted celebrity, William was known for keeping his head down, self-consciously trying to avoid the attention he attracted. He was still coming to terms with the trauma of losing his mother two years earlier in a tragic car crash in Paris. Like all her friends, Kate had followed the story closely, deeply saddened by the princess's death, which had prompted an outbreak of mass mourning around the world. The loss to Prince William and Prince Harry was almost unbearable, and when William returned to school, he threw himself into his studies as a distraction. He had pleasantly surprised his teachers at Eton when he passed each of his twelve GCSEs, excelling in English, history, and languages. Throughout his school life, William was well aware of how different he was. He would joke on the weekends that he was "off to WC," which baffled his friends at first until they realized he didn't mean the toilet, but nearby Windsor Castle "to see granny."

With her stunning transformation, it wasn't long before Kate caught the eye of the best-looking boy at the school and began dating Harry Blakelock, an upper sixth former, in the fall of 1998, when she was in the lower sixth. It was her first proper romance and Kate was smitten. Tall, incredibly good looking, and popular, Harry had a reputation for being quite a catch among the girls. "It was well known that Kate was dating Harry when he was in the upper sixth, although it has stayed a secret until now. They were together for most of Harry's final year," recalled a friend and former pupil. "Harry was a boarder in B1 and he was very sporty and captain of his year's rugby team. He was an excellent scrum half and a good cricketer. He played in the First Eleven, and he was also very good at hockey. He was what you'd call a model pupil — top of his year and very clever. Kate was in the lower sixth and it was her most serious relationship at Marlborough. It fizzled out when he left school and took a gap year [year off]." Kate was heartbroken, according to her friends. She desperately wanted to make the relationship work, but Harry was planning to travel overseas and they both agreed it would be quite impossible to be in a relationship when they would be on opposite sides of the world.

The summer of 1999, before she started the upper sixth, was one of mixed emotions for Kate. She was crushed and bruised from the breakup with Harry, but her attention soon turned to new possibilities. Her friend Emilia d'Erlanger had introduced Kate to some of her out-of-school friends. The niece of the tenth Viscount Exmouth, Emilia was fantastically well connected and part of William and Harry's friendship group, known as the "Glosse Posse," so called because most of the aristocratic "members" resided in Gloucestershire, where the Prince of Wales has his country house, Highgrove. The Glosse Posse would meet on weekends and during holidays when they were invited to Club H, William and Harry's "den" in the cellars of Highgrove. Complete with a set of turntables on which they played vinyl records, a bar stocked with non-alcoholic beverages, and a portrait hung in the bathroom of their ancestor Edward VIII, who threw the monarchy into chaos when he abdicated in 1936, the get-togethers were a great deal of fun.

Being so close to Emilia and Alice, who was also a member of the exclusive group, it was only a matter of time before Kate met

William, and that summer they were introduced. "We all knew as teachers that that year group was moving in royal circles, they were friends," recalled Mrs. Patching. Another of Kate's teachers described Kate as "on the fringe" of the royal set. "I was aware that William was friends with Mark Tomlinson and Emilia d'Erlanger. It doesn't surprise me that she met William while she was at Marlborough. It was certainly within the bounds of possibility, put it that way."

Their very first encounter is not something Kate has ever spoken about; indeed, it has always been believed that Kate first met William when they were freshers (freshmen) at St. Andrew's. When she returned to school in September, there was much talk about the summer holidays. Alice told friends that she had met up with William and that he had asked for her number, but Kate kept quiet about their own meeting and threw herself with gusto into her final year.

During her upper sixth, Kate, like William, was given the honor of serving her school. The prince was made a member of Pop, a select group of prefects at Eton, and Kate was appointed head of house. "Marlborough did some big social days out in London, and as a prefect, one of Kate's jobs was to promote the school. She was an ambassador for the school and a very good one," said Mrs. Patching. "Catherine had a good relationship with everyone. She was very well-mannered, she was aware of social situations. She had a real confidence in herself. She felt secure at Marlborough. She was successful and diligent and hard-working. When she got to the upper sixth, she had a lot more responsibility. She was able to go into any sort of social situation and speak to anyone."

As a prefect, Kate enjoyed the use of a special common room and was also allowed to hand out punishments to others, but she rarely did. In fact, when she caught older pupils having a forbidden cigarette on the playing fields beyond the central quad, she turned a blind eye, not wanting to be seen as a tattletale. She herself had never been part of the more hedonistic set that experimented with boys, smoking, and alcohol. Apart from having to join Mrs. Patching on one of her "punishment runs" — for little more than having her lights on late — Kate was never in trouble. She performed well in class, and though she wasn't a natural academic, her hard work got her good grades in her chosen subjects — chemistry, biology, and art. Kate was determined to go to a university, aware that she would need top grades to be selected for one of the best in the country. She would also need an array of extracurricular activities to add to her university application. Although her passion was still for sports, she enrolled in the Duke of Edinburgh Gold Award program, which entailed volunteering in the local community, learning a new physical skill for a year, and participating on a four-day trek in the wilderness. According to Mrs. Patching, it was "a huge achievement" for Kate, who was one of the few pupils who made a point of completing the paperwork so that she could go and receive her medal at Buckingham Palace. It was a fitting end to a very happy school life. Now all Kate needed were her grades.

CHAPTER 4
A CHANGE OF HEART

Kate flew down the stairs as soon as she heard the letterbox clatter. It was Thursday, August 17, 2000, and the whole family had been waiting for the postman to arrive. The brown paper envelope that would seal Kate's future lay on the doormat. "Open it," squeaked Pippa, who had raced downstairs behind her sister. Kate tore it open and read the typed letter twice. She smiled, looked up at her family, and announced the good news. She had achieved two A's and a B, exactly the grades she needed for her first-choice university, Edinburgh. She skipped with joy, threw her arms around her sister, and rushed to phone Emilia and Alice, who had also applied to the Scottish university. For most of the upper sixth, the three best friends had imagined their lives together as students in the Scottish capital. Kate hoped desperately that they had gotten their grades.

Some 8,000 miles away in the Belize jungle, Prince William was also celebrating. The eighteen-year-old prince was on exercise with the Welsh Guards in the South American jungle when he received an e-mail from his housemaster at Eton, Andrew Gailey, telling him that he had achieved an A in geography, a B in history of art, and a C in biology, and most important, a place at the University of St. Andrews to study for a degree in the history of art. His father had already sent an e-mail of congratulations, and back at home Charles told reporters he was delighted with William's results: "I know how hard William worked to achieve these excellent results and I am very proud that he has done so well." St. James's Palace issued a statement confirming the happy news. "Prince William is obviously delighted and relieved that he has got into St. Andrews and is very much looking forward to becoming a student in a year's time."

St. Andrews University is steeped in royal history — the Scottish King James V studied there in the early sixteenth century — but of course when the Palace announced that Prince William was going, the university became world-famous overnight. The compact coastal town of St. Andrews is "a destination rather than a place one stumbles across, because it is so remote," according to the university's former vice chancellor Brian Lang. The population is tiny, just 18,000 residents, and the town is dominated by students. With the news that William was going to be studying there, its popularity rocketed and the university's registrars recorded a 44 percent rise in applications. Coincidentally, the university had just shot up the league table to become the only Scottish university in Britain's top ten elite colleges, ahead of Edinburgh. Delighted to be charged with the education of a future King, a spokesman said, "We are pleased for Prince William as we are for all successful applicants to the University of St. Andrews, and look forward to welcoming him to our community next year," adding that the university would be a "unique, nourishing, and challenging" place to study.

Like Kate, William had initially wanted to study at Edinburgh, where the history of art degree program is considered one of the best in the country. Whereas his father and his uncle Edward had studied at Cambridge, William had been eager to break the mold. He didn't want the academic pressure of studying at Oxford or Cambridge, and he had loved Edinburgh when he visited the campus. The city was considered the party capital of the British Isles and some of William's friends from the Glosse Posse were heading there. But despite William's enthusiasm, both his housemaster and his father had urged him to reconsider. Edinburgh is a large, fast-paced city, where the protection of the prince would be complicated. On their recommendation, William had gone to visit St. Andrews, a smaller, more sheltered university than Edinburgh, where the history of art program also enjoyed a first-class reputation. The Queen's cousin James Ogilvy, the son of Sir Angus Ogilvy and Princess Alexandra, was a former student. He had loved studying there and urged William to take a look. After an informal visit, William agreed it was the right choice.

Kate, however, was set on Edinburgh, and according to her residence house tutor, Miss Gall, who helped Kate complete her Universities and Colleges Admissions Services (UCAS) form, and Jasper Selwyn, the career adviser at Marlborough College, it was the first choice on her UCAS form. "As far as I am aware she had a place confirmed at Edinburgh," said Mr. Selwyn. "She was accepted through the usual UCAS routine. In those days you applied for five courses and got acceptances and rejections depending on your grades. You chose one firm place and one insurance. Kate's firm choice was Edinburgh and that was confirmed." Miss Gall insisted that it was not just the fact that her friends wanted to go that made Kate enthusiastic about going. "She wouldn't have applied to Edinburgh just because her friends were going; it was because of the course. She wanted to read history of art," she said. The arts faculty is regarded as one of the best in Britain and in their final year, the history of art students are given highly coveted work placements at either a gallery or a museum to prepare them for life as a postgraduate.

Although the course was prestigious, the social life was another attraction, and with only six hours of lectures a week, the students, who at the time had the biggest students' union in Britain, were known to spend more of their time in coffee houses or bars, or throwing dinner parties, than studying. Emilia and Alice couldn't wait to move to Edinburgh, but upon receiving her grades, Kate had a dramatic and sudden change of heart. She decided to turn down her place at Edinburgh, take a gap year — a year off — and reapply for St. Andrews.

It was a bold move and very risky, and

rather out of character for Kate. There was
no guarantee that she would get a place in
the history of art program at St. Andrews,
which was oversubscribed now that William
had confirmed his place. Kate was con-
vinced it was the right thing to do and
already had an idea for the first part of her
gap year. Her cousin Lucy, an undergraduate at Bristol, was studying Italian in Florence and had been badgering Kate to join
her, tempting her with the city's historic
art, the opportunity to learn Italian, and the
great social life to be had. It suddenly
seemed too good an opportunity to miss.
Having discussed the idea with her parents
and after outlining her evolving plans for
the rest of the year, she enrolled in a three-
month course to study Italian at the British
Institute in Florence. The program started
in September and ended at Christmas.
There was a voluntary expedition to Chile
that had caught Kate's eye, and she intended to do some research on that as soon
as she sent off her new UCAS form. Her
friends were rather taken aback — it was
unlike Kate to let them down. Knowing they
were going to be undergraduates together
in Edinburgh had kept her, Emilia, and Alice going through their exams, and she knew
that Pippa was planning to apply the next

year. Her decision was rather mysterious, according to her housemistress, Mrs. Patching: "After she left school, Catherine made some different decisions, but why she made those decisions I don't know."

Jasper Selwyn believed that turning down a place at Edinburgh, which was deemed one of the best universities in the United Kingdom, was unusual. "Edinburgh was a very popular choice, St. Andrews less so, probably because it was smaller." Another senior teacher at Marlborough who oversaw the reapplication said that the school was fully supportive of Kate's decision, even if it was somewhat surprising. "The school would have been aware of her reapplying and they would have been involved. She would have reapplied at the end of August or the beginning of September; it was a fairly smooth system. Everything was set up to help her. She decided to reapply, which is fair enough."

Kate was required to turn down her place at Edinburgh formally through UCAS, so Marlborough advised her to write a letter to the university directly as a matter of courtesy. Once she had reapplied to St. Andrews, she packed her bags for Florence. She did have the required grades to get into the history of art program, and it was now more a matter of whether she would be able to gain admission. It seemed every girl in America wanted to come to St. Andrews to search out the prince. Kate would have read the papers. She would have known that William was going and that there was every chance they could be in the same program at the same time if she got a place to study there.

As usual, her parents were wholly encouraging and knew that when Kate set her mind to something, generally it happened. Some royal watchers have claimed that Carole persuaded her daughter to apply to St. Andrews. Society journalist Matthew Bell penned an intriguing article in the *Spectator* after Kate graduated. "Some insiders wonder whether her university meeting with Prince William can really be ascribed to coincidence," he wrote. "Although at the time of making her application to universities it was unknown where the prince was intending to go, it has been suggested that her mother persuaded Kate to reject her first choice on hearing the news and take up her offer at St. Andrews instead." Bell, who claimed he had "a reliable source who knows Kate very well," fueled a frenzy of speculation. The truth is Kate did change her mind and reapplied to St. Andrews, knowing that the prince was going there, but only she truly knows whether her change of heart was because of William.

William had also been allowed some time to unwind before embarking on his vocational gap year. It was July of the new millennium and France had just won the European Football Championships, England having failed to even qualify for the quarterfinals. Despite this bitter blow to national pride, William was enjoying the summer, riding around the country lanes near Highgrove on the new Honda motorbike his father had given him for his eighteenth birthday. The present marked a coming of age, as did his new romance. Rose Farquhar, a student at the nearby Westonbirt School in Gloucestershire and part of the Glosse Posse, had been friends with William for some years. Like William, she had just finished her A-levels, and when one of their nights out had become amorous, they saw no harm in embarking on a summer romance.

However, idyllic as it was — both the summer and their romance — the courtship was brief, for William was to embark on an action-packed year off. Ideally, he had wanted to ride polo ponies in Argentina, but Charles had devised a more educational gap year for his son that was to be both fun and challenging. That August, William left the United Kingdom and headed for Belize for a taste of army life. There, William took part in an operation, code-named Native Trail, deep in the jungle, where he was trained by the Welsh Guards in survival skills, learning how to treat a snakebite and kill a chicken for food. Immediately afterward, he flew to Rodrigues, an island off the coast of Mauritius, a paradise of white sands and warm turquoise waters, a welcome contrast to the humid rain forest of South America. But William wasn't there solely to work on his tan; the Royal Geographical Society operated the Shoals of Capricorn project, and the prince was to spend most of the trip learning about the endangered coral reef. Determined to stay under the radar, he checked into a no-frills guesthouse for a month as "Mr. Brian Woods."

Meanwhile, Kate had arrived in Tuscany in September and was enjoying the dizzying charms of the Renaissance city of Florence. It was her first time living overseas without her family, and Carole had been on the phone to her niece Lucy to make sure everything was in place ahead of Kate's arrival. By a stroke of luck, a room had become available at the apartment Lucy was renting, and the British Institute, which oversees students' accommodation, offered Kate the room for $750 a month.

The apartment was situated in a residential block in the center of town, a stone's throw from the British Institute on the Via della Spada, one of the choicest roads in the city and conveniently located above a delicatessen where the girls could grocery shop. Each morning, just after 8:30 A.M., Kate pushed open the heavy door onto the bustling street, bought herself a cappuccino, and made her way through the beautiful Florentine palazzos to the British Institute. It was balmy and magical, and after her lessons from 9:00 A.M. to 12:00 P.M., she took advantage of the warm afternoons to stroll around the cobbled streets, soaking up the city and its Renaissance treasures. Being in Florence was invaluable, given her choice of university degree, and she relished the opportunity to familiarize herself with the countless masterpieces that were on display around the city in galleries, museums, cathedrals, and churches.

Ever the ambitious student, Kate had signed up for an intermediate course, but languages were not her forte, and after a couple of weeks she dropped down to beginner's Italian so that she could spend less time studying and more time enjoying the delights of the city. She had brought with her a professional camera with a long lens and set about compiling a portfolio of work. Mostly, she shot scenes of city life, spending hours on the busy Ponte Vecchio capturing the hustle and bustle of the Florentines and the city's myriad of tourists as the afternoon sunshine dipped into early evening.

Sharing a house with Lucy and her two other roommates meant Kate was rarely homesick. But several weeks after she arrived, her cousin moved into another apartment in the city. But by then Kate had forged new friendships, and though she was never lonely, she was still pining for Harry. Those who knew her during her time in Florence say she was still heartbroken after the breakup and often talked about her ex-boyfriend. "When Kate arrived, she was really hung up about this boy from Marlborough called Harry," recalled a friend. "She spoke about him all the time. I think he might have broken her heart slightly. He seemed to have blown hot and cold with her when they were at school, and she was always talking about how she could get him back. He was the only boy she talked about, and I don't even think it was that serious.

They definitely didn't sleep together. I got the distinct impression she was still a virgin."

With her wavy brown hair, button nose, and athletic physique, Kate was a hit with the boys and known as "pretty Kate." But she didn't date anyone during her time in Florence, nor did she engage in flirtations with the many handsome young Italian barmen who would ask her out. "Italian bar men would love Kate, and the irony was that because they always fancied her, the rest of the girls used to get free drinks, but Kate would only have one glass," said her friend. "Whenever she went to a bar, the Italians would fall over themselves to serve her. She would handle their compliments very gracefully but would never rise to it. She was very demure, and partly because her Italian wasn't very good, wouldn't respond." Kate found the attention amusing and would giggle at their over-the-top pickup lines, but she simply wasn't interested. "She was very unassuming and young for her age and not really interested in boys," added the friend. "She would attract male attention, but she was shy around boys. When they approached her, she would always get very embarrassed. She never seemed comfortable with the attention. She had an aura about her, and everyone who met her adored her. She knew she was good-looking, but she wasn't arrogant about it."

Although she socialized, Kate wasn't a big drinker, and when her friends went to the famous Caffè Giacosa, the home of the Negroni cocktail, Kate would make a solitary glass of wine last all evening. Occasionally, she would go to the Art Bar next to her apartment, which was famous for its fresh fruit cocktails, but she would never drink to excess. "She'd get giggly and silly after a few glasses, so then she would stop," said a friend. "She was never interested in getting really drunk. She wasn't really a party girl. There was lots of socializing among the British Institute pupils, who were all very well-to-do, posh public-school kids. They would all get rather drunk and silly, but Kate didn't enjoy alcohol. She wasn't uptight or boring, she was really fun and lovely, but going out and getting wasted really wasn't her thing. She never, ever let herself get out of control. While others were often doing drugs around her, she wouldn't be anti or judgmental, in fact she was quite interested in what drugs did to you, but she would never ever try them. I never saw her smoke, either." She rarely went out clubbing but loved to dance and would sometimes go to a member's club called the Blob just behind the Piazza della Signoria.

Although alcohol and drugs did nothing for her, Kate was passionate about food and loved to shop at the *rosticerria* (rotisserie) opposite her apartment that sold delicious home-baked lasagnas and pasta dishes to take out. On Sundays, Kate and her apartment mates treated themselves to a leisurely brunch by the river and then went shopping. The designer boutiques Valentino and Versace were on the road parallel to theirs, but Kate didn't have the money to shop at such expensive boutiques. She had arrived with just one suitcase, and her staple outfit was fitted jeans and V-neck sweaters, which she wore smartly with a Ralph Lauren shirt. "She was very horsey and public school in her fashion," according to one of her girlfriends. "She always wore her hair curly, not straight, and she was curvier than she is now." That might have been because of her love of cooking and the fact that she often prepared dinner parties for her friends in the open-plan kitchen. She would spend hours browsing the local food markets for fresh produce, and like her mother and sister, she was a good cook.

When her parents came to visit in October

2000, they checked into a boutique hotel and treated Kate to dinners at some of Florence's most fashionable restaurants. "Her father, Michael, was quiet, but Carole was very gregarious and would not stop telling Kate how beautiful she had become," recalled a friend. "She had rosebud lips and this amazing mane of hair and she was gorgeous. When they were at dinner, Carole would exclaim to the waiters: 'Look at my English rose. Isn't she so beautiful? What do you think of the waiter, Catherine?' Kate would be cringing in the corner, but she knew it was true."

Like her peers, Kate spent much of the time thinking about the future and pondering what university life might bring. Her friend recalled that she had set her sights on St. Andrews and was waiting to hear if she had been accepted to study there, "She was going off to university, but she had deferred her place. We talked about the fact that William was going to St. Andrews." The prince was a popular topic of discussion after it was speculated in the press that he might be enrolling at the prestigious John Hall Pre-University Course in Florence to brush up on his history of art, before going to St. Andrews. Prince Charles had hosted a lunch at Highgrove that August for the mayor of Florence and a number of well-known Italian dignitaries, who suggested that William, soon to be a history of art student, should visit the city. There was quite a buzz about an imminent royal visitor among the aristocratic crowd in Florence, among them Princess Anne's goddaughter Lady Eloise Anson, who was taking a fine art course and was a popular fixture at the riverside bars. "There were a lot of very well connected posh English girls straight out of boarding school and lots of girls who knew Prince William, or claimed to know him. And there were people in particular who would brag about him all the time, especially as we thought he was going to be coming out to study on the John Hall course," recalled a former student. Kate, however, appeared nonchalant and didn't tell a soul that she had already met William.

While she waited to hear if she had been accepted at St. Andrews, she learned that she had qualified for a place on a volunteering expedition to Patagonia in Chile that was organized by the UK-based company Raleigh International, which coordinates community and environmental projects in South America. Kate had found out about the program through the career department at Marlborough, and being an avid explorer, when she realized she had a whole year to fill before going to her university, had applied for the $4,500 trip. At school she had loved adventuring and hiking, and the Duke of Edinburgh Gold Award had prepared her well.

She felt she was more than equipped to apply for the overseas adventure, and after a preliminary interview, she took part in a tough assessment weekend in the countryside in Oxfordshire, where she had to carry out survival exercises and sleep underneath a tarp, with only a ration pack for sustenance. Some weeks later, she was informed she would be heading to Coyhaique, the small capital of Region XI, where Raleigh is based, at the start of the new year. By coincidence, it also happened to be the very same destination to which William would be heading in October.

Prince William returned home from Rodrigues at the end of September, but he had an onerous task to carry out before he left Chile. The British media had agreed to leave William alone during his gap year in return for some controlled access to him, and on September 29, William gave his first solo press conference at his father's Gloucestershire home. While Charles hovered protectively, William, dressed in his jeans and a sweater that he tugged at nervously, faced the press gang. The reporters asked him about his trip to Rodrigues and how he was enjoying his gap year, while the photographers snapped away. For someone who hated the limelight, William handled the situation admirably. He had learned from his mother that saying too much could backfire badly, but he also knew he had to give the newspapers "a line." The reporters got their story, and pictures of the suntanned prince graced the pages the following morning.

But Fleet Street had missed its scoop. Just days later, on October 1, 2000, William boarded a British Airways plane going from Gatwick to Santiago. The trip had been kept top secret, and St. James's Palace only announced the prince was leaving at the very last moment. Malcolm Sutherland, who was in charge of the expedition, said, "The whole aim was to get him out to Chile on expedition just a few days before announcing it. It was a very well-kept secret." Mr. Sutherland went to Clarence House, Prince Charles's London residence, where William and Harry had their own private living quarters, to meet with the prince ahead of his departure. In the privacy of William's apartment, he warned the young royal that Raleigh was not for the fainthearted. He would be working and living with 103 young volunteers from all walks of life. Some were part of Raleigh's "at risk" program and included former drug addicts and recovering alcoholics. Others, like William, had just finished their A-levels and wanted a stimulating challenge. Kate was one of the latter, but unlike William, who was fast-tracked, she had to endure the grueling selection process.

William was in Chile for three months. From the moment he arrived, he threw himself into his new surroundings and got to know the other people on his trip. According to Logistics Manager Graham Hornsey, who has led an impressive thirty-five expeditions and came to know William well, the prince proved to be a very grounded and decent young man: "William coped very well, and what struck me about him was how normal he was. He said he wanted to be treated like everyone else, and he was. When you saw him cleaning the toilets, it wasn't for the cameras, he really did clean the lavatories." During his time in Tortel, a small coastal town, William oversaw the construction of a fire station, and he tracked huemul, an endangered species of South Andean deer in the Tamango National Park. The most challenging expedition of all was sea kayaking up to 12 miles a day through the deep ocean fjords of Patagonia. In the remote wilderness of the Patagonian countryside, William could be himself. For the first time he didn't need to wear the electronic tag that enabled his protection officers to monitor his every move. On the snowcapped mountains, he was free — and he reveled in the moment.

Kate boarded a British Airways flight to Chile just days after William landed back in Britain, having completed his time there. Once again their paths had come tantalizingly close to crossing, and it was one of the many coincidences that would come to define their romance. According to Mr. Sutherland, Kate could not have known William was going to Chile when she applied for the program, because her application would have been submitted before he left in October. "That's the bizarre thing about it. Her application would have been well and truly complete before the announcement by St. James's Palace that William was going out there," he said.

Kate arrived at base camp in Coyhaique on a bitterly cold day in January 2001. Before she left, she had received a letter from St. Andrews confirming that she had a place there and was able to enjoy a lively family Christmas at Oak Acre. Delighted and relieved to know that she hadn't jeopardized her chance of studying, she looked forward to the next part of her gap year. She had spent the holidays shopping for all-weather clothes and equipment suitable for extreme climates, and she had spent a small fortune acquiring everything on the checklist.

Arriving in Coyhaique, Kate donned her navy blue Raleigh fleece and took part with gusto in the ice-breaking games. According to Mr. Sutherland, she fitted in from day one. "I remember her well; she was level-headed, she kept her head down and got on with things. She didn't make a name for herself for the wrong reasons. She got stuck in with the rest of her team. She was rather like William actually, reserved but in a nice way. There was no arrogance about her. She would pool together and make things happen. She made friends quickly and gravitated towards the people I suppose she could relate to." Although she didn't stand out as one of the big personalities of the team, Kate did make an impression, and Graham Hornsey recalled her being a "big achiever. . . . She was proactive when it came to projects. It was largely down to the Venturers to set their targets and Kate aimed high."

Unlike William, Kate didn't take part in the sea kayaking or tracking the endangered huemul deer. Instead, she conducted a marine survey on the south coast with British and Chilean scientists. An adept amateur sailor, she quickly mastered how to use the small, uncomfortable — but powerful — inflatable Zodiac boats to navigate the choppy, freezing waters in order to survey the flora and the fauna of the inlets. There were no sanitary facilities, and Kate washed in a bucket of cold water and survived off ration packs. Robin Vincent Smith, the assistant logistics manager on the trip, recalled how competent Kate was despite the difficult conditions. She knew how to pitch a tent and make a campfire and was able to cope with walking long distances. "It was cold and wet and we were sleeping in tents on the beach. We would get up very early in the morning and make porridge on a campfire, then get into the Zodiacs and drive out to the fjords in Puerto Yungay. We'd go quite a distance and they weren't the easiest boats to drive or particularly easy places to reach, but I remember Catherine and her group learned to navigate the boats quickly. We

127

were in the middle of nowhere in very extreme conditions. It was one of the hardest expeditions I have done; even lighting campfires was hard work because it was so wet and damp. The waters were choppy, and we used to wear oilskins and rubber suits because the regular hiking clothes were just not good enough to keep us warm and dry."

Although some of the volunteers protested and even broke down, Kate never complained, even when she had gone without a hot shower for weeks on end. "She was mature enough to cope with the experience. You could just tell that she was very with it," said Mr. Sutherland. Like William, she spent her free time reading, listening to music in her tent, and writing letters home. She struck up friendships, and according to Rachel Humphreys, an interpreter on the trip, she was popular with the boys: "She had a certain presence. She was a very mature girl, attractive and popular, particularly with the boys. But she was always in control of herself and impeccably behaved."

Understandably, the prince was a topic of much interest, having left Chile only a few weeks before the new recruits arrived. But though some were curious about his time in Chile, Kate didn't ask about the prince at all. "People were very respectful of William and the fact that he wanted the trip to be private," said Mr. Sutherland. "It was the only time he was going to have a normal experience, and there was a feeling among the volunteers that they weren't going to talk about it. William loved being in Chile, he loved the fact that it was so remote and cut off. He merged into the masses and was part of the team."

For Kate, the highlight of the trip was teaching Chilean children at a local primary school once a week in the village of Tortel, where, like William, she was involved in building one of two fire stations. Despite not speaking Spanish, Kate found other ways to communicate with the children, drawing them pictures and acting things out. "Kate loved it and made it a lot of fun," recalled Mr. Sutherland. "She was very patient in the classroom, and she had a very easygoing approach. . . . She also loved the final part of her tour, trekking in the Patagonia hills. She seemed to really enjoy the solitude and being out in the wilderness. That was a parallel between her and William. Actually I think they are both very similar. They are reserved but in a positive way and very thoughtful. You can see why they work so well together."

When she returned home at the end of

March, Kate was tinged with sadness that the adventure was over. It had been a long, tough but rewarding ten months, but now she had to settle back into "real" life. She had helped contribute to the cost of the trip, so with her savings account somewhat depleted, she needed to secure a summer job. Although her parents were generous and Kate never wanted for anything, money wasn't just handed out and Kate knew that she was expected to earn her keep. Her father suggested she apply for a job working at Ocean Village Marina in Southampton, where he had heard there were positions for deckhands on board Challenger boats. Despite the fact that Kate's sailing experience only extended to family holidays in Norfolk and, once they had come into money, Barbados, she loved being out at sea, and according to Sir Chay Blyth, the former round-the-world yachtsman and then–managing director of the hospitality business, Kate got a job as a deckhand from June until the end of the summer. "Kate applied the usual way and would have submitted her CV and been interviewed, although she would likely have come via a recommendation."

During the warm summer of 2001, while William was on a four-month work placement at the Lewa Downs conservation park in Kenya, Kate was causing something of a stir in sunny Southampton. Working for the BT Global Challenge Yacht, where Princess Anne is the patron and the famous sailor Ellen MacArthur came up through the ranks, was prestigious. Kate was privileged to be working with seasoned professionals, several of whom had sailed around the world, and fortunate to be in the company of many students, who, like her, had taken summer jobs ahead of their fall university studies. Each morning and evening, she was required to wash down decks, and in no time at all, she had amassed an army of male admirers, due to her habit of hosing down the yacht wearing the briefest pair of shorts. With her long, tanned legs and tumbling brown hair, Kate stood out and was so eye-catching she would often bring the parking lot to a standstill as visitors admired her statuesque form. "Kate had a reputation for being very pretty and for wearing very short shorts, and she had a great set of pins," joked Sir Chay. "She was singled out for being a stunning girl, and she was a favorite with the crew, which was mostly male."

Kate spent four months working on different Challengers, but most of the time she was onboard the seventy-two-foot-long *Isle of Man,* earning $75 a day. The hours were long — she was on the deck at 7:00 A.M. and never finished before 6:00 P.M. She took her meals on the boat and slept in a sparse and very small cabin in a bunk bed she shared with a fellow female deckhand. Kate was under the joint command of South African–born skipper Cal Tomlinson and his British counterpart, David Melville. The boats were hired out by businesses eager to treat their clients to a day of luxurious hospitality, culminating in an afternoon racing on the Solent, the strait that separates the Isle of Wight from the mainland of England. As well as washing the decks, Kate was expected to help load the 660-pound catering boxes on board and wash and pack away the sails at the end of the day. "It was backbreaking work," said Mr. Tomlinson. "Kate mucked in and was very professional. She fitted right in, although she did stand out for being so pretty. She spoke well, she was very attractive, and she had an air about her. She was competent and confident but very unassuming. She was polite and respectful to whoever was in charge of her and neat as a pin. She never wore any makeup; she was naturally beautiful."

Greeting the guests as they came on

board, Kate was a very popular hostess. After instructing them to take off their shoes, she showed them through to the main deck, where they were offered a glass of champagne before lunch. Before they set sail, Kate was sometimes required to carry out an onboard safety demonstration. It was something her mother used to enjoy doing when she worked as a flight attendant, and Kate laughed at the fact that she was now doing the same thing. She didn't see the funny side, however, when some of the crew played a practical joke on her. "When she pulled the toggle, the thing inflated and a load of condoms fell out," recalled Mr. Tomlinson, who witnessed the moment. "She was mortified and very embarrassed. She took it more seriously than the others might have, but she wasn't thrown off her stride. She was angry at first, but she settled down, and I don't remember her ever getting her own back."

The Challenger crews were the life and soul of Ocean Village, and after work they socialized in Southampton, congregating at Los Marinos, a lively late-night bar at the local cineplex. Kate rarely went out, but when she did, she would often stay on the periphery. "Ours wasn't a party boat and Kate wasn't out partying every night," said

First Mate Paul Horsford. "She wasn't aloof, but she wasn't part of the 24/7 Ocean Village lifestyle. I don't remember her drinking at all. She was always very professional and very private, and very careful with what she said. We got along very well and spoke about most things. I was a lot older than her and her skipper, so we mostly talked about sailing."

Kate loved being on the open water, and as an amateur sailor she was eager to learn more. Over the course of the summer, she learned how to heave a line, throwing a long thick rope to a neighboring yacht for hours. Astonished by how far it could be thrown out to sea, she loved competing against the others to see who could heave the farthest. "She was keen to hone her big-boat skills and develop herself as a sailor," said Mr. Tomlinson. "She made no bones about that. She was a naturally competent person and you could tell she had been sailing before. She was no fool . . . and had a good head on her shoulders. She was keen to learn and she had the right attitude."

Although she didn't integrate much with her colleagues socially, Kate did strike up a friendship with a fellow deckhand named Ian Henry, who escorted her on the rare occasions she did go out. "He thought he was in with a chance. He was a nice, good-looking guy and he had his own car, which was a rarity for a crew member," recalled one of Kate's team. "He was sweet on Kate, but somebody was delegated to tell him to back off because she wasn't interested. As far as I know she wasn't seeing anyone." Mr. Henry never spoke about the alleged romance to the press, insisting he and Kate had only ever been "very good friends."

With university just weeks away, the deckhands joked with Kate, asking if she planned to make a beeline for Prince William. "Towards the end of the season, the onboard conversations turned to the future, and she told us she was going to St. Andrews," said Mr. Tomlinson. "We all knew William was going there, and we asked if she would be seeing him. She told us she was going to be in the same hall as him and when some of the crew teased her and said, 'Are you going to go for it?' she just smiled and shrugged her shoulders. That was the last that was said about it. We had no idea at the time we were looking at the future Queen of England."

Although Kate gave nothing away to her colleagues, she was more candid with Mr. Horsford, who had become avuncular during their time together.

"We spoke about Prince William," Mr. Horsford revealed. "I said, 'Obviously you might meet him,' and she said, 'I've already met him once or twice before.'" The admission surprised Mr. Horsford. He and Kate had worked together all summer, and although she had talked about going to St. Andrews, she had never mentioned knowing William until then. Bragging wasn't her style, and she was intuitive enough to realize that if she wanted to stay friends with the prince, discretion was the way forward. It was exactly the foresight that ensured that when they did next meet at St. Salvator's Hall, William trusted her from the start.

Carole Middleton poses proudly with her baby daughter who was as good as gold and known as Catherine until she went to university. (© Rex Features)

Kate described her time at St. Andrews Prep School as "some of my happiest years." Here she is (*first on left*), age 13, with her classmates and favorite tutor, Kevin Allford.

Kate (*top row, center*) loved sports and played Goal Defense for the school netball team. Her mother Carole also played Goal Attack in a teachers' and parents' team.

Kate (*far right*) loved her time at Marlborough College and made friends for life. A boarder at Elmhurst house, her favorite tutor, Ann Patching, says she was popular and talented. (© Solo Syndication)

Kate (*top row, fourth from left*) was a skilled hockey player and made the school's top team together with her younger sister Pippa. (© ExclusivePix)

Kate's first boyfriend Harry Blakelock was in the year above her at Marlborough School. When they split up, Kate was heartbroken. (© Rob Rich/SocietyAllure.com)

Kate spent three months in Chile working for the voluntary organization Raleigh International just like Prince William. She is remembered for being a team worker and a competent sailor.

RIGHT: It was at St. Andrews University in Scotland where Kate, who was voted the prettiest fresher in her year, first caught William's eye. He invited her to breakfast and their friendship grew from then on.

LEFT: Having discovered a passion for pasta in Florence during her gap year, Kate and her friend Laura Warshauer enjoyed pasta parties in St. Salvator's Hall.

RIGHT: Kate and her friend Olivia Bleasdale, one of the "Glosse Posse," dress as schoolgirls for a Harry Potter themed party in their first year at St. Andrews.

LEFT: Fresh faced and make-up free Kate was nicknamed "beautiful Kate." Some girls were jealous of her close friendship with William and were unkind to Kate.

RIGHT: Kate dated Rupert Finch, a popular rugby player and third year law student, when she was a fresher. They were known as the golden couple at St. Andrews.

Kate and William enjoy a day out at the Beaufort Polo Club in June 2005. They didn't know if their relationship would survive post-university, but they were determined to make it work. (© Rex Features)

LEFT: Kate caught Prince William's eye when she took part in a charity fashion show. She daringly decided to turn her see through skirt into a dress moments before she strutted down the runway. (© Malcolm Clarke/Daily Mail/Rex Features)

The hard work pays off and Kate receives a 2-1 degree in the History of Art. Her proud parents, Carol and Michael, were in the audience along with the Royal Family, who had come to see Prince William graduate at the same ceremony. (Kate © Newsphoto/ Alamy; William © Anwar Hussein/ WireImage/ Getty Images)

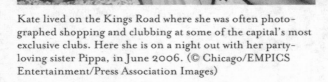

Kate lived on the Kings Road where she was often photo-graphed shopping and clubbing at some of the capital's most exclusive clubs. Here she is on a night out with her party-loving sister Pippa, in June 2006. (© Chicago/EMPICS Entertainment/Press Association Images)

ABOVE: As a royal girlfriend Kate was followed everywhere by the paparazzi. On the morning of her 25th birthday there were rumors the couple were about to announce their engagement and Kate had to battle her way past the cameras to drive to work. (© Mark Cuthbert/Getty Images)

RIGHT: William draws Kate in for a tender embrace on the slopes of Klosters in January 2006. Happy and in love, the usually camera shy prince throws caution and royal protocol to the wind and kisses his girlfriend. (© Scott Hornby/The Sun/News Syndication)

RIGHT: The pressure of being in the limelight was sometimes too much for Kate and William, who seemed distant from each other at the Cheltenham Festival Race in March 2007. Weeks later William announced they had split up. (© Stephen Lock/Rex Features)

LEFT: Newly single, Kate took part in a charity dragon boat race, but when the event turned into a media circus she pulled out at the eleventh hour. (© Max Mumby/Indigo/Getty Images)

BELOW: At the Concert for Diana in August 2007, William and Kate were secretly back together but they sat in separate rows in the royal box to avoid being photographed together. Kate danced with her sister Pippa and brother James instead. (© Alpha)

CHAPTER 5
AN "UNDIE" GRADUATE AT ST. ANDREWS

Standing amid the throng of excited freshers in Younger Hall, the very place she would eventually stand in her graduation ceremony, Kate listened as Brian Lang, the principal and vice chancellor of St. Andrews University, delivered his welcoming address.

After telling his nervous students that they would need to work hard and behave themselves, his tone softened: "And if you do work hard," he said, "you will enjoy a good social life here." He paused. "In fact, look around you. You could, at this very moment, be looking at your future spouse." The undergraduates glanced around and exchanged shy smiles. Even if they weren't looking at their future husbands and wives, these would likely be their friends for life.

It was early September, the weather was still mild, and Kate and her fellow undergraduates planned to make the most of the late summer before the temperature

dropped and the small coastal town prepared to shiver through winter. Despite being so exposed to the elements, St. Andrews
University is an attractive option for many
students — it has an excellent academic
reputation and is well known for caring for
and nurturing its students. As the town is
so remote and relatively small, the university
community is well integrated within the
town. Along with all freshers, Kate had
already signed the Sponsio Academica, an
oath of commitment to respect university
life, preserve its reputation, and look out for
other students. And this year, most unusually, students had also been asked to sign a
confidentiality agreement on enrollment.
There was already a united feeling of common purpose in the hall, and when Brian
Lang ended his talk, as he did each year, by
quietly asking the students to respect each
other's privacy, there was an added degree
of poignancy to his request. Everyone in the
hall knew that very soon, their lives would
be touched in some way by the arrival of
the most famous undergraduate the university had seen in many years.

Like everyone else present, Kate knew that
William Wales — as he was to be known —
had not yet arrived, having made a decision
to join his fellow students after Freshers'

Week. The university hierarchy was nervous about the media storm that would greet Prince William's arrival and, together with the Palace, had made an agreement with the press that they could have limited, managed access to the prince if they left him alone for the rest of the time. William himself was well aware that even with this agreement in place, his participation in Freshers' Week might provoke a media frenzy and spoil things for the other students, and anyway, he was doubtful of the benefits of the pre-term partying, later saying, "I thought I would probably end up in a gutter completely wrecked, and the people I had met that week wouldn't end up being my friends anyway."

For Kate, the end of Vice Chancellor Lang's speech marked the beginning of a hectic week of partying, meeting her "university parents" — older pupils who were in charge of looking after freshers — finding her way around the town, and settling into her residence hall. After a year of freedom and adventure, she was ready to begin life as an undergraduate. In between parties and Orientation Week events, Kate made Room A-31, her first-floor, corner bedroom, feel homey and welcoming. A practiced photographer, she put up a collage of photos — all framed with neat white borders — that she had taken of her family, friends, and travels in her gap year, with room to add more as she charted her university days. She and her roommate, Sarah Bates, got to know each other, chatting about their school days and people they knew in common. Sarah was also a boarding-school girl but very much into shooting, hunting, and fishing, and though the two young women got along well, their social lives took slightly different routes.

Kate had picked her accommodation wisely. St. Salvator's — or Sallies, as it is nicknamed — is a beautiful, Oxbridge-style residence hall and one of the last at St. Andrews that continues long-standing traditions, such as a formal dinner at High Table once a week. Most of the rooms have glorious views of the lawn, the North Sea, or St. Andrew's Castle, and the facilities — the well-resourced library, the stained-glass wooden-paneled dining hall, the pool and ping-pong tables, and an old-style common room, complete with open fire, a grand piano, and daily newspapers — allow the students to get to know each other. Kate soon found her way around and was often seen relaxing in the common room, curled up in an armchair, a cup of tea in hand, either reading newspaper articles her father rather touchingly mailed to her or getting to know her fellow hall mates.

Kate had to make an effort to get to know people, but as Freshers' Week drew to a close, William moved into Room B-31 on the floor above her, surrounded by a ready-made group of friends, some of whom were, like him, Old Etonians. Known immediately as the "Sallies Boys," they included Fergus Boyd, Ollie Chadwyck-Healey, Charlie Nelson, and Oli Baker. It certainly didn't take them long to spot "Beautiful Kate," as she had been crowned by the other Sallies residents at the end of Freshers' Week. She was initially more reserved than many of the other young women, but her natural beauty was apparent. Tanned from a recent holiday in Barbados with her parents, fit from her regular early morning run or swim, and dressed in her comfortable Hennes jeans, fitted sweater, and signature cowboy boots, she radiated an outer freshness and an inner confidence.

It took William a couple of weeks to summon up the courage to ask Kate to join him and his friends for breakfast. He immediately remembered her, and they quickly discovered they had plenty in common besides their mutual friends. They were both

141

health conscious, always opting for a breakfast of muesli and fruit over the cooked option; they discussed sports and skiing trips; they compared notes on their gap year experiences in Chile; and they talked about the different courses they planned to take in the history of art program. Kate got along well with the rest of the Sallies Boys, and within a couple of weeks, she was hanging out with the "Yahs," as the other students called them, sitting side by side on the long benches in the canteen eating meals with them, socializing in hall or going for drinks at Ma Bells or the West Port, the most popular student haunts in town.

Both Kate and William became friendly with an American student, Laura Warshauer, who lived down the corridor from Kate and was at St. Andrews for a year to study history of art. In shock after hearing the horrific news that many people in her hometown, New York City, had been killed in the catastrophic 9/11 terrorist attacks on the Twin Towers, she was comforted by her fellow students, including both William and Kate. Laura was a talented musician, composing and singing songs on her guitar. William would pop into her room to listen to her jamming, and Kate borrowed a tripod and camera to help Laura make an audition tape to send back to the States. But music wasn't Laura's only allure. "Will would often come to my room in search of cookies and hot chocolate," she remembered. "I was known for always having food supplies, and I would often cook for us in halls." Having developed a love of pasta in Florence, one of Kate's favorite pastimes was to join Laura for her popular lasagna parties, at which everyone would gather around and eat "on the floor of the halls just outside my bedroom door. Will, Ollie, and Fergus turned up once and brought plastic wine glasses from Woolworth's. Will seemed to really enjoy it."

As the term took shape, Kate immersed herself in university life. Her courses were stimulating and she was hardworking, eager to learn more about the art of Renaissance Europe, twentieth-century paintings, and critical approaches in art history. She was a diligent student and often took notes for William when he was unable to attend lectures, going over them later in the comfort of the common room, as the autumnal evenings gathered in around them. It soon became clear to others that they enjoyed a special connection. According to a former student, lots of people made jokes about it: "We would joke to her, 'Bet you'll be wearing a tiara soon!' " Others were less kind: "Some of the girls in her year weren't very nice to her. There was a lot of bitching behind her back. Kate hated that, I think because she was bullied at school. She wasn't at all bitchy, she was always very lovely to everyone, but the other girls, and most of them were society 'Yahs,' thought they should be with William and they were jealous that Kate was so close to him."

If, for a relatively quiet student like Kate, surviving the hurly-burly of Freshers' Week had been tough, then navigating her way through the university's infamous "Raisin Weekend" — the wild, carnivalesque first-year initiation during which academic "mothers and fathers" dress up and chaperone their "children" through a weekend of partying, culminating in the largest outdoor shaving-cream fight on the planet — was scary. As Michael Choong, a close friend of both William and Kate, remembered, "Raisin Weekend starts on Sunday morning with a champagne breakfast, and drinking continues through to the early hours of Monday, when the foam fight starts at noon in the Quad. Kate and I ended up at the same party on Raisin Weekend because my academic mum knew Kate's academic mum. It was the first time I met

Kate. We were both nervous but also excited. It was like a rite of passage into St. Andrew's society. It was a huge amount of fun. Kate was quite shy, not overly gregarious. She didn't wear much makeup, she was in jeans and a blouse. We all ended up swapping clothes, covered in felt-tip all over our faces and all over our arms. It was an entire weekend of parties . . . The first semester was full of trepidation, you were finding your feet, it was all about discovery. I remember from Freshers' Week onwards, we basically just ended up going out for twenty nights in a row."

When it came to socializing, William kept a low profile. Having declined to join in the Raisin Weekend festivities, he preferred to spend the evenings with his friends in Sallies, enjoying dinner parties rather than nights out at the clubs in the town. William was, naturally, cautious about those who tried to befriend him and had a built-in system of vetting people, planting red herrings to catch anyone he suspected of selling stories about him. He kept his distance from the many clubs and societies on offer to the students, although he did join the water polo team, and in order to keep his swimming technique up, swam each morning, with Kate, at the luxurious Old Course

Hotel. Within a few weeks of the first semester, their friendship was firmly established, and as Laura Warshauer noticed, "They had each other's backs and looked out for each other."

This was certainly true during Oli "Hairy" Baker's party in October of the first term. As Laura recalled, "Kate and I were eating brownies. Kate was never a big drinker, she didn't need alcohol to give her confidence. Will was getting really hit on by this girl at the party, and it was getting quite uncomfortable because he couldn't shake her off. He was being really polite, but this girl just didn't get the hint. All of a sudden Kate came up behind him and put her arms around him. He said 'Oh, sorry, but I've got a girlfriend,' and he and Kate went off giggling. He mouthed 'Thanks so much' to her in a really exaggerated way, but Kate was the only girl in the room who could have done that. And that was just a month after we started university."

Kate, however, was a long way from being William's girlfriend. She had attracted a number of admirers in Sallies: "Guys would go the canteen for breakfast and eye up Kate," remembered Michael Choong, and she had already turned down Al (Alexander) Smith, a first-year student who took a

146

psychology course with her. They had become friendly during Freshers' Week, and like most of the boys in their year, Al had developed a crush on Kate. "It started off as a flirtation before Al plucked up the courage to ask Kate out," remembered one former student. "She turned him down, albeit very nicely. He was a little bit heartbroken but they stayed good friends."

Al Smith recalled Kate as being bubbly and beautiful. "Kate and I met in the first week. We were academic siblings — my friend was our joint academic father. We went out a few times as a group to some local bars and had a lot of fun. Kate was very striking and beautiful. She was bubbly and open and very likable. A lot of boys fancied her and asked her out. We got to know each other well. She was a very conscientious student and always turned up for lectures in her first year. She got good grades and gave up psychology at the end of her first year to concentrate on history of art."

Another first-year student, Sam Butcher, a devoted rugby player, also had designs on Kate. "Sam was charming and very sociable and came from Blackpool," recalled a former student. "He was very popular and he really fancied Kate. He sent her a saucy text and asked her out, but he didn't get a reply."

Kate had her romantic sights set elsewhere. Rupert Finch — otherwise known as "Finchy" or "Blue Hat Wonder" — was a handsome fourth-year law student. Never without his blue Oakley cap, Rupert was part of a boarding-school group that lived in Flat 2, The Scores. Tall, swarthy, and extremely desirable, he and Kate soon became an item. According to Michael Choong, "All the blokes loved Kate and all the girls loved Rupert. They were a golden couple. He would have crazy parties at his house, and all-night drinking sessions following nights at Ma Bells, when the vodka bottle came out." Kate had found herself a popular, older boyfriend, and while she was focused on her studies and committed to her hockey training and fitness regimen, she was enjoying a lively social life. The first term was going well for Kate.

Despite being happy to be going out with Rupert, it soon became apparent to those around her that Kate was wary of the other female friends in William's life. Unsurprisingly, he had no end of students interested in him. Many girls had gone to extreme lengths to meet him, even trying to change their degree program in order to attend history of art lectures. But being linked with women was no ordinary matter for the future King of England. He knew from past experience that any whiff of romance was pounced upon by the press and had the potential to cause both him and the young woman distress. Their families would be hounded and their every move charted. His summer romance with Rose Farquhar had remained secret — and did so for many years — but his more recent relationship with Arabella Musgrave, a member of the Glosse Posse and the daughter of Major Nicholas Musgrave, who managed the Cirencester Park Polo Club in Gloucestershire, was headline news. William had dated Arabella the summer before he started at the university, and the press had gotten wind of the romance, which came to a natural end when William left for Scotland. He wanted to be free to have fun, and one of the first girls he spotted was the Texan heiress Meghann Gunderman — known as Gundy. When William asked her out — something he did not do lightly — it came as somewhat of a shock when she declined his advances. This seemed to make him want her more. One student remembered, "I heard William ask her out on a date, but she wasn't interested at all and she turned him down. He kept saying, 'Why won't you go out with me?' She wasn't having it."

Soon after this setback, while auditioning for a part in an adaptation of J. D. Salinger's novel *Franny and Zooey*, William met Carley Massy-Birch, an English language and creative writing student in the year ahead of him. Having enjoyed performing in school plays, William had noticed posters around town inviting male students to audition for one of two parts in the play. Accompanied at a distance by his protection officers, he bicycled to the Byer Theatre and, according to one of the directors, Andrew Sands, "He gave an audition and read from the script, as everyone else did. And it was quite a hard piece — he was in the bath talking to his mother. He wasn't nervous, he looked really good, and he delivered an amazing recital. Zooey is a bit of a fragile existential type and William got into it — he did it very well." William didn't end up getting the part — the play was only on for four nights in the tiny theater, and the production team felt that it would be unfair to the theater's regular audiences if the auditorium was packed with hordes of press every night.

William was already on the fringes of the thespian set. His close friend Fergus was a talented actor, and William loyally went to see whatever he was appearing in. However, after his audition he became more involved, smitten by Carley, an active member of the Drama Society. Raised on a farm in Axminster, in Devon, she described herself as "a country bumpkin." She was also extremely modest, as she was often praised for her sharp intellect and her arresting natural beauty. Unlike Meghann, Carley was eager to go out with him, and William was soon bicycling to her house on Crail Lane, where they got to know each other better over coffee and cakes at Cherry's café at the end of her road. Often, Carley would cook supper for them, and they were frequently seen drinking pints of cider at the Castle pub on North Street.

Whereas things between Rupert and Kate were pretty straightforward, being together was more complicated for William and Carley. As the first term drew to a close, Carley felt unable to continue, unsettled by the covertness of their relationship and also by William's inability to truly forget Arabella. And it wasn't just Arabella herself whom William appeared to be pining for. He missed his friends from home, weekends in Gloucestershire, and clubbing in London. Here, in the small town of St. Andrews, even though the press was generally respectful of his privacy, William found himself under the public gaze wherever he went. He was still rattled by the embarrassing furor when his uncle Edward's TV company, Ardent Productions, breached the media ban and tried to film him covertly during the first term, and he felt constantly spied upon. There were countless students — particularly ones from overseas — who would spend a fortune on new wardrobes and drink only at the most fashionable bars in the hope of spotting him and the well-meaning townspeople, who would stop and openly stare if they saw their future King bicycling to a lecture. Toward the end of the first term, William began to have serious doubts about life as an undergraduate and vowed to talk to his father as soon as he returned home for the Christmas vacation.

But before any big decisions needed to be made, there were parties to enjoy, including the most talked about one of the term. Both William and Kate were part of a select group invited by the Scottish heiress Hermione Wemyss to her parents' castle in Fife for a charity promises-style auction and party. The atmosphere inside Wemyss Castle was "insane," according to one guest: "There were van Dycks that had been sprayed with cobwebs." Laura Warshauer recalled, "Everyone was dressed up as school kids, and it was a Harry Potter theme. Kate was adorable in a pink sweater with a white buttoned-down shirt, a baseball cap, and a little skirt." Kate had volunteered her services as a girl Friday and lined up on the castle's grand staircase with the other "promises." As Laura recalled, there was a tangible connection between William and Kate as she came down the stairs. "They really had eyes on each other that night and William, dressed in a sweeping cape, bid $300 for a date with Kate. They spent the rest of the night dancing together, and though it was very innocent and nothing happened, there were sparks." At the end of the evening, Kate was driven back to the residence hall with William by his protection officer, but they went back to their respective rooms. The next morning, they both left St. Andrews — William giving Kate and Laura a lift to the airport — to return home for Christmas.

The holidays passed quickly. For Kate, it was a chance to recharge her batteries, catch up with her friends, get the gossip from Pippa and James as to the goings on at Marlborough, and spend a relaxing Christmas and New Year's Day with her parents. For

William, things were more turbulent, as he talked his future through with Prince Charles and his former housemaster at Eton College, Dr. Gailey. They listened carefully to William and concluded that quite apart from the problems associated with feeling hemmed in at St. Andrews, William was not being inspired by his history of art course of study. After much discussion — in which his father shared his own difficult experiences of adapting to undergraduate life at Cambridge, and his grandfather, Prince Philip, issued a characteristic warning to "knuckle down and not wimp out" — it was decided, in conjunction with the university administration, that William would return to St. Andrews in January 2002. He was to remain in Sallies, where he was actually happy and comfortable, but would switch to pure geography, a subject he had excelled in and enjoyed while at school and had already been studying at St. Andrews as part of the broader Scottish system. This seemed like a good compromise, and William felt decidedly more optimistic about his undergraduate days ahead.

Returning to St. Andrews at the end of January 2002, a couple of weeks after her twentieth birthday, Kate learned that she had been chosen as one of the models for the upcoming Don't Walk fashion show. Back in November, Kate — along with two of her close friends and another four hundred or so hopefuls — had auditioned for the charity show that was taking place at the end of March and was one of the most important fixtures in the St. Andrews calendar. A fellow student, Charlie Moretti, more used to directing serious plays and building atmospheric stage sets, had been "tasked with rebooting the fashion show," the purpose of which was to raise money for charity — in 2002, for breast cancer and juvenile diabetes. Until now the show had been low key, with a bunch of students getting donations from local shops and railroading their friends to model, but with his characteristic theatrical flair, Charlie had decided to change all this and stage a more upscale show. He approached local and national designers and, somewhat ambitiously, got the national press involved. "All they wanted to know was whether William was going to be there, but I wasn't allowed to say because of the media deal," he recalled.

Kate passed the audition because of her natural good looks and fabulous figure, but she was also — as Andrew Sands, a member of the production team, testified — "in the right crowd," able to "bring the rich play cats to the show." There was no doubt in anyone's mind that the evening would have an edge if William were to attend, and though Charlie Moretti played water polo on the prince's team, they needed as many open avenues as possible. They all knew that Kate was as close to William as it got. Indeed, at the start of the second term, when it came to sorting out accommodations for the second year, William had asked Kate, Fergus, and Olivia Bleasdale to share a house with him — an invitation Kate had accepted. In the weeks leading up to the big night, there was much anticipation as to whether or not William would come.

Andrew Sands choreographed the show and decided who would walk down the runway: "The show was at the Student Union, which was very unglamorous. It's where the local disco The Bop was held. It was an uninspiring 1970s building. It was a blank canvas, and we created the mood we wanted. We had an uncomplicated central runway with tables around it. The top tables were closest to the catwalk and were offered to people in the show and sold out immediately. Kate was given a table, and she invited William and his good friend, Adam England, along with some others. It raised an eyebrow that she had invited William and definitely caused a bit of a stir." The price of the tickets was not prohibitive — between $23 and $38 each, with a table of up to ten people costing $300.

Preparations for the show were time-consuming, and Kate had to attend several rehearsals, during which she was taught to walk like a model, had her clothes fitted, and was paired up with appropriate runway partners, one of them being Fergus. Charlie had managed to secure donations from the fashion house Chloe, as well as some well-known French labels and some new, younger designers, among them Sophie McElligott and Charlotte Todd. Kate was given one of Charlotte's sheer skirts to wear, along with about eight other changes, from black underwear to more formal creations. This was a new world to Kate, but as Andrew Sands remembers, nothing was too much for her: "She was actually a great model, she put up with a lot of diva tantrums that always accompanied the show. She was always on time, smiley and polite, and wasn't diva-ish at all. She wasn't political and didn't try and befriend people on the committee, which plenty of others did. She was amazingly confident and didn't ask for huge amounts of guidance or fish for compliments. She wasn't nervous or panicky on the night, she was very self-contained."

When it came to the evening itself, Sophie Butler, the local hairdresser who did Kate's hair for the show, was backstage with the models: "We worked really hard before the show. On the actual night, it was really just tonging and putting in the colored straw ribbons we braided into the hair, which I had bought from a florist. Backstage, Kate was with a few of her friends who were also in the show, and lots of Red Bull was being drunk, so it was all very excitable. I just remember her being a lovely girl. She was happy to do anything and everything she was asked to do. She was so beautiful and natural, she did stand out and she really made an impression."

And maybe it was because Kate knew William would be there, in the front row, that just before it was her turn to take center stage, she decided to dispose of the chunky knitwear she was supposed to be wearing over Charlotte Todd's see-through long skirt and instead, as Andrew Sands recalled, "hoisted the skirt up and made it a much better-looking dress, which she wore over her black underwear." Whatever she did, it worked — as she shimmied down the runway, her long, curled hair braided with ribbons, her slender waist, washboard stomach, and toned legs visible through the sheer dress, William barely knew where to look. "Wow," he whispered to a friend. "Kate's hot!"

The show was a huge success and the mood was upbeat at the various after-parties, the first — for all those involved in the show — at the West Port and then a series of more-exclusive house parties around town. Both Kate and William ended up at the same party at 14 Hope Street, where, according to Andrew Sands, "They kissed at the end of the night. They were both standing up in the corner of the living room, and I recall seeing them out of the corner of my eye. It was dark, there were lots of people, and the music was playing very loud. Everyone pretended that they weren't taking much notice, but it went round St. Andrews like wildfire afterwards. It wasn't cool to make a big deal of it, you couldn't be seen to be acting like he was different from anyone else, but word got around."

Other people at the party report that Kate was seen pulling away as William leaned in to kiss her. She may have been momentarily concerned that anything more intimate than their already close friendship might muddy the waters when it came to living together.

There was also the matter of Rupert, although her relationship with him had cooled over the Christmas vacation. But whatever the nature of the advance, this was the moment that seemed to mark a shift in their relationship, the possibility of something stirring. As Charlie Moretti concluded, "I think the fashion show made them the couple they are today. . . . I was always certain they would be together and maybe the fashion show was the crystallizing moment."

A few days later, on March 30, 2002, the Queen Mother died at the great age of 101, and William, who was extremely fond of his great-grandmother, returned to London to be with his family. The Queen Mother had links with the university — Queen's College was named in her honor, and in 1929, 72 years before William took his place there, she had been awarded an honorary degree of doctor of laws. In fact, the Queen Mother had sent William off with the immortal words, "If there are any good parties, invite me down." As William fondly recalled, "I said yes, but there was no way. I knew full well she would dance me under the table." It was a sad time for Queen Elizabeth II and her family — just seven weeks earlier, Princess Margaret had passed away: the death of both her mother and sister, in this, the year of her Golden Jubilee. Kate, along with the rest of the nation, was touched by the sight of William and Harry walking behind their great-grandmother's coffin from Westminster Abbey, with echoes of the pain of their mother's death etched on their faces.

Back at St. Andrews at the beginning of the summer term, William and Kate settled back into lectures, and Kate found herself socializing more and more with William's close circle, with intimate and increasingly intricate dinner parties being a favorite evening source of entertainment. Wanting to earn some extra money to fund her summer vacation, Kate secured herself a job at The Doll's House Restaurant, a popular bistro in town. Michael Choong took a friend and her parents there. "It was a cute little place in town. There weren't that many places to go out and The Doll's House was lovely. It had rustic wooden painted furniture decorated with dolls and doll's house furniture. We had a picture taken with Kate while she was working there. She wore jeans and a dark shirt and a black apron. It was a bit awkward having her wait on us, but she was very friendly and smiley and just got on with it." By now she had a close group of female friends, with whom she would spend her time. Among them was Olivia Bleasdale and Fergus's girlfriend, Sandrine Janet; Lady Virginia "Ginny" Fraser, the daughter of Lord Strathalmond, who knew Kate from her former school, Downe House; Mel Nicholson, who was dating Oli Baker; and Bryony Gordon who was studying geography with William. By now, Kate's relationship with Rupert had fizzled out. He was graduating at the end of the year, and they both knew, deep in their hearts, that their relationship was over. With William waiting on the sidelines, Rupert never really stood a chance.

As the undergraduate exams came to an end and the students were able to set aside their studies for the balls and festivities to mark the end of the academic year, Kate reflected on her first year at the university. As she packed up her room in Sallies, she looked at the photographs that told the story of the past ten months at St. Andrews and wondered what she would add during her second year. Living in the same house as William would, she knew, require the utmost discretion, so any photographs of life inside 13 Hope Street would have to be kept privately. She knew that there would be other restrictions on her freedom —

much more than the Sponsio Academica or the confidentiality agreement required. But these were sacrifices Kate was prepared to make. William was by now one of her best friends. As she said good-bye to him and her other close friends and flew home for the summer, little did she suspect just how adventurous her second year would turn out to be.

CHAPTER 6
THE BUBBLE BURSTS

During the summer vacation, while Kate was working as a waitress at the Henley Royal Regatta and William was undertaking official royal engagements, back in St. Andrews, Apartment A at 13 Hope Street was undergoing radical internal redecoration. The well-maintained two-story, top-floor apartment was being fitted with bulletproof windows, a bombproof front door, a state-of-the-art laser security system, and floor-to-ceiling reinforced pine shutters. At the same time, Special Branch officers were informing residents of the quiet street that come the start of the academic year, new tenants were moving in and there would be increased security — and an initial flurry of activity — in their neighborhood.

And so, in September 2002, just before the beginning of their second year, William, Fergus, Kate, and Olivia returned to St. Andrews to settle into their new home. William's room, situated on the first floor between the galley kitchen and the high-ceilinged living-dining room, was the largest of the bedrooms and looked out onto the wild garden and the back of the Student Union on Market Street. Kate had a smaller bedroom, which she personalized with her usual flair — photographs taking pride of place. With its open-plan living area, the apartment was ideal for entertaining, and the quartet soon established themselves as great dinner party hosts — Kate and Olivia mostly responsible for the cooking and William and Fergus, the shopping.

Now that they were free from the regimen of eating in the university hall, it wasn't long before dinner parties became the craze among Kate's social set. The local Tesco grocery store had never seen anything like it and had become a locus of great excitement, a frisson of expectation in the aisles, buzzing with students and local people, who, at certain times of the week, "shopped to spot the prince." Dressed in his characteristic different shades of cream and white, Fergus stood out wherever he went, and if Fergus was browsing, shoppers could be pretty sure William was not far behind him. Andrew Sands remembered, "Tesco's was a bit of meeting place, and people would get seriously dressed up to go there. It's where the great and the good met up, often while they were buying groceries for that night's dinner party."

As the early evenings closed in and the weather turned, the apartment mates fell into the rhythm of term routine. William and Kate discovered that they were content to spend much of their free time in each other's company. After a morning swim or run, they would go off to their different faculties but return home as soon as they could to catch up. Studying was an important part of Kate's daily routine, and she rarely missed a lecture in either the core subjects of nineteenth- and twentieth-century history of art or the new courses on offer to second-year students. She had chosen to take a course in the history of photography, which enthralled her. While she maintained her flawless attendance, she would hurry back to study in the apartment or relax with William, spending the long evenings listening to music or watching films, occasionally venturing out for a drink at the West Port or Ma Bells. Discovering just how compatible they were, just how much they had in common, and all they had to talk about came as a surprise to them both, and as their friendship deepened, something shifted, and within a few months things began to fall quietly into place.

Of course, where William was concerned, this was not exactly straightforward: though he was enjoying a freedom that no royal before him had ever had, the tricky business of living a normal life while being in line to the throne continued to be difficult to navigate. Nothing illustrated this more in that autumn semester than the sudden collapse of Paul Burrell's trial in November 2002. Princess Diana's former butler had been accused of stealing over three hundred items from the estate of the Prince and Princess of Wales, but during the trial, an astonishing and unexpected out-of-court intervention from the Queen meant that the case against him no longer stood. William was as shocked as anyone when this happened, not knowing what to think of the man with whom he, his mother, and his brother had once been so close. Through all this, Kate was there to support William — especially during the unpleasant aftermath of revelations and counteraccusations, all played out in the frenzy of the media.

It was around this time that journalists thought they had spotted a new woman in William's life. He had recently started walking to the library and lectures with fellow geography student Bryony Daniels. Tall, with waist-length hair, she was extremely attractive, and the fact that the media assumed she was William's new girlfriend was no bad thing for the prince. "She was the cover for a long time because she was often seen with William and they were photographed walking together in town. He let the press think that she was his girlfriend because it was the perfect ruse," explained one student. "Bryony used to cut out the press clippings about them being an item and put them on the fridge. It was very convenient for William, but I think there was a bit of Bryony that wished they were dating."

Kate needed no warning that any obviously romantic connection to William would be seized upon by the press and that their bourgeoning relationship had to remain beneath the radar. And so, while life inside 13 Hope Street was changing for both of them, they made sure that they were rarely seen together in public. Charlie Moretti recalled that they would never hold hands while walking on campus as many of the students did. "They had some lectures together, so you would see them on campus, but they were never openly affectionate. They were never touchy or feely in public."

According to Kate's lecturer and head of the History of Art Department, Professor Peter Humfrey, none of the lecturers knew that the couple had become close, and even on campus, Kate kept her head down. "She was extremely discreet, she wasn't the type to make a big show, she was very quiet and in retrospect I can see that it was perhaps a deliberate policy." Kate kept busy, and together with her friend Katherine Munsey and other second-year students, she got involved with the Lumsden Club, a group set up to rival the long-established, archaic, all-male Kate Kennedy Club. Andrew Sands observed the group at close quarters, full of admiration for Kate's dedication to its charitable aims: "She spent a lot of time with the girls from the club. Kate was one of the key figures in it. They organized charity events, including a garden party in the summer that became one of the things to go to. That went down well because it was all very much in good spirit — their opening event was huge, and they raised loads of money. The idea was that everyone bought a ticket and brought a toy to the event that would be sent off to a hospital or an orphanage." Between this, her studies, part-time work at The Doll's House, and hockey practice, Kate's life — on the outside at least — continued as usual.

However, though there may not have been a whole lot of difference in Kate's routine and activities, her close friends noticed a change in her behavior. Never having been one to party hard, Kate was nevertheless sociable and outgoing and in the previous year had spent a lot of time out and about with Rupert and her friends. Now, here she was going straight home after lectures or hockey practice and more often than not staying in for the entire evening. For William, the domesticated routine of living with his apartment mates — shopping, cooking supper, watching a movie, listening to music, even doing the housework — was exactly the normality he craved. This must have been bliss for Kate, the man she was falling in love with, wanting nothing more than a quiet night at home, no external distractions, night after night.

Dinner parties were a good way of socializing and enjoying each other's company without having to go out into town and risk being spotted together. Katherine Munsey, a mutual friend of Kate and William, was considered to be the queen of entertaining, astonishing her guests with a fine attention to detail: "She would go to extreme efforts and had the silver brought up from London when she was throwing a really big event," remembered Andrew Sands. "She was very stylish and so were her dinner parties, which would consist of courses and courses. They would take it in turns to host at each other's houses, which always entailed lots of drinking and lots of fun."

At Hope Street, Kate was in charge of the cooking and occasionally William attempted to make a dish, but as Kate recalled some years later, she was often required to come to the rescue when the meal risked being spoiled: "I would have to wander in and save something that was going."

One thing William could be relied on for was supplying copious bottles of Jack Daniel's for the popular after-dinner drinking games, a favorite of which was called "I've Never." This entailed one player admitting something he or she had never done and then asking the others if they had. Anyone assembled who had done the deed had to take a drink. One of their friends recalled, "William and Kate loved the game, but it went a bit wrong on one occasion when Carley came for dinner. She and William were still friends, and she lived across the road in Howard Place. She could literally wave to William from her sitting room, where she would sit knitting by the window, which rather grated on Kate. When it was Carley's turn to play, she announced, 'I've never dated two people in this room,' knowing full well that William was the only one who had, because Kate was sitting next to him. He shot Carley a thunderous look and said under his breath, 'I can't believe you just said that' before drinking his shot. Kate didn't speak to Carley much after that, but we were in shock. We knew they were together, but it was the first time William confirmed his and Kate's relationship."

A few weeks later, in the middle of November, William invited Kate — along with fifteen other friends, including Olivia Bleasdale and Ginny Fraser — to a shooting weekend at Wood Farm in Sandringham. Crammed into a six-bedroom cottage, Kate got her first taste of one of William's regular shoots and the advantages of being across the estate from Prince Charles, who sent over a home-cooked meal for them. This was to be the first of many such weekends, Kate having to get used to the routine of the shoot and the braces of pheasants hanging around the kitchen waiting to be cooked and eaten.

The rest of the second year passed gently by, both Kate and William busy with their coursework and summer-term exams. To the astute observer, there were glimpses of something developing between them — they were seen lying side by side in the spring sunshine during the breaks in a rugby match in which William was playing; they danced together at the Kate Kennedy Club annual May Ball — but they managed to keep the depth of their relationship under wraps. Some of their friends knew the true state of affairs, of course, and others had suspicions — but crucially, the public had no idea.

Ever alert, however, the press thought that something might be up. William and Kate had been spotted walking to lectures together, and the media suspected that Kate was too pretty to be just a friend. When William attended her belated twenty-first birthday celebration in June 2003, a reporter door-stepped her father, Michael, and asked him what he knew about their relationship. He was politely evasive: "We are very amused at the thought of being in-laws to Prince William, but I don't think it's going to happen." Kate had told her parents that she was growing close to William, and she also confided in her sister, but she swore them all to secrecy, insisting nobody was to utter a word to anyone else. The relationship hadn't fully developed, and she didn't want anything to upset this delicate early stage.

Carole had pulled out all the stops for Kate's party, renting a large tent for the garden and hiring caterers to help prepare a sit-down dinner for family and friends. The occasion was nearly overshadowed when Ginny Fraser, one of Kate's St. Andrews friends, sent out invitations to her own twenty-first party on the same date, causing a headache for members of their clique, who were put in the uncomfortable position of having to choose whose party to attend. According to one of their friends, "It caused a real divide and a bit of a social rift. Kate was very upset, as she had sent her invitations out first and invited Ginny. She cut Ginny off a bit after that."

Among their St. Andrews friends, twenty-first celebrations were big occasions. Kate and William were still talking about Meghann Gunderman's lavish party, which had been held at a Scottish castle and was rumored to have cost $150,000. The party had a Gone with the Wind theme, and, a fan of fancy dress, Kate had decided to make her party 1920s themed. Although some of her friends elected to go to Ginny's party over hers, William promised Kate he would be there to celebrate with her, and when his Volkswagen Golf crunched up the gravel driveway, followed closely by his security team, Kate's heart leaped. Her parents had treated her to a flapper-style cocktail dress, and she looked incredible, having spent the day preparing for the party with Pippa and Carole.

Not wishing to draw attention to his belated arrival, Kate discreetly slipped out of the cocktail reception to greet William at the front door, where she introduced him for the first time to her parents. Dressed in a smoking jacket and with his hair slicked down in a nod to the theme of the night, he quickly got into the swing of the party. Glasses of Pimm's and lemonade and flutes of champagne were served on the lawn before supper, where William was seated at Kate's table. According to one guest there that night, "There were lots of Marlburians as well as St. Andrews friends, but there was quite an overlap. Lots of them knew each other, and William knew quite a few people there, which made it very relaxed. We all gave him his privacy, and he kept himself to himself. It was a sit-down dinner and dance, and William looked very dapper; he seemed to be having a lot of fun — we all were."

Kate, along with a handful of their friends

from St. Andrews, including the Sallies Boys, had been invited to William's twenty-first, which took place a couple of weeks later, on June 21. They had all been asked to dress up for the Out of Africa–themed birthday party at Windsor Castle. For Kate, this was the first time she would be in the presence of so many of William's family, including Queen Elizabeth II and Prince Charles, who had both gotten into the spirit of the party and were wearing colonial dress. Kate spent most of the night chatting with the St. Andrews crew and was pleased when William introduced her to some of his friends from Eton as well as the Glosse Posse she had heard so much about. In turn, they were curious about the girl William introduced to them, having heard him talk so much about his new friend at St. Andrews. William, however, had given no hint that they were dating.

In fact, on the day of his birthday, he had given an interview in which he claimed he was single. "There's been a lot of speculation about every single girl I am with, and it does irritate me after a while, more so because it is a complete pain for the girls," he said. "These poor girls, whom I've either just met or are friends of mine, suddenly get thrown into the limelight and their parents get rung up and so on. I think it's a little unfair on them, really. I'm used to it, because it happens quite a lot now. But it's very different for them and I don't like that at all. If I fancy a girl and she fancies me back, which is rare, I ask her out. But at the same time, I don't want to put them in an awkward situation because a lot of people don't know what comes with knowing me, for one — and secondly, if they were my girlfriend, the excitement it would probably cause."

His comments about being single hadn't unnerved Kate; she knew by now that William had a habit of planting red herrings, particularly to put the press off the scent, but something happened that night that did unsettle her. From the start of the evening, William had seemed rather preoccupied with Jessica "Jecca" Craig who had flown in from Kenya to celebrate his milestone birthday. William had first met Jecca, the daughter of British conservationist Ian Craig and his wife, Jane, in 1998 in Kenya during his school holidays when he worked on the game reserve. He returned during his gap year when rumors emerged in the press that he hadn't just fallen in love with Kenya but also with the Craigs' attractive daughter, who was just his age. William was upset about the story and eager to quash the reports, so he instructed his press aides at the Palace to insist Jecca was just a friend. Kate didn't know whether they had been romantically involved or not, but she noted that Jecca had been seated at the head table next to William, whereas Kate had to raise her glass to toast the prince from afar.

There was a mere mention of Kate being one of the prince's guests in the papers; a far bigger story had detracted from any of William's girlfriends there that night. A gate-crasher dressed as Osama bin Laden had managed to foil Palace security and not only gained entry to Windsor Castle but took to the stage while William was thanking the Queen and Prince Charles. The prince thought it was a prank organized by Harry until security men wrestled the intruder to the floor and arrested him.

Kate pushed the niggling sense of doubt she had felt since that night to the back of her mind and reassured herself with the fact that William had instigated something rather promising for the start of their third year. Having enjoyed living in Hope Street, William had decided that for his third and fourth years, when he didn't have quite as many lectures as previously, he would like the "space and freedom" and privacy of the countryside. Toward the end of the summer semester, he had invited Kate, Alasdair Coutts-Wood, and Oli Baker to move with him into Balgove House on the Strathtyrum Estate, about one-quarter mile from St. Andrews. Kate was thrilled. The house was set in stunning grounds, with glorious views from the bedroom windows — acres of lawn, orchids, and fuchsias instead of the concrete back of the Student Union. With the Palace still reeling from the security breach at William's twenty-first, it was subjected to the security measures necessary for a modern-day prince, and unmarked police cars patroled the estate while William's protection officers took up residence in the assorted outbuildings. Kate took on the role of homemaker, dressing the windows with pretty red-and-white gingham curtains, while William installed a champagne fridge and a huge oil painting of his grandmother in the impressive dining room.

The most significant advantage of the cottage was the privacy it afforded William and Kate, far from prying eyes. Not only was the long driveway framed by hedgerows, but the couple had the seclusion provided by two acres of wild meadow, hidden behind a six-foot stone wall. William joked that it was like a miniature Highgrove, and with its crab-apple trees, blooming rhododendrons, and patches of wild poppies, it was an impressive substitute. For the first weeks of the term, while the weather was still warm enough, they would pack a picnic hamper and spend pleasant afternoons stretched out on a blanket, sharing a bottle of chilled white wine, their only company an occasional pheasant. It was during these quiet, reflective moments that Kate was able to confide in William how painful she had found the recent death of her grandfather, Ron. He had died at the age of seventy-two, after suffering from motor neuron disease for some years. According to Carole's brother, Gary Goldsmith, who was interviewed by the *Daily Telegraph,* "He was up a ladder in his sixties cleaning a gutter for an old lady when he fell off it and broke both of his heels. He had to crawl into the house to phone an ambulance for himself. It was through that trauma that he believes he developed motor neuron disease. It was the erosion of a healthy man."

Denise Allford, Kate's former teacher at St. Andrews Prep, recalled how Ron's health deteriorated after the fall: "It was a terrible accident, and although he recovered physically, the shock really affected his system."

Jean Harrison, Carole's second cousin, who had known Ron and Dorothy since she was a girl, attended the funeral. "The wake was at the local pub in the village," she recalled. "Dorothy was very proud of Carole and Gary and how well they had done. They paid for most of Ron's funeral, and I think she was very happy about how well they had done, but she was devastated by Ron's death. The whole family was. Kate was at St. Andrews at the time, and although we didn't know she was dating William, it was obvious from some of the things that were said that she was seeing someone quite important."

Having recently lost his own great-grandmother, William well understood Kate's grief and gave her a shoulder to cry on. The shared experience only brought them closer.

It was this natural empathy and deep friendship that ensured they were so happy and relaxed in one another's company. Their romance was by now in full swing and made all the more exquisite by the fact that virtually no one knew of their love for one another. Of course, their close friends were aware, but they were protective of their romance and bound by the university pledge not to talk to the press. And so their third year as undergraduates began, a scaled-down version of the earlier years — smaller classes and tutorials and, when not entertaining, a quieter, more secluded home life. After the unsettling events surrounding his twenty-first birthday, Kate and William's relationship was back on track.

Their new home quickly became their castle. The cottage was spacious and rustic, with a large open fireplace. Michael Choong spent time there: "The house was really lovely. It had an Aga, a breakfast table, an outside area for a barbeque and a fire pit — perfect for entertaining." The pièce de résistance was an impressive dining room, complete with a long mahogany dining table with seventeen chairs, the oil painting of the Queen, and an oversized Union Jack flag.

Being out of town meant that Kate and William could go exploring more easily. William had a car at St. Andrews that he had kept in the police station for safety when living on Hope Street, but now the Golf was always within reach and he and Kate could explore further afield, driving out to the sea and walking along the beach or up on the cliffs. Michael Choong observed other parts of their routine at close quarters: "They would have barbecues in the summer and invite other students over. When people heard Will was having a party, there would be lots of people turning up in taxis. The parties were good fun and would go on 'til late at night. The protection officers were always there, but they were very cool. They just allowed us to get on with being students. I remember turning up once with sacks of ice for drinks, and they helped me unload it from the boot. We called them by their first names and they were always very friendly." Wanting to give William time with his friends, Kate made a point of not being at all the parties and would visit her girlfriends instead. "One of her closest friends was Mel Nicholson, who was going out with Oli Baker," recalled Andrew Sands. "They spent a lot of time together and used to go to Pizza Hut in town, where we'd see them huddled over a pizza having a very serious conversation." Determined to get the best grades she could, Kate applied herself to her studies and was very much in charge of domesticity in the cottage.

Around Christmas time in December 2003, rumors began to surface in the press that William and Kate were an item. Kate had already confided in her mother that their close friendship had blossomed into a serious romance and that she and William had fallen in love. With Kate's blessing,

Carole told Michael, James, and her brother, Gary, during the Christmas holidays that the relationship was serious. Pippa, who by now was in her first year studying English Literature at Edinburgh University, having enjoyed a gap year like Kate, knew exactly what was going on; the sisters spoke at least every other day, and Pippa had been to stay with Kate and William at Balgove House. Not everyone in the family had been able to keep the secret, however. Unbeknownst to the family at the time, Gary broke his niece's confidence, later telling the press that "When Kate and William first began dating, Carole telephoned the immediate family to warn them that the relationship would likely to become public. I was so delighted that at a business meeting I pushed a piece of paper across the table to a colleague that read, 'I think I'm going to be the uncle of the future Queen of England.' "

Nevertheless, it was not until several months later in the spring that the romance was revealed to the world. William had invited Kate to join a select group of his friends on a skiing holiday at Klosters, and she had readily accepted. As this was the royal family's favorite resort in the Swiss Alps, a place to which they returned annually, it wasn't entirely surprising that William and the royal party were photographed on the slopes. Skiing holidays, rather like the family's church visit on Christmas morning, have always attracted the press, but this time they got more than they bargained for. Jason Fraser — a paparazzo who seven years earlier had snapped William's mother in the arms of Dodi Al-Fayed aboard the *Jonikal* — managed to get a shot of William gazing lovingly at Kate as they glided up the mountain on the ski lift. The photo confirmed the rumors that had been around for months, and the *Sun* was prepared to pay the highest price for the picture that confirmed there really was a romance between them. "Finally . . . Wills gets a girl," was the headline above the sensational front-page picture, published on April 1, 2004.

The Palace was furious, accusing the newspaper of breaching the press embargo that protected Prince William while he was at the university. They argued that the agreement did not just apply to the periods of the year that he spent at St. Andrews itself. Clarence House refused to comment on the *Sun*'s claims and issued a statement that made it quite clear the matter was not open for further discussion: "We don't discuss the nature of William's relationships with his friends. There may be speculation about other women he is photographed with. We're not going to get into a debate about the nature of his friendships." Returning to St. Andrews, after their holiday Kate and William were more cautious than before, and their close friends threw an even tighter net around their privacy. Charlie Moretti remembered, "When it leaked that they were dating, we all tried to protect them. We would text William and Kate if we saw any photographers hiding out. None of us wanted their lives to be any harder. St. Andrews gave them a few years of normality, and I don't think any of us wanted to ruin that." Vice Chancellor Brian Lang, who was in constant communication with the Palace, said the university community made a point of giving William and Kate space: "The feeling was that they should be left alone — no one wanted to single them out for special attention."

In fact, the press did stick to the agreement, and when Kate and William kissed in public for the first time after a rugby match in May 2004, there were no cameras or photographers to record the moment.

During the rest of their third year, the couple remained pretty much behind closed doors, rarely seen together in public. They enjoyed being alone, and the time, importantly, afforded Kate a glimpse into royal life. They were often away for weekends, during which William taught Kate to shoot. She was gradually introduced to life inside Highgrove, Prince Charles's estate in Gloucestershire, as well as Balmoral, the Queen's Scottish estate, and Sandringham, the Queen's residence in Norfolk. As she had with her son, Charles, when he was a student, the Queen allowed William, her grandson, to use Tam-na-Ghar, a 120-year-old cottage tucked away in the remote countryside of the Balmoral estate, as a getaway. Surrounded by rolling hills and wild heather, it made a perfect retreat for Kate and William. After their last class on Friday afternoons, they would drive the eighty or so miles from St. Andrews to Balmoral and spend the weekend walking across the moors or strolling by the River Dee, returning to the cottage to cook and eat in front of a roaring log fire. Sometimes friends would join them, and Pippa and James would often come up to spend time getting to know their sister's boyfriend. These were idyllic times for Kate.

But storm clouds were brewing, and it was in the summer of 2004 that their relationship encountered its first set of serious difficulties. After enjoying a holiday together with a group of friends on the island of Rodrigues, which William had been wanting to revisit since his gap year, they realized it would be some time before they saw each other. William had been invited to Nashville, Tennessee, to stay with his close friend Anna Sloan, who was studying at Edinburgh University with Pippa. Although there was no suggestion of a romance, Kate hated the idea of him being away with another woman, even if Anna was just a friend. She knew it was a flaw, but she was territorial when it came to William. When he returned from that trip, he barely had time to unpack his bags and see Kate before jetting off again, this time to Greece with Guy Pelly and some of their friends for a boys-only cruise in the Mediterranean. Kate knew William well enough to realize that he clearly needed some space, and before he went to Greece, they agreed to use the time apart to think about things. As with many couples who meet at university, the crunch time came as the prospect of graduation loomed.

It was as if real life had suddenly intervened and burst their bubble once they had left Balgove House for the summer vacation. Kate knew she had no option and was forced to give William his freedom, but the rest of the summer was agonizing as she questioned his commitment to her and tried to make sense of what was going on. In truth, William was experiencing some unease about being tied down, and having agreed to a break with Kate, he had the opportunity to play the field again.

He had always had a soft spot for Isabella Anstruther-Gough-Calthorpe, the younger sister of William and Harry's polo-playing friend Jacobi. With her intimidating triple-barreled surname, Isabella was just the sort of rival that Kate feared — astonishingly pretty, titled, and the heiress to a stately home and a banking fortune. During the summer, William made repeated efforts to take her out, on one occasion boldly turning up at the family's Chelsea home on the pretense of seeing Jacobi. Isabella, however, had no aspirations to date a prince and, despite his amorous advances, declared that she was not interested in dating William.

In order to take her mind off things, Kate accepted an invitation from Fergus Boyd to join a group of university friends at his family's holiday home in France in the Dordogne. Among the group were Kate's friends Ginny and Olivia. She hadn't told them about the trial separation from William, but she was unusually subdued and they asked her what was wrong. At first she brushed off their concern, but one evening, she could no longer keep it to herself, confiding to them that she and William were taking a break. "She was debating whether or not she should text or call him. She got quite drunk on white wine and really let her guard down," recalled one of the group. "She said how sad she was and how much she was missing him."

However, the summer appeared to be a blip in their relationship, for while William had clearly needed time away, by October they were back together, returning to Balgove House for the start of their final year at St. Andrews. Kate had some conditions — the most heartfelt one being that he wasn't to contact Isabella again — and just as though nothing had happened, they slotted back into life as a couple. Later that term, Kate was invited to Prince Charles's fifty-sixth birthday party at Highgrove. William's father was very fond of Kate and already saw her as a future daughter-in-law. She was thrilled to be included. It was even clearer how much Prince Charles saw Kate as part of the family the following March, when she was included in his pre-wedding skiing holiday at Klosters, along with William and Harry.

However, whereas his father's wedding to Camilla Parker Bowles was just around the corner, William was in no hurry to tie any knots, as evidenced by the unguarded remarks he made to a reporter during an après-ski evening in a local bar: "Look, I'm only twenty-two, for God's sake. I am too young to marry at my age. I don't want to get married until I am at least twenty-eight or maybe thirty." Kate no doubt knew of William's thoughts on marriage — and maybe even felt the same way — but it can't have been reassuring to hear such a categorical, emphatic wish to remain single.

The runup to Charles and Camilla's wedding, meanwhile, had been beset by problems and was probably enough to put William off the idea, for the foreseeable future at least. Charles and Camilla had wanted a civil wedding at Windsor Castle, but when it was realized that if a license were granted, then any other couple could also be married there, the plan was scrapped. Instead, it was decided that they would marry at Windsor Guildhall, followed by a blessing by the Archbishop of Canterbury in St. George's Chapel in the castle. Although the British public had largely warmed to the idea of Camilla marrying Charles, there was speculation that the Queen would not be attending the nuptials. Charles was crest-fallen that his wedding was being labeled a "fiasco" in the press but had been reassured by William and Harry's supportive joint statement: "We are both very happy for our father and Camilla and wish them all the luck in the future." It had been difficult for them in the early years following the death of their mother, but they had more than accepted Camilla as part of their father's life: "We love her to bits," remarked Harry.

Against all the odds, the wedding was a success, even though it had to be delayed a day because of the death of Pope John Paul II. When Camilla emerged from the shadows of Capital Guildhall into the spring sunshine to spontaneous applause from the waiting crowds, it seemed the worst was behind them. And while the Queen and Prince Philip had not attended the civil part of the ceremony, they were there at St. George's Chapel — along with the other seven hundred guests. The most moving tribute that day came from the Queen, when for the first time she gave the couple her public blessing: "My son is home and dry with the woman he loves."

Kate was not at the wedding — protocol dictated otherwise — and this, more than any other time in her relationship with William so far was the starkest reminder that her boyfriend's family was beyond anything she had ever known. From the outset, Prince Charles and Kate had enjoyed a good relationship. But there were strict rules about who could and could not be invited, and Kate was not yet an official part of the inner circle and wouldn't be until she was a royal fiancée.

The Easter break seemed to pass in a flash, and soon Kate was back at St. Andrews to prepare for her finals, putting the final touches to her dissertation on Lewis Carroll, the author of *Alice in Wonderland* and a significant figure in the history of photography. According to her tutor, Professor Peter Humfrey, "Kate produced a good piece of work; it was very interesting." She had been a diligent student throughout her four-year program and was determined to get a good final grade.

Both Kate and William finished their finals at the end of May 2005 and launched themselves into the end-of-degree celebrations — including the traditional May Ball, which was organized by the Kate Kennedy Club and held at Kinkell Farm. For once Kate let her hair down, and not able to tolerate her drink, was carried out by Fergus

Boyd before the night was over. Knowing this was the last few weeks they would all be together, William was characteristically generous and threw several barbecues and cocktail parties at Balgove House, Kate doing the catering while William tended the bar. There were also William's social engagements and obligations outside St. Andrews, and he included Kate in several of these, most notably flying down to Oxfordshire to attend the wedding of his close friend Hugh Van Cutsem to Rose Astor. This was the first society event at which Kate and William would appear together, and their rumored attendance ensured that a number of paparazzi turned up at the parish church. William was an usher and had arrived ahead of Kate, who appeared rather nervous as she made her way to the entrance past photographers desperate to get an image of her. As they left the church, Kate and William were pictured walking into the distance, heads tilted, bodies turned toward each other and deep in conversation. Their closeness was there for all to see.

On June 23, 2005, Kate and William graduated from St. Andrews, both with a well-deserved upper second degree. It was a high-profile event for the university as the Queen and Prince Philip had traveled to the town to see their grandson receive his degree certificate, the first time they had ever attended a family member's graduation ceremony. There had been much preparation ahead of the royal arrival; the university had sent details of every student graduating to the Palace ahead of the day, and in a pleasant surprise, the sun was out. Vice Chancellor Brian Lang recalled, "The Queen was wonderful; she was the proud admiring doting grandmother, I remember hearing William say: 'Hello Granny, I'm so glad you could come.' We knew she hadn't been well, but nothing was going to keep her away from that day and she was very good company. It was such a glorious day — St. Andrews at its best. In the sun, this beautiful ancient medieval town was full of bright good-looking students. Everything went right that day, thank goodness, because we had the world's press watching us."

In addition to the Queen, who had been suffering from a cold on that day, Prince Charles and Camilla came to watch William, and of course Michael and Carole were there to proudly see their elder daughter graduate. As William knelt before the chancellor's wooden pulpit to collect his parchment, the flash of cameras was overwhelming as graduates and their guests

195

captured the moment that the future King of England was awarded his degree. Moments later, Kate was called to the stage as Catherine Middleton to receive her degree in the history of art.

At the end of the ceremony, echoing his words from four years earlier when the assembled graduates had listened as nervous freshers, Brian Lang delivered his final words to them: "You will have made lifelong friends. You may have met your husband or wife. Our title as the top matchmaking university in Britain signifies so much that is good about St. Andrews, so we rely on you to go forth and multiply." Poignant and, as it turned out, prophetic words.

CHAPTER 7
THE BREAKUP

It was a bizarre experience and one Kate still hadn't gotten used to. As she flicked through the news channels, there was her boyfriend, leading every story. On his first solo overseas tour, William was in New Zealand representing the Queen, and as he laid a poppy wreath in Wellington to mark the sixty-year commemoration of the end of World War II, Kate watched with a mixture of respect and disbelief. This was exactly the situation that made their relationship so surreal, and although she had been catching up with William by e-mail, there had not yet been a chance to talk on the phone for any length of time.

It was the first time that they had been away from each other since graduating a few weeks earlier, and their time together at St. Andrews already seemed distant. They had both agreed that they wanted to make their relationship work and didn't want to be apart for too long, so Kate planned to join William and his best friend, Thomas van Straubenzee, in Kenya in July. They were going to Lewa Downs, and never having been to Kenya before, Kate was looking forward to the trip, but she was also apprehensive. William's friendship with Jecca was still a sensitive subject, even though he had assured Kate they had only ever been friends. Kate and Jecca had met at William's twenty-first birthday party and then again more recently at the wedding of William's old friend Hugh Van Cutsem. The newspapers, which had already labeled Kate and Jecca "love rivals," had had a field day when Jecca, dressed in a poncho and cowboy hat, sat just a few pews ahead of Kate, rather more dignified in a cream suit and a black fascinator. Now, the very fact that William was taking Kate to Kenya was enough to allay any major fears on her part.

Kate fell in love with Lewa, where they stayed in the $2,300-per-night Masai-inspired Il Ngwesi Lodge in the middle of the Mukogodo Hills. It had spectacular views of the majestic snow-capped peak of Mount Kenya, which the couple enjoyed from their outdoor bathroom and the canopied four-poster bed that could be wheeled out onto the terrace underneath the stars.

Days were spent outdoors, too. Situated next to the Ngare Ndare River, Lewa Downs is the natural habitat of the lion, elephant, rhino, buffalo, and the biggest herd of the world's endangered species of Grévy's zebra. While William tracked the endangered beasts, Kate, Jecca, and Thomas were taken into the bush. Each morning, as dawn broke, they set off in the safety of a guarded 4×4 safari truck over the waking plains of the savannah. Kate had brought her camera and took advantage of being so close to the wildlife. There were also plenty of other things to do while William worked, and she played tennis on the clay court with Jecca or swam in the saltwater pool. At sunset, William would join his friends for cocktails while a chef prepared freshly caught fish. Dining al fresco as the African sun set was a magical experience and any previous coolness between Kate and Jecca soon melted.

Post-holiday, William's future was already mapped out. Like his brother, Harry, he would be enrolling at the Royal Military Academy Sandhurst in 2006. Before that, in fall 2005, he was to undertake a series of work placements, including two weeks of land management in the Peak District, on the Chatsworth Estate owned by the Duke and Duchess of Devonshire, followed by three weeks at the Bank of England and the head offices of HSBC bank. It was, he reluctantly told friends, "time to join the real world." Similarly, after four years as a carefree student, Kate also had her future to think about, and she duly sent out her CV to a handful of London art galleries so that she could put her history of art degree to some good use. Finding somewhere to live wasn't a problem. Her parents had bought an expensive apartment in Chelsea before she graduated and had given Kate the keys. Located on Old Church Street off the fashionable and sought-after King's Road, the two-bedroom pied-à-terre was perfectly positioned and had been beautifully furnished by her mother. The plan was for Pippa to move in with Kate when she graduated from Edinburgh.

Kate's apartment was only a short drive from William's living quarters at Clarence House. By now, she was a regular visitor, and when she pulled up in her VW Golf, Kate was waved through the cast-iron gates without needing to stop for a security check. She even had a parking space reserved next to William and Harry's in the gravel courtyard. Kate was beginning to get to know Harry, who had been at Sandhurst since May and was full of tales of the tough training he had had ahead of his older brother. Unlike Pippa, who had come to visit at St. Andrews, Harry hadn't visited his brother, but he had met Kate many times at Balmoral on shooting weekends. Although they got along well, it was rather crowded when all three of them were at Clarence House. Charles and Camilla had the run of the large, four-story building, while William and Harry shared a small wing, consisting of a functional kitchen with a dining table for entertaining, a living area, a bedroom each, and a small gym.

In between looking for a job, Kate filled her days shopping on the King's Road, meeting friends, and seeing William. Because of the ongoing intense speculation about the seriousness of her relationship with William, she had to quickly come to terms with the fact that she was a constant target for the paparazzi. She only had the benefit of the prince's protection officers when she was with him, and so she had to deal with the unwanted attention alone. It was like navigating an obstacle course, and it seemed there was always a photographer ready to pounce, whether she was leaving her apartment to go to the shops or heading to Buckingham Palace to swim at the pool, a privilege she now enjoyed. The paparazzi soon worked out where she lived, shopped, and worked out, and she was photographed nearly every day. William was aware of the situation and anxious about it. He had seen firsthand how his mother had been harassed by the paparazzi and was determined that Kate not be subjected to the same treatment. At his request, she was given a hotline to the press office at St. James's Palace and the mobile number of the Prince of Wales's head of press, Paddy Harverson. "We had been introduced to Kate early on, and we were instructed from the outset to give her every support possible," said a senior press aide. "She was obviously the subject of a lot of press interest and intrusion from the paparazzi. William said we had a duty of care to her and her family and so we advised her on how to deal with the cameras. We told her to smile at the photographers so that it would be a better picture. She was given advice on how to manage the media, and we were there to support her if there was a crisis."

At St. Andrews, the media agreement had meant that the couple was sheltered, but out in the real world, Kate found herself in new territory. She was polite, but she never posed for the cameras, having been told by courtiers not to engage with the media.

Earlier that summer, she and her mother had attended the Horse Trials at Gatcombe Park, Princess Anne's country house. With or without William, Kate's attendance at any event was now big news, and she was quickly surrounded by the press pack. Dressed in a cowboy hat, brown corduroy jacket, and fitted jeans, the photographers addressed her as "Kate" and asked her to pose for a photograph. "If I do it now, then I'll have to keep doing it," she explained. It was the first time she had ever addressed the media, and her response was smooth and calculated. It was the clearest indication yet that she was being given some very effective media training behind the scenes. Bizarrely, she had been advised to watch footage of the late Princess of Wales in order to learn how to deal with the paparazzi, notorious for being aggressive in their pursuit of a picture, taunting their prey in order to get a response. At the Palace, there was a concerted effort not to allow Kate to be exposed to the same ruthless treatment.

In a further show of support, Kate was also given access to the Prince of Wales's London-based legal team, Harbottle and Lewis. The lawyers were instructed to write to newspaper editors before the year was out to express their concerns about how much Kate was being photographed. When a German magazine, *Das Neue,* pinpointed the exact location of Kate's London home, William was livid. Although the intrusive photography was bad enough, this was, he fumed, an unacceptable invasion of Kate's privacy and posed a serious problem for the prince's security team. William was often at Kate's apartment, and now it was a matter of public record that his chauffeur-driven Range Rover could be seen parked in the narrow street. Panic buttons linked to the local police station were installed at Kate's apartment as an additional security measure.

When it came to going out in London, William and Kate had their own way of dealing with the paparazzi. As they had done at St. Andrews, they never held hands in public — in fact, they never acted like a couple. At a private black-tie gala dinner in Whitehall that October, they sat at separate tables in order to not be photographed together and, according to guests, barely spoke to each other all evening. It was the same during a night out at the Mamilanji nightclub in London a couple of weeks later. William was enjoying himself on the dance floor, while Kate sat with her friends. They arrived and left separately, according to the British show-business journalist Emily Maddick, who was at the club that night observing them. "William was in very jovial spirits, chatting and drinking," she recalled. "Close to midnight, he hit the dance floor with some of his friends. He was having a great time dancing to 'Don'tcha' by the Pussycat Dolls, and he knew the words. He was loving it, but Kate was sitting in the VIP area with friends, cradling a glass of white wine. She didn't seem in the mood to dance, and William left the club separately and said he was on his way to a house party. You would never know they were together."

They made a point of keeping a low profile, and although the press speculated that the romance might be on the rocks, the truth was William and Kate were tighter than ever. Not acting like a couple when they were out was their way of keeping private what was special, even though it was not always easy for Kate. By November, she was still jobless, but she approached her parents with a business proposal to launch a children's clothing line on the Party Pieces website. They talked the idea through that Christmas when she went home. Carole thought it was an excellent plan of action. Children's T-shirts had always sold well on the site, and she believed that a clothing line had the potential to be successful.

Kate loved being back with her family at Christmas, and even though they were no longer children, Kate, Pippa, and James still opened stockings on Christmas morning before making a start on the Christmas puzzle, a family tradition. Ever since they were little, Michael had dressed up on Christmas Day, and this year he donned a sumo wrestler's outfit, which had the family in stitches. On Boxing Day, the day after Christmas, Kate packed her bags and drove to Norfolk to join William at the Sandringham shoot. She had stayed at the royal estate several times with William and their friends for shooting weekends, but she had never been invited for Christmas when the entire royal family was in attendance. William thought it better not to stay in the main house, where Kate might find things a bit daunting, so he arranged for them to spend several nights at Wolferton Marshes, an isolated cottage on the estate. She was thrilled to be part of the festivities and was now an accomplished shot herself. Diana never enjoyed her stays at royal residences, complaining that William and Harry were "always out killing things," but Kate loved the sport and seemed to settle in well.

After seeing the new year in together, William and Kate boarded a plane on New Year's Day for Klosters. The trip was an early birthday present for Kate before William started Sandhurst, and this time he didn't care who saw them on the slopes, as he kissed her passionately. They would not see each other for five weeks once he enrolled at Sandhurst, and they made the most of every minute together.

On their return to London with the days ticking down, Kate threw a champagne send-off for William at Clarence House with his closest friends, and then on January 8, 2006, William left London to begin his army training. Driven down by his father, while closely followed by his security team carrying the prerequisite ironing board, he was welcomed by the major general. After signing into Blenheim Company, William was shown to his sparse, soulless room, which overlooked Old College. Not wanting to overshadow his brother's arrival, which was captured by the waiting media, Harry was not there to greet William but made his way to his room later. Now that he was in his third term, Harry took great pleasure in reminding his older brother that his higher rank meant that William would have to salute him.

While William knuckled down to intensive

physical and mental training, which would prepare him for his future career with the military, Kate started putting the wheels in motion for her new business plan. She worked on a business strategy and started sourcing reasonably priced, high-quality children's clothing. She traveled around the country looking at samples and flew to Milan where, using her basic Italian, she found a reliable manufacturer. That summer, the press reported that she had the backing of clothing label Viyella, which wanted to partner on the project, but the rumored venture came to nothing. Kate realized that starting a business was not easy, and she hit obstacles early on. She decided not to register the company with Companies House because it would mean publishing personal details as well as annual accounts. Her parents helped where they could, and Kate had some savings to get the business off the ground, but by the summer, she was operating the business at a loss. She confided to Jamie Murray Wells, an entrepreneur and close friend of William's, that she was struggling to break even. "The business is running into debt, but I really want to prove to my dad that I can do this without asking him for any money," she said. Kate decided that she might be better off working for a well-established fashion company instead. She was rumored to have been approached by the design house Ralph Lauren, which was interested in making her an ambassador. According to one former employee, it was "an idea, but it never took off." In the end, Lady Gabriella Windsor was appointed to the role. Kate was also rumored to have applied for a job at the Harrods store in Knightsbridge, London, as a buyer's assistant in the fashion department, but again, it came to nothing.

Although she was eager to carve a career for herself, not having the commitment of a nine-to-five day job rather suited her. As a royal girlfriend she was largely at William's beck and call, and she fitted in seeing him around his timetable. She also had a busy social life, constantly whizzing up and down the M4 motorway to London to see her friends. She was often spotted browsing in clothes shops in Kensington and Chelsea and attending glitzy nights out with William on the rare occasions he had time off from Sandhurst. They attended the Boodles Boxing Ball in June, a charity night for which some of their closest friends were competing in the ring, and the opening of a new shop at Bluebird, the fashionable restaurant and café on the King's Road, owned by the retail tycoons John and Belle Robinson, friends of the Middletons. Kate seemed to revel in her role, and even without William, she still mingled in royal circles. Earlier in the year, Kate had caused quite a stir when she was photographed in the Royal Box at the Cheltenham Gold Cup with Prince Charles and the Duchess of Cornwall. It was the first time she had appeared with the family at a public event without William, appearing happy and relaxed as she chatted with Camilla and her children, Tom and Laura. Kate's warm rapport with Charles had intensified, and the prince had grown even fonder of Kate. He loved it when William brought Kate to Highgrove for occasional weekends and had given them a set of keys and allowed them to share a room. "Charles was like any other father; he was very kind and hospitable towards Kate from the beginning," said a senior member of the household. "He was delighted William had found such a lovely girlfriend, and she was made to feel at home. Charles loved the fact that Kate enjoyed coming to Highgrove and to Birkhall in Scotland — where he would take her hill walking and deer stalking. It gave him great pleasure that they could share those pursuits." Birkhall, the eighteenth-century mansion that the Queen

Mother gifted to Charles when she died, holds a great deal of significance for the Prince of Wales. Charles would escape from Gordonstoun, the Scottish boarding school he hated, to see his grandmother at the three-story house on the Queen's 50,000-acre Deeside Estate when he was a boy. The place, he said, had a "soul-refreshing effect," and he refused to move the eleven grandfather clocks from the dining room. Nor would he refurbish the moth-eaten tartan curtains, despite Camilla's protests.

Camilla, meanwhile, took it upon herself to advise Kate on royal etiquette. The duchess was skilled in royal courtship, and she encouraged Kate to work her diary around William's engagements. Kate made sure she kept the weekends free so she and William could be together. Often they stayed at her parents' house or at Highgrove with Charles and Camilla. They also had a close-knit group of friends, and there was always a shooting party to be enjoyed in the countryside. That Easter, to celebrate William's success in making it through the notoriously tough first term at Sandhurst, Kate had arranged for them to go to Mustique, an island in the Caribbean, where the Robinsons owned a luxury villa. They generously waived the $12,000-per-week rental charge and told William and Kate to make themselves at home.

William had longed to visit the private island for some time; his great-aunt, Princess Margaret, had owned a villa there where she conducted a long-standing affair with her young lover, Roddy Llewelyn, in the 1970s. Better known now as a private playground for rock stars and A-list celebrities who want five-star luxury and complete privacy, the paparazzi are banned, and every visitor is vetted by the island's twenty-five-strong security team.

Described by the fashion designer Tommy Hilfiger as "endlessly social yet perfectly private," Mustique is the epitome of luxury. It has its own private airport, nine stunning beaches, and some of the world's most sumptuous villas, one of which has its own golf course. There is just one hotel on the island — the Cotton House — and a guesthouse. The Robinsons' hillside home, a five-bedroom stone mansion overlooking the famous Macaroni Beach and the sparkling turquoise Caribbean Sea, was quite simply paradise. The villa came with its own maid and gardener, as well as a cook who, alerted to the fact that the future King of England was coming to stay, had the couple's favorite foods flown in from St. Vincent ahead of their arrival. Kate and William loved it from the outset. They slipped anonymously into island life, zipping around on golf buggies and sunbathing on the tranquil beaches. With a health spa, world-famous equestrian center, and a busy tennis club, there was plenty to do. According to Elizabeth Saint, who runs the island's equestrian center where William and Kate went riding, "They love it here; they can be natural, and that's very precious for the island and everyone that lives here. We value their friendship. Mustique is a haven and sanctuary for them because no one ever talks about what goes on here."

In addition to riding horses along the shoreline, Kate and William played beach volleyball and chilled out by the infinity pool at their villa, beneath the shade of the poolside gazebos. They challenged the Virgin Group tycoon, Sir Richard Branson, to games of tennis, appreciative of the loan of his catamaran, on which they enjoyed romantic dinners à deux. Some evenings they ventured to Basil's Bar, a rustic beach shack on stilts overlooking the sea. Wearing his famed caftan, Basil Charles, one of the island's most exuberant characters, poured William's vodka and cranberry while Kate enjoyed a chilled piña colada. They danced into the night, and according to one merry-maker, William was so relaxed he joined in a karaoke night and sang along to Elvis Presley's "Suspicious Minds." "William and Kate loved Mustique and promised they would come back," recalled a regular visitor to the island. "They were left alone to enjoy their holiday and no one bothered them. They could be themselves, and they really got into the spirit of Mustique. It can be as pretentious as you make it, but William and Kate were very relaxed. They were always dressed down and often turned up at Basil's barefoot."

Back in Britain, the romantic getaway prompted further engagement rumors, much to the amusement of the pair, who had started a wall chart in the kitchen at Clarence House to document the number of times the press speculated they would tie the knot. There were, however, reports that aides had started earmarking potential dates for a royal wedding around the calendar of the senior royals. It is not unusual for significant events to be planned months in advance, but St. James's Palace Press Office denied an engagement was imminent, insisting there were "no plans" for the couple to get married. When William and Kate attended Laura Parker Bowles's wedding to

Harry Lopes in Wiltshire later that summer, there was no ring on Kate's finger.

If Kate was expecting a proposal, she didn't let her disappointment show. In fact, during the summer of 2006, the relationship seemed stronger than ever. The couple's fears about conducting their romance in the real world were largely allayed by packing in as many holidays as William's Sandhurst timetable allowed. In August, they headed to the party island of Ibiza to stay with Kate's uncle, Gary, who gave William, Kate, Pippa, James, and a few of their friends, including Guy Pelly, the keys to his $9-million Spanish villa, La Maison de Bang Bang. With gold engraving on the external wall, it is a fortress-turned-party-palace and a rather unlikely destination for royalty, but Kate and William had a ball. Gary, who knew the island well, chartered a yacht so that they could sail across the sea to nearby Formentera.

Surprisingly for such a popular vacation destination, William and Kate were able to explore the island in relative anonymity and spent a night at the Pacha nightclub without being recognized. "We organized a whole itinerary for them, including going over to a neighboring island on a boat. They've got mud baths and they were all rolling in the healing mud, which they thought was great fun, although it was particularly smelly," Gary recalled in a magazine interview. Tanned and toned in their matching white bikinis, Kate and Pippa performed expert backflips into the azure waters. Back at the villa, Gary arranged for William to learn how to mix music. "A friend of mine was teaching William how to mix on the DJ decks and he performed to the whole family. William loved the place. He said it was so much fun. Carole told me afterwards that they all had a brilliant time."

William had enjoyed being on vacation with Kate and her siblings, and just as Kate had been welcomed into the royal residences, William felt at home with her family, known by friends as the "En Masse Middletons" because they spend so much time together. It was entirely different from William's home life, and the couple often went to Oak Acre for Sunday-roast dinners. Carole made a point of stocking William's favorite red wine, and William was expected to help clear the plates after the meal, along with everyone else. Sitting around the family table and catching up over an informal meal was a treat the prince rarely enjoyed with his own family. He got along well with Michael and adored Carole, who apparently kept a picture of the prince on her mobile phone. William had been very supportive when Carole's mother, Dorothy, passed away in July after a four-month-long battle with lung cancer. Although he had never met "Lady Dorothy," he knew how close Kate was to her seventy-one-year-old grandmother, whom she regularly visited in Pangbourne. Her mother's death, four years after her father passed away, hit Carole hard. Dorothy had always been a strong, energetic, and charismatic woman, but when Ron died she was terribly lonely, according to Jean Harrison: "Dorothy was very sprightly, but she had always been very dependent on Ron, and she was immensely affected by his death. She never learned to drive, and without Ron she couldn't get about much. Then she got cancer, and it was Kate who called me up to tell me that she had died. She said that Dorothy had danced at her last birthday. It was obvious she was very close to her grandmother, and Dorothy would have been over the moon that Kate was dating Prince William, although Dorothy never told me. She knew how to keep a secret."

According to Gary, Dorothy was very proud that Kate was dating the prince. "To mum, Kate's relationship with William was like all her Christmases had come at once," he told the *Sun* newspaper. "We are from such humble stock, and then here is her granddaughter dating Prince William. She was so proud."

Dudley Singleton recalled how Kate took care of her mother at the wake, which was held at Oak Acre. William was not at the funeral service, during which Kate read a poem, and according to Mr. Singleton, at the reception afterward, Kate chatted with the local villagers and her grandmother's friends who had come to pay their respects. "I remember talking to her and she was very quiet. She was very upset as she was very close to Dorothy, but she was dignified in her mourning. There was no great show of mourning — she didn't wear her grief on her sleeve. Kate was going places at this stage, she was with William, but she still made time to talk to the villagers and no one was excluded."

Still, not for the first time in her life, Kate was at a crossroads. Another summer had passed, and as the year 2006 advance to its close, she had to admit she had no real vocation. Fortunately, a solution was around the corner, thanks once again to the Robinsons. Belle Robinson, who owns the Jigsaw clothing company with her husband, recalled, "She rang me up one day and said: 'Could I come and talk to you about work?' She genuinely wanted a job, but she needed an element of flexibility to continue the relationship with a very high-profile man and a life that she can't dictate." When an opportunity for an accessories buyer at Jigsaw Junior — the children's clothing division of the high-street chain — came up, Belle suggested that the job might suit Kate perfectly.

After a successful interview, she reported for her first day of work, arriving at the company's head office in Kew, immaculate in a crossover jersey dress and a pair of L.K. Bennett heels. Her four colleagues in the fashionable open-plan office were all female, glamorous, and ambitious, and each had been briefed ahead of Kate's arrival — not that she needed any introduction. By now she was a cover star, gracing the front pages of magazines and newspapers on an almost daily basis. Kate and William's recent holiday in Mustique had been major news, so the staff was well aware of her connections to their bosses. It was one of the reasons Kate was allowed to work a flexible week although she was expected to work from 9:00 A.M. until 6:00 P.M. Although Kate tried to blend in, her arrival most mornings was far from low key. These days she was driving a fancy silver Audi A3, the royals' car of choice, and had been given a discount on the luxury hatchback. It was more powerful than her Golf, but she could never outrun the paparazzi, who would stake out the entrance to the building, waiting for a picture. Belle recalled, "There were days when there were TV crews at the end of the drive. We'd say, 'Listen, do you want to go out the back way?' And she'd say: 'To be honest, they're going to hound us until they've got the picture. So why don't I just go, get the picture done, and then they'll leave us alone.' I thought she was very mature . . . and I think she's been quite good at neither courting the press nor sticking two fingers in the air at them. I don't think I would have been quite so polite."

According to another colleague, "Kate was pleasant from the outset and made friends quickly. We were aware of her connection to Belle and John, but she was never treated differently. She was very diligent and never late, and she had a very good work ethic. She made an effort to blend in and get on with the job."

Kate's job was to select children's accessories, and she was responsible for purchasing bracelets, necklaces, ballet slippers, hair

220

clips, and anything else that she thought would sell. She spoke to suppliers in the Middle East and worked closely with her team, making key decisions about the season's trends and what would sell both on the shop floor and on the website. It was her dream job, and she seemed to have a genuine talent for spotting eye-catching designs. She quickly became part of the team, and if not working out in the company gym at lunchtime, she would often eat lunch in the staff canteen. Kate's colleagues knew when William called because she would take the call outside so as not be overheard. "She was very cautious," recalled a colleague. "She got on with the people she worked with, and she was close to a girl she worked with called Katie Orme, but they weren't people she confided in. She never talked about William or their relationship; she was always very discreet."

Being a family-run company, there were often social occasions such as barbecues and cricket matches held for the staff members and their families. Kate once attended a company fashion show and tea party at the Hurlingham Club, but despite her efforts to just be one of the team, an enterprising photographer used a long lens to snap her drinking a cup of tea, and the photograph was published in a glossy magazine. As a buyer, Kate had the opportunity to meet fashion writers and photographers when she went to press days at the New Bond Street office, and she was happy to talk with them. "Kate and the other buyers came to see how the collection had come together," said a colleague. "Kate was very comfortable among the fashion press and people were naturally curious, but she was just pleasant and confident. I remember her chatting to members of the press. She was very interested in the work they were doing." According to her friend Emma Sayle, "Kate loved the job. She always said she had great fun traveling to fairs across the country, where she would hunt for ideas and inspiration."

Kate's four-day-a-week arrangement, which had apparently annoyed some of the staff, meant that she could attend William's Passing Out parade at the end of December. Kate and her parents had been given VIP tickets to the ceremony, which in itself predictably sparked a flurry of media activity. It was the first time Kate had attended an official engagement in the company of the Queen and senior royals, and the fact that William had also invited her parents made it even more significant. Dressed in a scarlet dress coat and a wide-brimmed black hat, Kate beamed as she watched William graduate as a second lieutenant. He would be joining the Household Cavalry's Blues and Royals regiment in the new year to train as a troop commander, like Harry.

In her elegant fitted brown coat and Cossack-style fur hat, Carole stood next to her daughter, occasionally whispering an aside and glancing at her husband, who was sitting next to William's private secretary and most senior aide, Jamie Lowther-Pinkerton. Kate looked on as William paraded outside Old College in his smart dark-blue tunic adorned with a red sash, signifying that his platoon had the honor of carrying the sovereign's banner. William found Kate in the crowd and smiled. "I love the uniform — it's so sexy," she whispered to her mother. The cameras were fixed on Kate, and a lip-reader was commissioned by one broadcaster to relay her every word. Unfortunately, it was neither William's uniform nor Kate's comment but Carole's unfortunate habit of rather innocently chewing nicotine gum throughout the ceremony that made the headlines in the newspapers the next day. She had been trying to quit smoking and was mortified that she had been captured chewing away. It was a taste of things to come, and Carole vowed she would not slip up next time.

Within a matter of weeks it was Christmas, and once again William and Kate prepared to spend the holiday apart. The Middletons had rented a country house in Perthshire, and Kate had invited William to join them for the new year celebrations. She had decided not to go to Sandringham for the Boxing Day shoot this year so that she could be with her parents, who had both recently lost a parent — for along with the passing of Dorothy, Kate's other grandmother, Valerie, had also died that summer from lymphoma.

Set on the outskirts of Alyth, Jordanstone House, an eighteenth-century manor house, was quite something. It was bitterly cold outside, a foot of snow adding a touch of magic to the scene. Inside, the Christmas tree lights glowed and log fires crackled in the spacious hearths. There was an all-weather tennis court, snooker room, an orangery, acres of surrounding parkland to explore, and four-poster beds in most of the thirteen bedrooms. William and Kate had been assigned the most luxurious of all, and she was looking forward to his arrival. However, when William telephoned on Boxing Day evening from Sandringham to tell her he wasn't coming, she was crushed. It was not like him to let her down at the last minute, and as it was only a few days before William was to relocate to Combermere Barracks in Windsor to start life as an army officer with the Blues and Royals, Kate was even more upset that she wouldn't be spending time with him.

William tried to make it up to Kate by throwing a small party at Highgrove to celebrate her twenty-fifth birthday, but she was rattled. The prince was in Windsor on her actual birthday, and when Kate left her apartment that morning, she looked tired and puffy faced. Dressed in a pretty black-and-white print Topshop dress and her standard knee-high black suede boots, she had not expected to have to elbow her way past close to twenty photographers and TV cameramen who had been camped outside her front door since 6:00 A.M. Kate's birthday had prompted a fresh barrage of speculation that there would be an engagement announcement, and there was a panic to get the first pre-engagement picture. These days, a good frame of Kate was worth up to $30,000. The Princess of Wales's former press secretary, Patrick Jephson, had fueled the rumor mill by claiming in a magazine article that Kate was set to be the next royal bride and that an announcement was imminent. To an observer, the signs were there. Bookmakers had stopped taking bets on when the couple would get engaged, and the High Street store Woolworth's had already started designing "Wills and Kate" wedding china. There was talk of Kate being given around-the-clock police protection — a step that historically accompanied an engagement — and there were police outside her home that morning to keep the press gang in check. Like the young Diana Spencer on the eve of her engagement to Charles, Kate was like a rabbit in headlights as she walked to her car. Usually unflappable, she looked genuinely shaken when some of the photographers chased after her as she accelerated out of the street.

The memory of the Princess of Wales still lingered — it was just weeks since the official inquest into her death had been published and concluded that the car crash in Paris was a tragic accident. When William called to wish Kate a happy birthday, she was close to tears, and the prince instructed his aides to issue a statement complaining about the level of harassment Kate was experiencing. His message to the press was unequivocal: leave Kate alone. "Ms. Middleton is a private individual and as such can expect to have the privacy and private life that would be enjoyed by any member of the public," the Palace insisted. Even Prime Minister David Cameron remarked about his "concern about the number of people on Kate Middleton's doorstep."

There was no engagement, and deep down Kate feared there might not be one in the future. She was increasingly miserable at having to cope with the downside of her fame without William present, which only compounded her sense of loneliness. The pang of uncertainty she had felt since New Year's Eve had not subsided, and although she and William spoke regularly on the phone, she knew they would not be seeing much of each other over the coming months. After several weeks in Windsor, William was posted to Dorset for a two-and-a-half-month tank commander's course.

They managed to see one another on occasional weekends, and in March 2007, Kate and William were able to spend some proper time together on a skiing holiday at Zermatt in Switzerland with friends. Tucked away in their wooden chalet, Kate felt bold enough to voice her fears about their relationship, while William did his best to allay them, but they both knew this was a rocky patch. A long-distance romance didn't worry Kate, but she did have a problem with William coming to London to party instead of spending time with her, which had became a pattern since he had moved to Dorset. It seemed to her that William would rather go out and enjoy himself when he had a free weekend than spend time with her. When the press reported that William had spent the night flirting and dancing with another woman on a boy's night out at Boujis, Kate was furious and told him so.

William, who can be headstrong and stubborn, seemed intent on having as much fun as possible, however, and when he was in Dorset, he often went out drinking with his platoon. For Kate, the final straw came as March drew to a close. William had been photographed partying at the Elements nightclub in Poole with two local girls, and to ensure her humiliation, his drunken antics were published in the tabloids. There were pictures of William dancing on a podium with a nineteen-year-old student, Lisa Agar, who claimed William was "touchy, feely, and quite pissed."

Kate knew that the worst thing was to back William into a corner, but the time had come when she felt she had no alternative but to deliver William an ultimatum. If they were together, she wanted his full commitment, otherwise the relationship was over. The strain between them was apparent at the Cheltenham races at the end of March. In their matching tweeds, Kate looked downcast and hid behind dark glasses, while William seemed distant from her. That Easter, early in April, they agreed to split, for the second time in their six-year-long courtship. Kate was heartbroken.

William had spoken to his grandparents and his father about his concerns in the weeks leading up to the breakup. When he canceled the new year celebration with Kate at the eleventh hour, his grandfather told him he had to make his mind up about marriage. The Duke of Edinburgh had enjoyed a long courtship with the young Princess Elizabeth before officially proposing two months after her twenty-first birthday. They would have married sooner had it not been for King George V insisting they wait until Elizabeth's coming of age. Charles, meanwhile, advised William not to hurry into marriage. Although he knew firsthand the dangers of procrastinating, he had also endured the pain of a very public divorce. The Queen advised William to take his time and not be rushed into marriage. The truth was, commitment frightened William and he had gotten cold feet. He was twenty-four,

loved his army lifestyle, and already said he
didn't want to get married "until I'm at least
twenty-eight, or maybe thirty." Apparently,
he had been spooked by talk of courtiers
looking for a suitable date for a royal wedding and china cups being made ahead of a
royal engagement.

Kate, however, was prepared to wait, but
no one was going to make a fool of her.
Fortunately, on the weekend of the split,
she was at home with her family, who as
always, was there to support her. Belle
Robinson, who had read the news in the
papers along with the rest of the country,
told her not to come into work that week,
while Carole, always a cool head in a crisis,
advised Kate to give William time. She reassured Kate that William would be back
and suggested they go on a holiday to Ibiza
with some friends. To make matters worse,
the papers that weekend were full of spite-
ful commentary suggesting that the breakup
came down to the fact that Kate was too
middle class for William and was not a suitable royal bride. Given her love and loyalty
to the prince, this must have stung Kate like
salt in a raw wound; and besides, it wasn't
true. Although Carole's family was proudly
working class, Michael's family could be
linked to earls, countesses, a former Prime

Minister — William Petty-Fitzmaurice, the first Marquess of Lansdowne, who served as Prime Minister in Britain from 1782 to 1783 — and royalty.

Genealogists are able to trace the Middleton lineage to King Edward III through Sir Thomas Fairfax, a wealthy aristocrat born in the seventeenth century. Fairfax was a parliamentarian general who served under King Charles I and was married to Anne Gascoigne, a direct descendent of King Edward III. They had twin sons who gave rise to two lines of descent. Nicholas Fairfax, the elder son, was distantly related to Princess Diana's family, the Spencers, and William Fairfax, the younger twin, was related to the Middletons. The discovery meant that William and Kate are in fact fourteenth cousins once removed.

But despite the family's distant connection with royalty, the Middletons came in for criticism, in particular Carole, who was labeled pushy and "unashamedly ambitious." Some commentators believed the royal family had lost its greatest asset since Diana. Others compared Kate to Camilla, fearing that like his father, William had just let his first true love slip through his fingers. Kate allowed herself the weekend to mourn the end of their romance. She was deeply touched to receive messages of support from Charles and Harry, who was preparing to go to Iraq, as well as the Duke of Edinburgh, who sent her his best wishes.

She mustered all her strength and took her mother's advice to show William exactly what he was missing. The prince had marked the end of their relationship with a night out at Mahiki nightclub, a Polynesian-themed bar in Mayfair, and Kate followed suit. The club, famous for its outrageously expensive and flamboyant cocktails, was managed by Guy Pelly. Dressed in a thigh-skimming minidress, Kate let her hair down and ordered a round of piña coladas. Michael Evans, who worked at the club, recalled that Kate was a model of decorum: "When Kate came to the club, she always queued and never expected free drinks." After hitting the dance floor, she spent the rest of the evening sitting on a swinging wicker seat talking to Guy. Until now, their friendship had been a touch frosty, but Guy had always been kind to Kate, protecting her from the jealous taunts of some snooty royal hangers-on who whispered "doors to manual" when Kate walked into the club — a derogatory reference to her parents' airline industry careers. He knew William better than most and assured her that the prince cared for her a great deal.

But Kate hadn't spoken with William, who was now drowning his sorrows back at the Elements nightclub with his new army friends. He could not have failed to notice the pictures of Kate in the daily newspapers. There she was, looking sensational, on front page after front page, enjoying nights out with her sister, with her friends, with people he didn't even know. She was photographed at a glamorous book launch in Mayfair with socialite Tara Palmer-Tomkinson and leaving a party to celebrate a movie about adult sex toys. It was a far cry from the tweed-clad young woman who had stood unhappily next to him at Cheltenham just a few weeks before. Far from appearing heartbroken, she seemed to be reveling in the attention she received from the many male admirers who were lining up to dance with her.

It seemed a case of what William could do, Kate could do better.

CHAPTER 8
WAITY KATIE

The weeks after the split were incredibly difficult for Kate and her family, and friends rallied around to support her. Fortunately, the media interest in her every move eventually died down, giving her some time to think about what she was going to do. Her life had come to a standstill; the man she hoped to one day marry had told her it was over, and now Kate was alone. For her, the future had always been William, and she had relegated every other part of her life to second place. She took her mother's advice and decided to turn what had happened into something positive. She now had an opportunity to think about herself and what she wanted to do. One friend from Marlborough, Alicia Fox Pitt, had been in touch to see if Kate wanted to take part in a charity boating challenge. A group of women, who called themselves the "Sisterhood," had decided to row across the English Channel to raise money for two children's charities, and Kate thought it sounded like an excellent idea for a worthwhile cause.

The criticism she had received in the wake of the split had wounded her, and she badly wanted to prove that she wasn't just "William's former girlfriend," as she was now referred to in the press, but a bright, determined, and driven young woman with a life of her own. Since the breakup in April, she had been inundated with interview requests and had been offered a multimillion-dollar book deal, but she would never dream of discussing her past with William. Secretly, she hoped there might be a reconciliation, but for the moment, she needed to focus on herself. She picked up the phone and called Emma Sayle, who was organizing the race.

"I first spoke to her in April on the phone after she and William had broken up," remembered Emma. "She said she wanted to be involved with something, and I told her about the race and she signed up in May."

Taking her place at the helm, Kate took the tiller and steered down the River Thames. Although she had learned how to sail a seventy-two-foot Challenger during her gap year, a dragon boat was an altogether different experience. Emma made

Kate her co-helm, and Kate, who as a child enjoyed sailing holidays in Norfolk with her family, had proved herself to be a natural. "The idea was to split the rowing between us," said Emma. "The boat was heavy but Kate was strong and well coordinated. She was able to deal with the currents and waves, and I was very impressed with how good she was."

The race, from Dover to Cap Gris Nez, near Calais, was quite a challenge. The Sisterhood — a group of twenty-one young women — was competing against the all-male "Brotherhood," and Kate was expected at every 6:00 A.M. training session without fail. Having taken a week's compassionate leave, she was now back at Jigsaw and the early morning starts on the river were not her usual choice before a full day's work. However, she soon found that rowing was a form of therapy, and on this hazy morning, as she steered down the River Thames past Chiswick and downriver to Hammersmith, with the frenetic exercise clearing her mind, there was time to reflect.

Since the split, Kate had gone through a noticeable transformation. It wasn't just the shorter hemlines and daring outfits — she was more spontaneous without William at her side and more outgoing. Behind the scenes, Carole had encouraged her not to dwell on what had happened but to live her life to the full. Pippa, who had just finished her finals, had made it her duty to take her older sister out, insisting that sitting on the sofa at home would do her no good. A steady stream of gilt-edged invitations to the best parties in town dropped onto the doormat of their Chelsea apartment, and Pippa kept a busy social diary for them both. They rarely strayed further than Chelsea, and evenings out entailed drinking at Mahiki, dancing at Boujis, or sipping champagne at a glitzy party. With their amazing figures, glossy hair, and matching smiles, they were a tantalizing and photogenic duo. Pippa, at five foot six the shorter of the sisters by four inches — Kate stands at an impressive five foot ten inches — was always the more outgoing, steering Kate around and fielding off the paparazzi. That season, they topped *Tatler* magazine's prestigious Most Invited list and, according to one newspaper, were now known not simply as the Middleton sisters but as "The Wisteria Sisters" because they were "highly decorative, terribly fragrant and have a ferocious ability to climb." William was certainly seeing a more tantalizing side to his ex-girlfriend and must have been reminded of the Kate who sashayed down the runway in her underwear and a see-through dress all those years before at St. Andrews.

Without the prince to take up all her time, Kate also had the chance to rekindle old friendships, and she was grateful for the chance to spend a week in Ibiza with Emilia d'Erlanger. Carole had arranged for them to stay at Gary's villa, La Maison de Bang Bang, and although she was "very low, spending huge amounts of time on the phone, walking around the pool," according to her uncle, she made an effort to go out to the fashionable Blue Marlin beach club, where she and Emilia drank cocktails and danced through the night. Kate loved spending time with her old best friend. It was, she said, the one good thing to have come out of the split.

Back in London, Kate forged a new friendship with Emma Sayle. They were spending a lot of time training together and got along well. They shared a love of sports: they both lived close to the King's Road and they had friends in common. In between training sessions, they would meet for coffee and got to know each other better. "She was very easygoing, and we all got on with her. She didn't have any airs or graces," Emma recalled. "We got to see a very different girl from the Kate you read about in the papers. She was lots of fun and really relaxed when she was training. She didn't make a big deal about the fact that she used to date William; in fact she kept it very quiet. A lot of the girls didn't know who she was at first, which really helped her settle in. She was very dedicated and always on time for training. She was also very fit and worked out at the gym. I remember she dropped down to a size six while we were training. She was devastated when she and William split up."

No doubt the emotional upset was another contributing factor to Kate's dramatic weight loss. By mid-May, however, William and Kate were back in touch and regularly talking on the phone. At the end of the month they secretly met up at Clarence House and at a pub close to Highgrove, where William told her he wanted to get back together. Kate didn't want to rush into anything. She had been badly hurt and told William she needed some time. According to Emma, "She was in touch with William the whole time she was training with us. She was very honest and open with me, and she always referred to William as the love of her life. He was the most important person in her life and that was very obvious. She would always speak about him very lovingly; to her he was just William. They had a very normal relationship and were very much in love. She said it was the best relationship she ever had and that when it's the two of them, it is perfect. It's when they are in the public eye it gets so complicated."

Back at Jigsaw's head office, Kate's colleagues noticed that she was spending more time on her mobile phone, talking in private outside the office in the parking lot. The start of June 2007 marked a pivotal moment. Kate and William had been invited to a party thrown by their mutual friend Sam Waley-Cohen at his family's seventeenth-century manor house, and according to one guest, they spent "hours" deep in conversation. "There's an idea that I was like Cupid with a bow and arrow. People love the idea that somebody put them back together, but they put themselves together far more," Mr. Waley-Cohen recalled of the night in an interview with the *Mail on Sunday*.

William pleaded with Kate to give their relationship another go, and by the time he invited her to a party on June 9 at his barracks in Dorset, she had made her mind up. Dressed as a nurse — a rather sexy one in fishnet tights and a short dress, for a Freakin' Naughty–themed fancy dress party

— William followed her around "like a lost puppy," according to one guest who said they stayed on the dance floor most of the night. As the clock struck midnight, William leaned in and kissed Kate. "They couldn't keep their hands off each other," recalled the eyewitness. "William didn't care that people were looking. His friends were joking that they should get a room." William didn't need any persuading and took Kate by the hand and led her out of the party.

When she returned to training the following week, she was noticeably happier, according to Emma, one of the few people who knew about the reconciliation. The clandestine reunion didn't stay a secret for long, however, and before the month was out, the *Mail on Sunday* reported that the couple was back together.

At the Palace the news came as no surprise. For some weeks, eagle-eyed courtiers had been observing Kate's Audi coming and going from its reserved spot at Clarence House. She was in residence whenever William was home from Dorset, and as well as spending some quality time with him, she had been helping him finalize the running order for a concert he and Harry had planned to commemorate the life of their mother. The summer of 2007 marked the

241

tenth anniversary of the princess's death, and the concert was to be a celebration of her life. While Harry had been in Canada on military training exercise, William had overseen and approved the all-star lineup for the Wembly concert. The night before, Kate had slipped unnoticed into Clarence House to help William make the final tweaks to his speech.

The princes had reserved the entire Royal Box for their family and friends, but in order not to deflect from the purpose of the day, William and Kate agreed not to sit together. Instead, Kate sat next to James and Pippa, now nursing her own broken heart after breaking up with her long-term boyfriend, JJ Jardine Patterson. Before the start of the concert, William had been quizzed about his on-off relationship with Kate during an interview with the NBC *Today* show and had managed to field the question well. A worldwide audience was tuned in to watch the concert, and he desperately didn't want it to be eclipsed by speculation about him and Kate.

Later, while Harry openly kissed his on-and-off Zimbabwean girlfriend Chelsy Davy in the front row, William and Kate were careful not to make eye contact, though when Kate sang along to Take That's "Back for Good," she allowed herself a momentary glance at William. It wasn't long until they could be together, away from the gaze of the media at the VIP after-party. According to one eyewitness, William couldn't take his eyes off Kate's revealing white lace dress and knee-high boots. They danced to the Bodyrockers' hit "I Like the Way You Move," which, according to friends was "their song," and they were later spotted canoodling in a dark corner. However, determined not to be photographed together, they went home separately at 4:00 A.M. the following morning.

Just days after the concert Kate was back at the helm, and with race day fast approaching, the Sisterhood's challenge was now headline news. With rumors buzzing that the couple had reunited, the paparazzi attended every training session, and the Palace was concerned that the event was becoming a "media circus." Once again, Kate had become the story, and when she appeared on the cover of *Hello* magazine posing with her teammates in their dragon boat beneath the headline, "Posing Exclusively for *Hello* with Her Crewmates," alarm bells rang at the Palace. Fully made up and beaming for the camera, Kate was accused of double standards in the press. One of her lawyers, Gerrard Tyrrell, had complained to the Press Complaints Commission about the level of harassment Kate was subjected to, yet here she was seemingly happy to take part in a promotional photo shoot. The late *Daily Mirror* journalist Sue Carroll suggested she was being "driven by the oxygen of publicity," while *Daily Mail* columnist Richard Kay noted that "the Sisterhood's practice sessions had become a magnet for publicity." The timing was unfortunate. The issue of the paparazzi's relentless pursuit of Kate had formed part of a landmark report by Parliament's Culture, Media and Sport Committee, titled "Self-Regulation of the Press." The report, published in July 2007, concluded that with regard to Kate, "harassment was evident" and editors could no longer use paparazzi pictures of her. The watershed moment had been her twenty-fifth birthday, when she was besieged by photographers outside her London home. The committee described Kate as the victim of "clear and persistent harassment" by the paparazzi. It was a major victory for Kate, her lawyers, and the Palace, but her participation in the now very public dragon boat race posed a serious dilemma and threatened to undo all their efforts in protecting Kate. She could not have it both ways, and according to Emma, the Palace advised her to pull out of the race.

"When the magazine came to photograph us at one of our training sessions, I'd already told them Kate wouldn't be in the picture, but when the day came, she was actually relaxed and wanted to be in on the team photograph. The magazine cropped Kate out and put her on the front page and made it the 'Kate Story' with a whole six pages about her on the inside. Kate was devastated. At the next training session, there were forty photographers and it was a nightmare. The whole thing was becoming a media circus, and Kate said she was under a lot of pressure to pull out by Clarence House. I thought it was a great shame and I actually told her I thought she was making a mistake . . . because it was the one chance Kate could prove to the world who she really was."

While her "sisters" rowed twenty-one miles across the English Channel that August, Kate paddled with William in the warm waters of the Indian Ocean off the coast of Africa. They had flown out to the luxury island of Desroches in the Seychelles for what they both knew was a make-or-break holiday. The prince had booked a $750-per-night private bungalow, and in order not to be recognized, they checked in as Martin and Rosemary Middleton. It was the perfect escape, and they spent the days swimming, taking kayaks out to the coral reef, and dining together on the terrace of their private villa. It was the first time they had been alone since their breakup, and they spent much of the holiday hidden away in the privacy of their beachfront bungalow. They had plenty to discuss. William was nearing the end of his training with the Blues and Royals and would be graduating as a troop commander in September, which effectively meant he was qualified to go to war like his younger brother, who was being posted to Afghanistan at Christmas. Harry had been due to go to Iraq that summer, but the tour of duty was canceled after Islamic militants vowed to kill him. It was exactly the reason that William, as heir apparent, could never be posted to the front line, despite his determination to be treated the same as every other soldier. As the future head of the Armed Forces, he would be assigned to work for each of the forces instead.

Kate knew that William wanted to serve in the military more than anything else. She understood that it was his means of having a sense of purpose — to serve his Queen and country meant everything to him, and she respected and supported him. But she had to think about her own future, too. She knew William was committed to the military, but what about his commitment to her? She needed some assurance that one day they would marry, if they planned to stay together. They had weathered their most serious split to date, and she needed to know that they shared the same aspiration — ultimately to be together. There on the paradise island, William promised Kate that he was in the relationship for the long term. For the very first time they talked seriously about marriage, and with the ocean before them and beneath the night sky, they made a pact to marry. "They didn't agree to get married there and then; what they made was a pact," a member of their inner circle explained. "William told Kate she was the one but he was not ready to get married. He promised her his commitment and said he would not let her down, and she in turn agreed to wait for him."

William was due to spend six months on attachment with the Royal Air Force (RAF) and the Royal Navy, and he would be away for much of the time. Kate listened carefully. She knew the sacrifices the future would entail, but she loved William and was prepared to wait for him. They sealed their secret deal with a kiss.

Back in England, William completed his tank-training course while Kate used the new chapter in her life to assess her own career. She had been working at Jigsaw for nearly a year, and although she was happy, she wasn't doing a job she was passionate about. Her real interest was in photography, and so, after talking to Belle Robinson, she handed in her notice in September. Kate had acquired an impressive portfolio of her own photographs during her travels, and she had started collating her work. According to Emma, "She talked about going abroad and pursuing a career in photography. She was considering going to Paris and also New York."

Now that she and William were back together, heading overseas was a less attractive option, so instead she approached the esteemed celebrity photographer Alistair Morrison, who was based in Windsor and whose work she had admired at the National Portrait Gallery in London. Mr. Morrison invited Kate to his gallery: "She was interested in photography and the history of art and she got in touch with me," said Mr. Morrison. "I was based in Windsor, and she was at her parents' home a lot, which was just down the motorway. She would often come to visit me at the gallery. I think I was seen as someone who could look after her interests and be discreet." When Kate said she wanted to curate an exhibition, Mr. Morrison suggested that she start with a series of his celebrity photographs. Kate's timing was fortuitous, and she was available to start work immediately. She spent several weeks coordinating the photographs and then worked on planning a party to launch the exhibition. She asked the Robinsons if they would allow her to use The Shop at Bluebird in Chelsea. "Catherine organized everything from the invitations to the selection of work and put together a guest list for the launch which included collectors, my list, the Bluebird's list and her own, including her family and friends," said Mr. Morrison.

Carole, Michael, and James came to the opening party, but William stayed away until the end of the evening, not wishing to upstage his girlfriend. "Prince William joined us for dinner," confirmed Mr. Morrison, who was so impressed with Kate's work he continued to mentor her afterward. "I encouraged her to pursue her photography, specifically some wonderful landscape work that she had done over her travels. At the same time I introduced her to my printers, as she was naturally keen to see some good quality prints of her work. She has a natural eye for landscape composition and uses light very well, often focusing on images heavily dominated by skies at all times of the day. Color was always her preference. Most of her work is a mixture of many locations and is almost exclusively sky dominated. I encouraged her not to generalize but to think about documenting one area through a number of different landscapes."

By now Kate had pretty much moved out of her Chelsea apartment and was mostly living at Clarence House. The prince, who had moved from Dorset back to Combermere Barracks in Windsor, was in London more frequently, and once again rumors of an engagement circulated. As 2007 came to a close, a public opinion poll in Britain found that 80 percent of Britons believed that Kate would be a good addition to the royal family, while courtiers at the Palace reverted to the forward-planning diary for potential dates. There was no doubt that Kate was back in the fold when she joined the royals' annual festive pheasant shoot at Windsor Park just before Christmas. She had been criticized by animal rights campaigners after being photographed deer hunting with Prince Charles in Scotland, but Kate had no intention of giving it up. She enjoyed the sport and often hunted with William, something she loved because it was a quiet and peaceful time for the two of them to be together.

The new year heralded a fresh start for the couple. They had celebrated Kate's twenty-sixth birthday at the beginning of January with a quiet dinner at Clarence House, a far happier and settled occasion than the year before. Once again, however, her birthday coincided with William leaving, this time for a four-month pilot-training course at RAF Cranwell in Lincolnshire. William had been looking forward to his secondment (temporary assignment) with the RAF. He had dreamed of being a pilot ever since he was a little boy and his uncle Andrew had regaled him with stories of flying helicopters in the Falklands. Now he was training for his own pilot's badge — known in the RAF as "wings" — on a fast-track course that entailed early morning starts and late-night cramming for exams. His career, according to his aides, was "his number one priority" and once again, they tried to dampen rumors of an engagement. Kate was prepared for the time apart and was reassured by the sheer intensity of the training, which left little time for William to party and misbehave. In March 2008, they flew to Klosters, and this time Pippa joined them. The sisters loved challenging one another on unmarked slopes. They were both better skiers than William, and Kate even outshone the protection officer who accompanied them down the slopes. Gliding expertly down the ski run, she conjured memories of Diana, who used to delight in outskiing Charles on the very same mountains.

This was not the only echo of the late princess. Back at home, Kate had joined the prestigious Harbour Club in Chelsea, where Princess Diana also used to work out. On Friday afternoons, she went shopping for groceries at the King's Road branch of Waitrose before driving to Clarence House to prepare for William's arrival from RAF Cranwell. The prince called her when he was en route, and Kate would always have a hot bath ready for him and a home-cooked dinner in the oven. Although their living space there was small, she had overseen a small refurbishment, and the Osbourne and Little wallpaper she had selected made their living quarters far more homey.

One friend, who was invited over for supper, recalled a scene of marital bliss: "Kate cooked and let William enjoy a glass of wine. Every so often he helped her stir and taste a sauce. They were very sweet together, very tactile, and they had a habit of finishing each other's sentences." They had been advised by Charles to stay away from nightclubs after their last visit to Boujis had ended in an unseemly scuffle among the paparazzi, who were desperate to get a picture of the couple now that they were back together. Because they were seen so rarely in public these days, photographs of William and Kate were worth a lot of money. When Kate had left Boujis she was nearly knocked over as she tried to get into a waiting car.

There had been another concerning episode when Kate and her family celebrated James's twenty-first birthday in April. Party promoter Ed Taylor, a friend of Kate's, had arranged a VIP table for them at Raffles nightclub on the King's Road, but unfortunately James downed one too many shots, and according to photographer Niraj Tanna, who was there, "Michael had to literally carry James to the car. He was all over the place and couldn't stand up properly. Carole was jumping up at me trying to push my camera so I couldn't take the photograph. James was swerving on the pavement, and then he started urinating on the street. That's when Carole started going mad and jumping up at my face trying to push the camera so I couldn't take a frame." Kate, who was said to be mortified, had left the club through a back entrance.

But it wasn't just James, however, who had come under scrutiny. William was at the center of an escalating argument in the press after it was reported that he had flown a Chinook helicopter to his cousin Peter Phillips's stag party on the Isle of Wight hours after graduating from RAF Cranwell. The two-hour sortie had been cleared by his senior flying officers, but there was a furor over the fact that the prince had been allowed to fly a $15-million helicopter to a stag party when there was a shortage of Chinooks in Afghanistan, where the aircraft is used to ferry in supplies to British troops. Questions were asked about why William had been allowed to use the aircraft as a taxi service. The RAF insisted the flight was a "legitimate training sortie which tested his new skills," but the episode descended into farce when it also emerged that William had made a number of practice flights to High-grove, Windsor Castle, and to Oak Acre, the Middletons' family home.

Carole and Michael, who had no idea William was arriving by air, ran into their garden after hearing an almighty noise in the adjacent field, only to discover it was William "buzzing in." The storm over the flights blew over a few days later, however, when William flew to Afghanistan in a top-secret overnight visit to see British troops. The trip had been planned for some time, but the Ministry of Defence was accused of staging a public relations exercise to save face.

Harry had recently returned from serving on the front line in Afghanistan after finally realizing his dream to fight for his country, but William was only able to make a fleeting visit to meet with RAF servicemen in Kandahar. Nonetheless, his mission was significant because he brought home the body of a British serviceman who had been killed in combat.

Kate had been invited to the graduation ceremony at RAF Cranwell on Friday, April 11, 2008, to watch William get his wings, and she watched proudly as they were pinned onto his pristine uniform. As she chatted with Camilla and William's private secretary Jamie Lowther-Pinkerton in the audience, Kate seemed very comfortable, her presence in the front row signifying that she and William were back on track. The following month, William asked if she would attend his cousin Peter Phillips's wedding on his behalf because he had been invited to the wedding of Batian Craig, Jecca's brother, in Kenya. It was a year since their breakup, and the fact that Kate was representing William at a family wedding was a sign of just how serious the relationship was.

Peter was marrying his Canadian fiancée, Autumn Kelly, at St. George's Chapel in the grounds of Windsor Castle on May 17, and all the senior members of the family were attending. Harry and Chelsy, who were back together after a romantic reunion in Botswana, had been invited, and Kate was grateful, for she didn't know many of the guests. Her friendship with Chelsy was lukewarm; they were completely different characters, and the bubbly Zimbabwean got along better with Pippa. Kate had made an effort to befriend Chelsy, inviting her clothes shopping, but Chelsy had turned the offer down, leading to a coolness between them. On this occasion, however, they bonded, because they were both nervous about meeting the Queen. Although she was a regular guest at the royal palaces and had been to Sandringham for the Boxing Day shoot, this was, rather surprisingly, the first time Kate would be formally introduced to the Queen. Understandably, without William by her side, she was shy and later recalled, "It was amongst a lot of other guests and she was very friendly." The Queen had made a point of coming over to say hello to Kate, but according to Lady Elizabeth Anson, the introduction was brief: "There wasn't much time to speak. Meeting someone as far as the Queen is concerned is having tea with them, so for the Queen, this was an introduction rather than a proper meeting."

Despite the brevity of their encounter, the Queen was interested in Kate and wanted to learn more about the young woman who looked set to marry into her family one day. William had sought his grandmother's advice during their brief separation, and the Queen was pleased that they were now happily back together, but she was concerned that Kate did not have a career. Although she was working on her photography, it had been six months since Kate quit Jigsaw, and there seemed to be no urgency on her part to return to work.

For the Queen, who carries out hundreds of engagements and travels around the country conducting official duties practically every day of the year, the idea of not working was unthinkable. Even during holidays, her red government boxes, containing confidential parliamentary papers for her to read, are always close at hand. She has a strong work ethic and has raised all of her children to follow her lead, putting duty ahead of self. At the time, a source close to the family said, "The Queen has no idea what Kate does. Privately, she is very concerned about what the repercussions could be if Kate is not in a stable job as and when William is ready to propose. The Queen is very close to her grandson, and they of course discuss Kate. Her Majesty is very aware that it's a serious and long-term relationship. Although they are not yet engaged, it seems more likely than not that Kate will be a royal bride one day, and the Queen is of the opinion that Kate should be working. She believes in a modern monarchy and feels very strongly that the royals should be leading by example. Swanning from one five-star holiday resort to another is not the prerequisite for a young woman possibly destined to be Queen."

To observers, Kate did seem to be having rather frequent holidays, and the press, much to her frustration, had taken to calling her "Waity Katie" because she seemed happy to wait on the sidelines for a marriage proposal. This label stuck, and it hurt

Kate, who felt she was in an impossible situation. The truth was she was in limbo. While Pippa was enjoying working for a London-based events company and James had started up his own business, Kate's career was on the back burner. It was impossible for her to commit to a full-time job while juggling her life around seeing William, who had started a two-month-long assignment with the Royal Navy at the start of June. The prince was following in royal footsteps when he enrolled at the Britannia Royal Naval College at Dartmouth. His great-grandfather, King George VI, had trained at the base, as had his grandfather and his father. Whereas William had a clear purpose to his life, right then flying naval helicopters and diving with nuclear submarines, Kate was becoming increasingly frustrated with her own lack of career.

Mr. Morrison was still encouraging her to curate an exhibition of her own work. He genuinely believed in her ability to take compelling photographs, but Kate was worried she might face a further backlash: "As with most young artists, the obstacle for Kate was confidence, and I think she was worried about being knocked. I encouraged her to look at her work and to edit it without asking for other people's opinions. I thought she could put together an exhibition, but she was worried that people would say that she was only being exhibited because of who she was. I think there was a fear of being criticized as well. I don't think the title 'Waity Katie' was fair. She wasn't lazy and just waiting for William. She was very aware of what she was capable of doing, and she went ahead and did it. She found opportunities to work in art and photography."

Kate was not, however, prepared to take the risk of showing her work and then be accused of cashing in on her royal connections. And while she was trying to forge her own future, her family watched helplessly from the sidelines. The concerns, at the highest level at the Palace, were privately being referred to as "the Kate problem" and had already made front-page news in the British press.

Carole wanted to put a plan in place before any further damage was done to Kate's reputation. She needed someone to shoot a new catalog for Party Pieces and help set up First Birthdays, a new section on the site. Kate was perfectly equipped to do both. Photographing princess outfits and treasure chests was quite different from shooting landscapes, and Kate described the work as "rather surreal" to her friends, but according to Mr. Morrison, it was an important technique for Kate to master and a happy compromise. "Still life is actually a good discipline. Kate may well have preferred doing landscapes, but this was part of her visual growing up. Working for Party Pieces was also a sensible stopgap opportunity for her. They are a very close family and very supportive of each other. Carole and Michael knew that Kate was going to be in a no-win situation, and I'm pretty sure they discussed the repercussions of being in the public eye. Carole's advice to all of the children was: 'You must prepare yourself.' I think she knew they weren't going to get patted on the back, and Kate particularly was always going to end up being criticized. People were always going to say that working for the family was easy."

James had recently launched a do-it-yourself cake-making enterprise — Cake Kit — within the Party Pieces operation, and Kate helped to coordinate a new website. It was a perfect arrangement that would keep them both out of the headlines, especially James, whose penchant for going out to fashionable London nightclubs and joshing that he would one day be "the brother of the future Queen" had been generating column inches in the press. There was no chance of them being spied on at Party Pieces' Bucklebury-based head office, and although it wasn't the most inspiring of jobs, the photography kept Kate busy and earned her some money. Most important, it gave her the flexibility to work her schedule around William. "This wasn't really a career choice. It was about being with the person she loved, who happened to be the heir to the throne," said Mr. Morrison. "Kate had to prepare herself for what that meant. It wasn't about being Waity Katie, it was about being with William. Quite simply, they loved each other, wanted to be with each other, and had to filter themselves through the fog of expectancy."

It was a sentiment echoed by her family and friends, and working for the family firm was considered the perfect solution. There was only one minor setback when Carole authorized a picture and biography of Kate to be posted on the website. It was designed as a positive PR move, but it backfired when the press accused Kate of breaching her own privacy, and within hours, the picture of her was removed from the website.

With her schedule now flexible, on June 16, 2008, when William was invested into the Order of the Garter at Windsor Castle, Kate was there to watch. The ancient ceremony saw William appointed a Royal Knight of the Garter, one of the highest honors bestowed by the Queen upon her most-trusted and dutiful "knights," among them Prince Philip and Prince Charles. William was invested in Windsor Castle's Garter Throne Room and then "installed" during a service at St. George's Chapel. Seeing him in his ornate velvet robes and hat of ostrich plumes, Kate, who was watching the procession with Prince Harry, couldn't resist a giggle. Later that month, she had plenty of time to plan William's twenty-sixth birthday, a small celebration at Highgrove for a group of their friends. When William left the country to spend five weeks aboard HMS *Iron Duke* in the Caribbean at the end of the month, Kate kept herself busy at work.

The Queen had quietly suggested to William that Kate get involved with a charity, and they both considered it an excellent idea. Party Pieces already had a connection with Starlight, a children's charity in the United Kingdom, and Carole regularly sent out complementary "prince and princess"–themed birthday party bags to hospices and children's wards around the country. Before he left for the Caribbean, William and Kate attended the Boodles Boxing Ball in June at the Royal Lancaster Hotel in London, where they took a table at the black-tie gala with some of their friends. The charity night, which involved a series of boxing matches between former Etonians and Cambridge graduates, was followed by a champagne dinner and raised $180,000 for the charity. Charlie Gilkes, one of the couple's friends, organized the gala, and Kate had arranged for cystic fibrosis sufferer Bianca Nicholas, who had sung that night, to meet William and Harry, which had thrilled the aspiring singer. Kate thought highly of the charity, which grants terminally ill children a "once-in-a-lifetime wish," and she arranged to meet with Chief Executive Officer Neil Swan of the charity to see how she could help more. He recalled, "Kate was working with Party Pieces at the time, and she came up with a clever idea for a party bag that doubled up as a coloring-in gift. She also designed some Starlight-themed crayons and other bits and pieces to go in the bags. To us, she was just Kate, and we would go and have meetings with her at Party Pieces, and sometimes she would come to us. She came up with lots of creative ideas for parties that we were arranging for sick children, and she did a lot of work below the radar."

Wanting to learn more about the work of the charity and how it helped hospices and children's hospitals around the country, Kate began making secret trips to the Naomi House hospice in Hampshire, close to her family home. She would drive to the hospice bearing gifts for the children, with whom she would spend hours reading and playing. The press never found out about the visits, which Kate wanted to keep below the radar, according to one senior source at the charity: "We are used to working with high-profile people, and it is in our interests to keep the visits secret. A few of us were aware of the work Kate was doing in hospices at that time, but we were asked to keep it quiet."

Kate found the visits deeply rewarding and grounding, and it gave her great pleasure to know that she was able to bring a ray of happiness to some seriously ill young people. "It upset us a lot when we read in the papers that Kate was work-shy when she was actually doing a lot of charity work that no one knew about," said one of her friends.

Kate recognized that her profile afforded her the opportunity to do something worthwhile. In September 2008, she joined forces with her friend Sam Waley-Cohen and co-organized a charity roller-skating disco to raise funds for a new ward at the Oxford Children's Hospital. Sam's brother, Tom, had been treated at the hospital for a rare form of bone cancer before his death, and Kate, who had been at Marlborough with Tom, was profoundly affected when he passed away at the young age of twenty. She helped Sam plan the event at the Renaissance Rooms in Vauxhall, South London, and oversaw the guest list. "Kate has been fantastic in using her contacts to get people along — she persuaded loads of people to commit. Her involvement has obviously raised the profile," Sam told the *Daily Mirror* after the event. The night was a sellout and raised $150,000, largely thanks to Kate, who whizzed around the skating rink in a pair of canary-yellow hot pants and a shiny green sequined halter top. On her final lap, she fell flat on her rear, spread-eagled in a most unladylike manner.

This, however, wasn't the only thing to knock Kate off her feet. William had announced, quite suddenly, that he wanted to join the RAF and become a search-and-rescue pilot, and the news had come as a surprise to Kate, the royal family, and the courtiers at the Palace. The prince had completed his military assignments with all of the Armed Forces, and now he was at a crossroads in his career. There were two real options; returning to the Household Cavalry or quitting the forces. The press had speculated that, having finished his assignments, the prince would be under pressure from the Palace to start carrying out more official engagements, but it wasn't what William wanted to do. He had seen his father struggle to carve a niche for himself as a king in waiting, and he didn't want the same fate, not yet. He had loved his time serving with the RAF, and now that he had his flying badge, he wanted to use it. The news that he was to join the RAF was made official on September 15, 2008. "The time I spent with the RAF earlier this year made me realize how much I love flying," William said. "Joining search and rescue is a perfect opportunity for me to serve in the forces operationally."

With that single decision, Kate's life was turned upside down. She had expected a proposal once William had completed his military training, but instead, she was forced to accept that there would be no engagement anytime soon. Kate would have to wait even longer.

CHAPTER 9
PRINCESS IN THE MAKING

Kate was still coming to terms with William's about turn. It was late October 2008, and they had flown to Scotland for some downtime. William had recently completed an exhilarating charity motorbike ride across Africa with his brother, so this was the first opportunity he and Kate had to spend some time together.

He knew that his decision to join the RAF affected hugely on Kate's life and that she needed some reassurance.

The reality was that William would train for eighteen months, and after that he would be expected to serve with the Search and Rescue Force for a minimum of two years. He would be based at the Defence Helicopter Flying School in Shawbury, Shropshire, for a year before being posted to a remote base somewhere in the United Kingdom. The question was hanging: Was Kate prepared to join him? She supported his desires and ambitions, but privately she was crushed. Essentially, William was asking her to be an army wife — without the nuptials. Her frustration was understandable. She had loyally supported William ever since he enrolled at Sandhurst, but the pact they had made in Desroches suggested that his military training was coming to an end and marriage would be the next step. Now that he was joining the RAF, Kate could see that he would be married to his job for several more years.

William was optimistic that he and Kate could make the relationship work. They had coped successfully with long periods apart before. Kate knew there was no point in trying to change William's mind — he was strong willed and determined.

At twenty-six years old, the prince was not too young to marry or become a working royal, but he didn't want to commit to either just yet. At the same age, the Queen had already been married for five years and had ascended the throne following the death of her father. Charles had given up his career as a naval officer when he was twenty-seven, five years before he married Diana, to devote his life to official duties. William, however, had been allowed a very different upbringing. Both Charles and Diana had wanted to raise their sons as "ordinary," within the confines of royal protocol, and as they grew into young men, William and Harry worked hard to pursue careers independently of their HRH (His Royal Highness) titles. The military gave William the chance to live a "normal" life outside of the bubble of royalty, which was about the most important thing to him. The idea of flying Sea King helicopters to rescue ships or mountain hikers in distress was, for the prince, the epitome of this privilege.

For Kate, it was a step backward. It seemed that everyone was getting married except for her. Just days before William had made his announcement, they had flown to Austria for their friend Chiara Hunt's wedding. Her best friend, Emilia d'Erlanger, was engaged to her long-term boyfriend, David Jardine Patterson, and Oli Baker, their friend from St. Andrews University, had recently proposed to his university sweetheart, Mel Nicholson. William and Kate's former apartment mate Fergus Boyd was getting married to Sandrine Janet the following May, and William and Kate had accepted an invitation to Nicholas Van Cutsem's wedding to Alice Hadden-Paton in the summer. As she neared her twenty-seventh birthday, Kate's plan to be married with children by the time she was thirty was looking increasingly unlikely. And it wasn't just Kate who was unsettled about the future. Carole was also "jittery" about the absence of a ring on her daughter's finger. "Carole is very concerned that it might not happen," revealed a friend. "She is concerned about Kate's position and that there might not be a wedding at all."

Kate had promised William in Desroches that she would stand by him, and she wasn't about to go back on her word. When she attended Charles's sixtieth birthday party at Highgrove that same month, it was a clear indication that despite William's unexpected career decision, she was sticking with her prince. Days after the party, William was posted to Barbados to spend ten days with the Special Boat Service.

While William spent Christmas at the royal estate in Norfolk, Kate and her family flew to Mustique as they had the year before. It was Kate's third visit that year, causing the press to christen her the "Queen of Mustique," a title once reserved for Princess Margaret.

On the island, the Middletons were treated like royalty. It was their second trip as a family, and they knew many of the local residents, including the tennis coach, Richard Schaffer, and the island's yoga instructor, Greg Allen, who came to teach them on the terrace of their villa every morning. According to Greg's partner, Elizabeth Saint, who took the family horse riding on the beach, "They love to ride, and Greg did yoga with them on a daily basis. He went to their house and taught them there. They love Mustique, and on the island everyone is very protective of them. They walk on the beach in their flip-flops, play tennis, and do their yoga. They don't want people hassling them and taking their pictures."

In the privacy of the luxury villa, Kate and her family relaxed and enjoyed the services of the in-house chef. One source who enjoyed a supper with them recalled, "There was always lots of chilled white wine, Carole's favorite drink. They are amazing hosts and enjoyed having a big table of people for dinner. They quickly made friends in Mustique, and it was always an open house. They are a lot of fun, and they aren't afraid to poke fun at themselves. One of Carole's favorite dinner party jokes is to put on her best air-hostess voice and announce incoming flights as they come in. It had everyone in fits of giggles."

Kate was home in time to go to Scotland to see the New Year in, and this time she and William stayed with Charles and Camilla at Birkhall. Kate had helped Charles choose a Labrador puppy for William's Christmas present, and the four of them spent many happy hours traipsing over the hills with the energetic pup in tow.

They were back in England in time for Kate's twenty-seventh birthday, a small celebration at her family home. William drove to Oak Acre, where Ella, the newest addition to the Middleton family — a sweet black cocker spaniel puppy belonging to James — was bounding excitedly around the kitchen. Unusually, the prince had arranged to stay the night, so his protection officers booked into a nearby guesthouse. It was the last time he and Kate would be together before he moved to RAF Shawbury.

On January 11, 2009, Flight Lieutenant Wales drove himself to the Defence Helicopter Flying School in Shropshire, three hours from London. After a couple of weeks living at the base, which had far from luxurious living quarters, he moved to a nearby farmhouse on the grounds of a stately home, prompting comments that William was being given special treatment. The Ministry of Defence however, insisted that he was being treated "like any other officer." Very few of his fellow officers, however, were living in such luxury. Complete with a tennis court and an outdoor pool, the farmhouse was a more comfortable option when Kate visited, and there was a bedroom for Harry, who had just split up with Chelsy and was being posted to the same base to train with the Army Air Corps in the spring.

Often, William would drive the 130 miles from Shropshire to Bucklebury for the weekend. He and Kate enjoyed time together, mostly away from the public gaze. As his schedule was unpredictable, the paparazzi never knew when William was going to visit, and the locals were protective when they saw the couple in the village. They were able to drink and eat traditional pub lunches at the local Bladebone Inn without being disturbed, and William often shopped at the local Spar store for newspapers and Kate's favorite Haribo candy. Nothing was ever reported about them going about their daily lives, which was how they liked it. "In the village we are very protective. There's a lot of camaraderie towards the Middletons," reported resident Lynda Tillotson. Martin Fiddler, who owns the local butcher shop added, "William and Kate are often here, but no one makes a deal of it and we leave them be. We have known the Middleton children for years and they are part of the village life."

During the week, Kate immersed herself in her work and added another string to her bow, selling online advertising for the company. She cold-called companies, asking if they wanted to advertise on the site, and introduced herself as "Catherine from Party Pieces." She also attended marketing fairs and used her new connections to boost the website's profile. She consulted Sir Richard Branson about a potential online partnership and was often in London for development meetings. She was still involved with Starlight and making regular visits to the Naomi House hospice, and quite remarkably, the trips had still not been leaked to the press.

It wasn't just her charity work that Kate was keeping below the radar; both she and William were making an effort to maintain a low profile. They stunned their friends in May 2009 when they decided not to go to Fergus and Sandrine's wedding at the Château de Boumois in the Loire Valley, despite having RSVP'd their attendance. According to one former St. Andrews student, they canceled at the last minute, citing William's work commitments. Kate had no real excuse for not being there, and their absence was the talk of the reception. William and Fergus were close friends, and it was out of character for him not to be at such an important occasion, especially when all of their friends from their university days were there. According to one source, William was worried that there would be too many guests they didn't know, while Kate apparently didn't want to have to face the inevitable question: "When will you two be next?"

Not being seen and photographed together seemed to relieve the pressure because it gave the press less chance to speculate on the state of their romance. These days the couple rarely went out and had become rather reclusive, apart from attending the occasional polo match. The paparazzi were at the couple's favorite nightclubs in June, hoping to catch the prince celebrating his twenty-seventh birthday, but together with Harry and a couple of their friends, they were in Cornwall. Kate had found a private house to rent near the seaside town of Fowey, so they spent the weekend surfing and enjoying pints in a local pub, where they watched England play rugby against South Africa. There wasn't one photograph of the weekend in the newspapers.

It was a great relief to the Queen and

Prince Charles that William and Kate were going out less. Britain was going through its worst economic recession since the 1930s, and the Queen didn't think that partying at expensive nightclubs projected a favorable image for the royals. Her view was that the family should be setting an example, which did not mean running up expensive bar bills at Boujis. There was also the thorny issue of privacy, which never seemed to go away. The Queen had recently asked her lawyers to consult the Press Complaints Commission about greater privacy for the royal family while they were in royal residence. The paparazzi staked out Sandringham House with alarming frequency, and she wanted this intrusion to end. William and Kate had been photographed shooting on the estate a number of times, and the Queen had not escaped the long lens, photographed some years previously, wringing the neck of a game bird. She had instructed a leading privacy lawyer to write to national newspaper editors explaining that action would be taken if they published pictures of the family and their friends on the royal estates. William backed his grandmother enthusiastically, but though the Queen was prepared to take legal action in order to protect the family, she also believed that her grandchildren had to tow the line. According to one royal source, "The Queen cannot understand why William, Kate, and Harry choose to go to well-known nightclubs and then complain about being harassed. Her view is if you don't want to be photographed, don't go." Kate, who had never really enjoyed clubbing, was more than happy to pare down their social lives. Instead of nightclubs, they went to the theater, slipping in once the house lights were dimmed, and they enjoyed dinners out at restaurants, where they made reservations under false names.

The one negative effect of William and Kate ducking out of the limelight was that the media's attention switched to Kate's family. James was still recovering from the humiliating coverage of his twenty-first birthday party when he had suddenly found himself back under the spotlight in the summer of 2008. A picture of him dressed in one of his sister's dresses had been leaked on the Internet, prompting taunts about his sexuality. Beer bottle in hand and red lipstick smeared across his face, James was clearly having fun with some university friends, but the photographs didn't seem so amusing when they were published in the *Daily Mail* beneath the headline, "Wild Side of Kate's Family." Shortly afterward, photographs of Pippa dancing in her underwear and wrapped up in a minidress made from toilet paper were anonymously leaked to the newspapers.

Carole was concerned that her family was coming under fire and that they did not have a public relations expert to guide them through the minefield of adverse publicity. Although Carole had generally taken care not to say anything in public, she had once let her guard down to a reporter from the *Daily Telegraph* during a day out at the races in November 2008. She told the journalist that she and her family felt "vulnerable." "I'm not a celebrity and I don't want to be one. Celebrities have minders and PR people. I don't want a PR person and wouldn't want to have to pay to employ one. I haven't asked for all this," she complained. She also said that James had found himself in a difficult situation while trying to promote his cake business: "James is very good with it all. He writes articles and has business projects which he wants to talk about, but then it's difficult when everything else is going on around him and people don't just want to know about his projects." Cake Kit was doing well. Gary had given his nephew a $16,000 loan and James had not been shy about promoting the business, but when he baked twenty-five cakes for *Hello* magazine's anniversary edition, one of which featured an image of Princess Diana, royal eyebrows were raised. It was the sort of publicity the Palace abhorred, and the newspapers accused James of cashing in on his royal connections.

This, however was not the only scandal to rock the family; the summer of 2009 saw the Middletons weather their greatest storm yet. On Sunday, July 19, the *News of the World*'s headline read, "I Called Wills a F——." Kate couldn't believe it. Her Uncle G — as he was affectionately known — who had looked after her when she broke up with William, had been filmed at his Spanish home by undercover reporters. Described in the article as a "braggart," he had been secretly filmed cutting up cocaine in his kitchen and rolling cannabis joints. Kate had never taken drugs, and she was equally horrified that Gary claimed to know how to organize prostitutes on the island. More worrying for Kate, he was incredibly loose tongued about her and William's relationship and talked openly about the holiday they had enjoyed at La Maison de Bang Bang. He was reported to have claimed that they would be announcing their engagement that year and joked that he would be giving Kate away. The Middletons were devastated, but as always, they stuck together. According to Gary, Carole telephoned him that morning. "The minute that story broke, Carole was on the phone apologizing to me on behalf of the family, specifically Kate, about me being suddenly thrust into the limelight," he later told the *Mail on Sunday*. It was a terrible time for the family, particularly for Gary, who had always had a love-hate relationship with his sister. "We are both headstrong and can bicker. But we are very close. We tease each other relentlessly," he said.

Whereas Carole was family oriented and sensible, Gary could be reckless. "The problem for Gary is that Carole never approved of Gary and his lifestyle," said a family member. Ultimately, Carole, who was in some ways more like a mother to Gary than a sister, forgave him and urged him to seek some help. Gary had been devastated when their mother, Dorothy, died. Perhaps that helped explain why he had fallen off the rails. He had made millions of dollars in IT recruitment, which afforded him his playboy lifestyle in Ibiza, but his marriage had collapsed. "Carole and Mike have an amazing relationship. They have nurtured three amazing kids," he said. "I should have taken more lessons from them on how to make the marriage work." Carole promised to help Gary, but first she needed to avoid the media storm and decided the best thing to do was to head to Mustique until the situation died down. William and Kate had actually been planning to go to Ibiza at the end of the summer, but in light of these events were compelled to cancel. They had no choice but to distance themselves from Uncle G for the time being. The Palace declined to publicly comment on the story, but William was as supportive as he could be, and when he and Kate attended the summer wedding of his old friend Nicholas van Cutsem, it was his turn to show the world he was standing by Kate.

In the summer of 2009, they returned once again to Mustique, and at the end of August headed to Scotland for the bank holiday weekend. Although Kate had been to Balmoral many times, this trip was significant because it was the first time she had been invited to the main house while the Queen and Duke of Edinburgh were in residence. The news was greeted with much excitement in the press, with unconfirmed reports that the Queen wanted to lunch alone with Kate. Kate had not been invited to Her Majesty's eighty-third birthday celebrations in June, but as she knew this was a matter of protocol, she did not view it as a snub. Until now, the Queen had met Kate only fleetingly at the wedding of Peter and Autumn Phillips, but she went out of her way to make her feel welcome, giving her permission to take pictures at Balmoral — a true gift to a photographer, with its turreted and Gothic-inspired architecture. As a woman who has lived her entire life in the public eye, the Queen rarely lets her guard down, and very few apart from her family and closest friends get to see the real Elizabeth. Now Kate was being granted an audience in a most intimate capacity. It was a generous move on the part of the Queen and an astute decision, given that the romance seemed to be very serious.

During her summer stay at Balmoral the Queen traditionally holds meetings with her most senior staff and her family, during which issues concerning the royal family — everything from overseas tours to marriages, birthdays, and state occasions — are discussed, and on this occasion, William was one of the subjects.

Once known as the "Way Ahead" group, started by the former Lord Chamberlain, the Earl of Airlie, in 1994, its gatherings are essentially an in-house royal forum and have proved to be very successful for planning the future strategy for the House of Windsor. The Queen, the Duke of Edinburgh, and their children were all invited, and William and Harry were recently asked to attend. According to one senior aide, "Philip traditionally chairs the committee, and there is always a twofold plan, the immediate future and the long term." The purpose of the summer 2009 gathering was to discuss the Queen and Philip's overseas tour schedule over the coming months. The Foreign Office had scheduled trips to New Zealand and Australia, Bermuda, and Canada, and the Queen felt that it was too much for her and the Duke of Edinburgh to take on, so she wanted to pass on some of her duties to younger members of the family. She was in robust health, but the four hundred or so engagements the previous year had taken their toll on the Duke of Edinburgh, who had been in and out of the hospital. William had been developing his philanthropic role, and he and Harry were planning to launch the Charitable Foundation of Prince William and Prince Harry, which was to serve as an umbrella organization for all of their charity work. William had said he wanted to be more than "just an ornament," and according to one well-placed courtier, the Queen felt now was the time to prove it. "The Queen is aware she is not getting any younger and she wants the new generation to start doing more. She sees Charles and now William as her substitutes, and she wants to get them off the bench," said the source. It appeared that a very subtle hand-over of power was being put in place. William was being lined up as a "shadow king" alongside his father for the very first time, and it was agreed that in the new year, he would go to Australia and New Zealand on behalf of the Queen. It was a momentous decision and a huge responsibility for the prince, as well as a key step in moving him to center stage alongside his father. It was an honor to be asked, and although he was excited to be representing his grandmother, it was a huge pressure and responsibility. William knew that it was a sign of things to come. Although his military career afforded him some relief from becoming a full-time royal, he would be expected to carry out more duties on behalf of his grandparents in the near future. His grandmother's Diamond Jubilee celebrations were already under discussion, and there was a strategy in place at the Palace not to overburden the Queen with official engagements.

Although there was no suggestion of Kate joining William, there were murmurs about creating a "princess-in-waiting role" for her. The Queen was pleased to hear that Kate was now so closely associated with Starlight. As well as her private visits to children's hospices, she was working on the committee for the "Maggie and Rose Art for Starlight" campaign, which involved running artwork shops for some of Starlight's children at the Maggie and Rose children's playgroup in Kensington. A number of leading artists had volunteered their time to teach the children, so Kate had helped organize the workshops. She was also involved in planning a gala dinner at the end of September to launch an exhibition of some of the children's paintings at the Saatchi Gallery. On the night itself, she walked up the red carpet with William. "We didn't know William was coming until about 6:00 P.M., when the sniffer dogs were brought in," recalled Neil Swan. "It was absolutely wonderful to have him there." It was an important night for Kate, and it had meant a lot to her that William and her family were supporting her, though Carole nearly upstaged both of her daughters in a stunning off-the-shoulder coral minidress. Party Pieces had donated a children's birthday party as one of the lots in the auction, but the greatest excitement was that William and Kate had arrived together. Even at a charity event, they were wary about being photographed together, and they refused to pose for the cameras. Society photographer Dominic O'Neill was asked to stay away from the event. "I got a note from the prince's office saying that Kate wouldn't attend the dinner if I was there," he recalled. "She was upset that I'd photographed her flat on her back at a charity roller-skating disco because the pictures had made the front page. There's definitely been a tightening up over the past year, and I suspect it is all preparation for a royal wedding."

But 2009 came to a close without an announcement. It was a continual cause of consternation for Carole, who was worried that her daughter was nearing thirty and still not engaged. She enjoyed a close relationship with William, and just before Christmas she had a quiet word when he came to visit. According to one family friend, she told him she was worried that an engagement might never happen. "Carole felt like she was treading water as far as her daughter's relationship was concerned. She put some pressure on William to let the family know where it was all leading. William spoke with her and assured her that the relationship was very much on track and that there would be an engagement soon." According to the source, they also discussed the longer-term future and children. "William said it was all on the cards and that when it did happen, Carole and Michael would be very much a part of their lives, and the lives of their own children. Carole trusted William and put her faith in him."

George Brown, who remained in touch with Michael and Carole, recalled, "It was a condition when they got married that they would be a part of the grandchildren's lives. Carole's a natural with children, and she will be a wonderful grandmother, and I imagine she'll want to be very involved."

Once again William and Kate spent Christmas apart, with the Middletons going to Restormel Manor, a holiday home in Cornwall. It was a relaxing, uneventful few days, that is, until Kate was photographed by a paparazzo while she played tennis on Christmas morning. When William heard, he was incandescent, considering it a flagrant breach of the PCC ruling that Kate was a private individual who should be left alone. He urged her to take legal action, and several months later, Kate won a record $15,000 in damages for breach of privacy.

It was a warning shot to the press: Kate was not prepared to have her privacy invaded, and she had the weight of the royal lawyers to help fight her case.

By the start of 2010, William was one step closer to flying Sea King helicopters. He had graduated from flying a single-engine Squirrel helicopter to a double-engine Griffin. Kate had jokingly taken to calling him "Top Gun." On January 15, she was at RAF Shawbury to see his father present him with his latest flying badge. It was a poignant moment for father and son; Charles had been awarded his wings in the very same hall. William had been told he would be posted to RAF Valley, a search-and-rescue base on the island of Anglesey in Wales in the new year, which would be his new home for some time. By now Kate had attended three graduation ceremonies, prompting royal correspondents to ask: "Why is Wills still flying solo?" At the Palace, courtiers were pondering the very same question. Planning had already commenced for Prince Philip's ninetieth birthday in June 2011, the Queen's Diamond Jubilee, and the 2012 London Olympics. No dates were being discussed for a royal wedding, however, because William hadn't given any indication as to when it might happen. His next period of training at RAF Valley officially ended in September 2010, which seemed an opportune time to get engaged before he embarked on a full-time flying career. Their closest friends had privately put bets on a 2011 wedding, but no one could be sure.

The question of marriage was even being debated on the other side of the world. William had flown to New Zealand twenty-four hours after graduating, and there was a great sense of excitement over how his five-day long tour would be received. The prince had been warned about the republican movement in Australia, but crowds of thousands turned up at every event to see him.

Dressed in his chinos and an open-necked shirt rather than a formal suit, William chatted happily to wellwishers and seemed entirely comfortable conducting walkabouts. With his good looks and natural charm, it was hard not to think of Diana, although William insisted he wasn't "anywhere near her level" when he visited a children's hospital in Wellington. The reception he received in Sydney was equally warm. When he arrived at Government House in Melbourne, he was swamped by female fans carrying banners with the message "We love Wills."

He was asked by one woman when he planned to marry Kate, and he teased, "As I keep saying, wait and see." It was a playful and somewhat telling response. Until now, William had never commented on the subject of marriage in public.

When he returned to Britain, William moved into his new home — a rather basic single room in the officers' accommodation at RAF Valley. That Easter, Kate and William holidayed with her family at the French ski resort Courchevel, prompting royal observers to speculate once again about an engagement. The couple was photographed kissing at a mountaintop restaurant and later, chasing each other down the slopes on snowmobiles. According to a ski instructor who sat at a table near the group during lunch one day, William referred to Michael as "Dad." "Prince William and Kate looked like a honeymoon couple. He held her hand under the table, stroked her hair, and kissed her cheek," instructor Meret Visser told the *Daily Mail.* "William was clearly very close to Kate's father. Every time he spoke to him, William replied, 'Yes, Dad.' Everyone in their group was laughing at this — it was clearly jokey. But William did look like part of the family." According to one family friend, it was a private joke emanating from

William's pledge to Carole.

Kate and William had decided that on their return from Courchevel, William would move out of his quarters at RAF Valley so that they could live together. With permission from his head of command, they rented a farmhouse on the Bodorgan Estate, owned by Lord and Lady Meyrick. The house, on the southwestern part of the island of Anglesey, near the Irish Sea, was only a twenty-minute drive from the RAF base. William had been told that, providing he passed his exams, he would be staying on at RAF Valley, news that pleased them both. The island was a perfect retreat from the paparazzi and incredibly beautiful. The farmhouse was surrounded by mountains and beautiful countryside, and was only a short walk from a small beach. This part of Wales could potentially be their home for at least two more years while William carried out a full tour of duty. Kate had moved all her belongings in by the beginning of June, but because the press was busy following William and Harry on their very first joint overseas tour to South Africa, no one noticed. William traveled home on his birthday and much was made of him turning twenty-eight, which was, after all, the year he predicted he might marry.

Although there was still no official announcement, the reality was that behind the closed doors of their new Anglesey home, William and Kate were already living the life of a married couple. By the end of June, Kate had given up working for Party Pieces and was immersing herself in her new life.

Anglesey was as normal as it was ever going to be for them both. The press agreed with the Palace not to photograph the couple's home because it was deemed a security risk. The farmhouse was well protected and could only be accessed by a private drive, making it virtually impossible to photograph anyway. As at St. Andrews, the locals on the remote island protected the couple, so they were able to go about their daily lives in relative peace. Since Kate's successful legal action in which she won substantial damages, newspaper editors were far more cautious about the pictures they published.

Their new home was idyllic, and with William at work, Kate filled her days taking photographs, walking on the beach, and compiling an exhibition of her work, having had the idea to stage a photographic exhibition and raise money for charity. Often, her only company was William's protection officers, an always entertaining group. Some, like Chris Tarr, had looked after the prince since he was a little boy and were full of stories. Michael and Carole visited from time to time, as did Pippa, and they all noted how happy Kate was in this phase of her life.

Although they had lived together as students at St Andrews, this time was different because it was just the two of them, a real road test for marriage. And it was proving to be a success.

William was, once again, being granted a privilege none of his predecessors had enjoyed. His father had spent most of his bachelor years refusing to settle down with one woman. He had proposed to Diana after a yearlong courtship, but he never got the opportunity to live with her before they married. William and Kate, however, knew each other's flaws and strengths, but the most important thing was that they knew they worked well as a team. Forever scarred by the pain of his parents' divorce, it was essential to William that when he married, it would be for life. Divorce had dogged the royal family for too long. From the abdication of Edward VII in 1936 that had nearly ruined the monarchy to the more recent divorces of Diana and Charles, as well as Prince Andrew and Sarah Ferguson, unhappy marriages threatened to seriously unhinge an otherwise solid establishment. Before William asked Kate to marry him, he wanted to be sure it was what she really wanted. By living together, Kate could decide whether it was, and as William later recalled "back out" if it wasn't.

William graduated as a fully qualified Search and Rescue Force helicopter pilot in September 2010 and joined Number 22 Squadron, C flight. It was a major achievement for the prince — he was now fully qualified to fly Sea King MK3 helicopters, which meant that he would be carrying out dangerous rescue missions and essentially saving lives. He spent the next few weeks familiarizing himself with the terrain and his crew before carrying out his first shift, during which he rescued an oil-rig worker who had suffered a heart attack at sea. It was a stressful but exciting job, and for the prince, incredibly rewarding. William was trained to fly in extreme weather conditions and was responsible for steadying the aircraft while lost climbers and casualties were winched to safety.

With his training completed, William and Kate were back in the spotlight as rumors circulated in the press once again that their long-awaited engagement would soon be announced. There was a flurry of activity to suggest that this time an engagement really was imminent. The *Mail on Sunday* revealed that the Royal Mint, which must secure the Queen's permission before manufacturing any new coinage, had started preparations for a commemorative coin to celebrate a royal wedding. The Palace claimed to have no knowledge of the coin, but for the first time, royal representatives changed tack on their stance about a possible engagement. Usually, speculation was accompanied by a denial, but on this occasion an aide seemed to suggest that there would be an announcement: "We don't know the date; only William and Kate know," he said. "I don't expect we will be told until the last minute. William plays his cards very close to his chest, that's his nature."

The following year seemed a good bet for a royal wedding; the year 2012 was likely to be dominated by the Queen's Diamond Jubilee and the Olympics. Bookmakers across the country stopped taking bets on a 2011 wedding after it was reported that senior courtiers had been in touch with Westminster Abbey about a possible ceremony.

Ironically, it was the madness of this media frenzy that provided the distraction that enabled William and Kate to slip out of the country to Lewa Downs in Kenya. However, before he escaped, William paid a visit to his grandmother at Buckingham Palace, deliberately arriving by motorbike so as not to be followed or seen. In this private visit, he asked the Queen's permission to procure a piece of jewelry from her collection.

And so it was that no one — apart from his grandmother — knew that William was traveling to Kenya with his late mother's diamond-and-sapphire engagement ring hidden away in the depths of his knapsack.

CHAPTER 10
A ROYAL ENGAGEMENT

As they jetted out of London's Heathrow Airport, bound for Kenya at the start of October 2010, Kate dared to hope that she might return from Africa with a ring on her finger, but as the holiday drew to a close, there was no sign of a proposal. There had been plenty of opportunities, each stage of their African adventure a potential setting for a romantic moment. But now on the last day of their trip, Kate's heart was heavy.

They had started with a trek to one of the most remote parts of the country, the rain lands of Ishak Bin, where they camped and cooked over a fire they built from forest wood. It was basic, remote, and most important, just the two of them — but there was no proposal. From Ishak Bin they traveled to Lewa, where they stayed at the same five-star lodge they holidayed in after their graduation. There they enjoyed game drives and on one occasion were lucky enough to spot a rare black hook-lipped rhinoceros, which was tranquilized and named in William's honor after he paid $9,000 to sponsor the beast and ensure it was safe in the wild. As the great animal lay breathing in the grass, he and Kate had touched it. But still there was no proposal, and so by the time they headed to Sarara for another safari with two friends from South Africa, Kate had given up hope. Instead, she threw herself into photographing the giraffe, elephants, wild dogs, buffalo, and vast open plains, which she planned to catalog when she got home.

The final leg of their holiday came as a complete surprise to Kate. William had booked a day and a night at the Il Ngwesi Lodge, a remote log cabin in the heart of the countryside near the great Lake Rutundu. He had stayed there before, so he knew it would be the perfect place to return with someone special. The lodge was basic and far from luxurious, but it was the remote location in the middle of the countryside that made it unique. And it was here that Kate's long-awaited dream came true. On the shores of Lake Rutundu, William got down on bended knee and asked Kate to marry him.

Even though she had thought about little

else for so long, when the moment came, Kate was speechless. Later, she declared that it was "very romantic" and a total surprise. As always where William was concerned, a degree of rationality applied to even this unique moment in his life, and he and Kate agreed to keep the proposal a secret until he asked Kate's father for her hand in marriage. He also wanted them to be able to enjoy the moment together before the news was made public. It was a secret he knew they wouldn't be able to hold on to for too long, knowing that within a matter of seconds of an official announcement, the news would go global. So when Kate signed the guest book the next morning, she gave nothing away. "Thank you for such a wonderful twenty four hours," she wrote. "Sadly no fish to be found but we had fun trying. I love the warm fires and candle lights — so romantic. Hope to be back soon."

When they returned home to Anglesey, Kate put her engagement ring in the safe. Had it been any other ring she might have been able to get away with wearing it on another finger, but Princess Diana's diamond-and-sapphire cluster was immediately recognizable. Although no one — not even his father or brother — knew of his intention to propose to Kate while away, William had spoken with Harry to make sure his younger brother was happy for him to have their mother's ring, as and when the time came.

Once they were back in Wales and William had returned to work, he invited Michael and Carole to Birkhall for the weekend. He had personally overseen everything from ensuring that there were freshly picked flowers in the guest bedrooms to organizing the menus. Just before supper on the first night, William took Michael into the drawing room, poured them both a large whiskey, and asked for permission to marry Kate. Without a moment's hesitation, Michael gave William his blessing. Before William could make the announcement, he knew that royal protocol meant that he had to ask for his grandmother's permission to marry Kate. He made Michael swear not to tell a soul about their secret engagement, not even Carole, explaining why it was of paramount importance that the news did not leak out before the official announcement from the Palace.

Michael kept his word; however, the weekend away didn't stay a secret for long. Carole had been photographed hunting in the Highlands, and the pictures, which were published the following week, caused a sensation. The fact that the Middletons were staying in a royal residence was seen as highly significant, prompting fresh speculation in the press that an announcement was just around the corner. The story traveled across the world like wildfire, with magazines in America buzzing with predictions that a wedding really was about to happen. *Vanity Fair* published an article predicting a wedding in 2011, while another tabloid publication in the States went further, dedicating its cover to the story: "Royal Wedding Is On!"

But despite the fervid speculation, there was no announcement from the Palace. When, weeks later, William and Kate were photographed in Gloucestershire at their friend Harry Meade's wedding, there were more rumors. Arriving arm-in-arm, smiling at the waiting cameras, they went through the front entrance rather than the side door. Later that evening at the reception, talk turned to when William and Kate would be walking down the aisle. "Maybe he'll get round to it some day," Kate told her friends, while William batted off jokes about how long he was taking to pop the question.

They knew they could not keep the engagement secret for much longer and agreed to make the announcement officially on Wednesday, November 3. The plan was abandoned, however, when Kate's only surviving grandparent, Peter, died suddenly the day before. William attended the funeral at the West Berkshire Crematorium before flying to Afghanistan for a Remembrance Sunday service with British troops, where he laid a wreath at Camp Bastion. Kate was deeply saddened not to have had the chance to tell her grandfather that she was engaged to William. She knew he would have been delighted for her.

On his return from Afghanistan on Monday, William and Kate agreed that they would make the announcement the following morning. The legally binding Royal Marriages Act 1772 obliged William to ask for his grandmother's consent. Providing she granted it, the Queen was then required to sign a notice of approval under the Great Seal of the Realm. Ironically, it had been made law by George III after his younger brother, the Duke of Cumberland, had secretly married the widow of a commoner. Now William and Kate, the first true commoner to marry into the royal family for several centuries, were about to write royal history.

It was Tuesday, November 16, 2010, and

the Queen, who had been reading briefing notes on her official duties for the morning over her breakfast of cornflakes, was thrilled to receive William's call, albeit a little surprised at the suddenness of the announcement. "The Queen had no idea that there would be an announcement that morning," said a source. "She was eating breakfast with Philip when William called to tell her the news. It was rather hurried, because William was apparently worried about it leaking out."

William enjoyed outfoxing the media, and this was one announcement he wanted to make himself. The last thing he wanted was a newspaper getting the scoop, as had happened with his father's engagement to Camilla. When William called from his private living quarters at Clarence House with Kate by his side, Charles was with Camilla at Highgrove, preparing to travel to Devon that morning. They were both over-joyed.

Harry, who was at his army base in Hampshire, turned the air blue with a string of expletives when the couple called to tell him the happy news. "It took you long enough," he joked. Kate then called her parents in Bucklebury. Of course her father knew, and Kate wasn't sure whether he had told her mother. Either way, it didn't matter. Kate told them to brace themselves for the announcement.

It was just after 9:00 A.M. when the couple walked across the cobbled courtyard to meet with William's private secretary, Jamie Lowther-Pinkerton. The former Special Air Service officer, known for his meticulous planning, congratulated the couple and told them the Palace Press Office would be ready to make the announcement by 11:00 A.M. The couple then went to see William's chief press officer, Miguel Head, and his team. "We were ecstatic when they came in to tell us," recalled an aide. "We genuinely had no idea they were secretly engaged, and they looked so happy when they told us. There was a palpable sense of relief. Then the hard work started, and there was an awful lot to organize in a very short time. Two hours later, we made the announcement."

In keeping with their modern courtship, the news was posted on the royal family's recently launched Facebook page, while Clarence House also tweeted the news, which was retweeted thousands of times and went viral within seconds. A press statement was issued to the world's media via e-mail: "The Prince of Wales is delighted to announce the engagement of Prince William to Miss Catherine Middleton. The wedding will take place in the spring or summer of 2011 in London."

It was the job of the Queen's private office, together with the British government, to decide on the date, which was no small task. Heads of state and diplomats around the world, along with foreign royals, would all need to be consulted. Although William had secretly hoped for a family wedding at St. George's Chapel in Windsor, like his cousin Peter Phillips, he knew that his wedding day would be akin to a semistate occasion. The only real options were St. Paul's Cathedral, where his mother and father had married, or Westminster Abbey, where the Queen had married Prince Philip, and her father, King George VI, had married Elizabeth Bowes Lyon.

Within minutes of the announcement, hundreds of journalists and reporters had gathered at Buckingham Palace. By lunchtime, TV crews from across the world were assembled at Canada Gate on the Mall reporting on the biggest royal story since the death of Princess Diana. The Queen was the first to comment publicly: "It is brilliant news," she told TV journalists at Windsor Castle. "It has taken them a very long time." Charles joked to reporters: "They've been practicing long enough." Camilla declared the news "wicked," while Harry couldn't stop smiling. "It means I get a sister, which I have always wanted," he said.

Prime Minister David Cameron added his personal congratulations, and Kate's parents held an impromptu press conference at the family home, where reporters and camera crews had gathered at the end of their driveway. They had spent the morning working on a brief statement at the kitchen table, assisted by members of William's press team, who had made themselves available by phone. Now that the engagement was to be made official, the Middleton family, at William's request, would be supported for the immediate future by the Palace's impressive PR machine.

Apart from his quip to one reporter nearly eight years ago on the weekend of Kate's twenty-first birthday party, Michael had never spoken to the media. If he was nervous, he didn't show it, facing the cameras with composure: "Carole and I are absolutely delighted by today's announcement and thrilled at the prospect of a wedding sometime next year," he said. "As you know, Catherine and Prince William have been going out together for quite a number of years, which has been great for us because we have got to know William very well. We all think he is wonderful and we are extremely fond of him. They make a lovely couple, they are great fun to be with, and we've had a lot of laughs together. We wish them every happiness for the future." Carole, dressed in a fleece top and designer jeans, smiled but said nothing. She had telephoned James and Pippa that morning to warn them that they would probably be contacted by the press, and to not say a word. Although the family had never had any instruction from the Palace about how to deal with the media, Kate had always advised them not to say anything to reporters. The wall of silence she had insisted on ever since she and William started dating was more important now than ever before.

As soon as the announcement was made, Scotland Yard's elite Royal Protection, known as SO14, had contacted the commander of the Royalty and Diplomatic Protection Department at Buckingham Palace and asked for a team of three officers to be made immediately available to Kate. The officer in charge would be Inspector Karen Llewellyn, previously responsible for protecting Princesses Beatrice and Eugenie, whose royal protection had been scaled down as a cost-cutting measure. The other two were Sergeant Emma Probert, who, like Carole, had worked as a flight attendant before a change of career, and one of Prince Harry's close protection officers, Detective Sergeant Ieuan Jones. Kate had met with the officers that morning and from that moment on was accompanied everywhere by the team. There was also a permanent police presence at Oak Acre, where uniformed officers brandishing semi-automatic machine guns patroled the grounds. It was, Carole later admitted to a friend, one of the hardest adjustments to this new life, not just for Kate but also for the family. Their friends in the village also had to get used to police convoys and SUVs with black windows driving through Chapel Row, as well as an unprecedented number of reporters who knocked on doors of neighbors and friends and visited the local shops in search of information about the family. Soon, there were guided bus tours taking over the narrow country lanes, with guides pointing out the couple's favorite pub, Kate's first school, and the family's former home in Bradfield.

It was William's parents who had set the precedent for celebrating royal engagements by granting a TV interview, and William and Kate knew that it would be expected of

them. The press aides at the Palace had
been liaising with ITN News all morning.
William wanted them to speak to the news
network's political editor, Tom Bradby, who
had interviewed him before. He was one of
the few journalists William trusted, and by
coincidence, Kate knew Mr. Bradby's wife,
Claudia, a jewelry designer with whom she
had worked at Jigsaw. Mr. Bradby was summoned to the Palace while he was walking
to Westminster that morning. "The phone
rang and it was Clarence House on the
line," he told the *Daily Mail*. "They're
engaged," said a voice. "It's out there. You're
on." He was told that the interview was set
for 7:00 P.M. that evening and that there
was no time to waste. While TV cameras
were set up at St. James's Palace, Kate and
William chatted with Mr. Bradby: "They
seemed in high spirits, happy and relaxed.
'Are you OK?' William asked Kate once or
twice. 'I'm fine,' she told him. 'I'll be looking after *you*!' "

Kate chose a royal-blue silk jersey dress
by one of her favorite designers, Brazilian-
born Daniella Helayel of Issa, and the color
perfectly complemented her ring. Meanwhile, her trusted hairdresser, James Pryce,
was called to the Palace to blow-dry her
hair. "I was doing a client when I got a call

from the Palace asking me to come and do Kate's hair. They told me that they had announced their engagement. It was hugely exciting and the most important blow dry I'd ever done. Kate just asked me for the usual." Kate had been dreading the interview, and afterward Mr. Bradby remembered her leaning back and sighing with relief, exclaiming, "I'm no good at this!"

While the film was taken to an editing room, there was another nerve-wracking appointment still to go — the official photo session — which meant coming face to face with Fleet Street's royal press pack. William led Kate into the stateroom with some trepidation, but it wasn't the lion's den she had feared. Kate introduced herself as Catherine and happily displayed her ring. "I'm sure you all recognize it," said William. Some of the journalists had covered Charles and Diana's engagement announcement nearly thirty years earlier, and the ring brought back memories of a young Lady Diana Spencer. Back then, in Charles and Diana's interview, when a reporter asked Prince Charles if he was in love, he famously responded, "Whatever love means." With his arm protectively around Kate, it was clear William knew exactly what love meant.

Like the late Princess of Wales, Kate was

statuesque and beautiful, with heavily made up eyes, but she seemed far more confident than Diana, who had been just nineteen when she and Charles got engaged. Although she admitted to being anxious, Kate managed to keep her nerves in check, and as she walked into the photo session, one step behind her fiancé, she appeared poised, almost regal, smiling despite the startling camera flashes.

The fifteen-minute interview was watched by a record 3 billion people across the world that evening. Incredibly, it was the very first time Kate had spoken publicly. She made a point of placing her hands on her lap so that she didn't fidget with her hair and spoke beautifully in a cut-glass accent. Some of her school friends noticed that her clipped tones were rather different from how she spoke when she was a young girl. "She has changed a lot, she's certainly grown into a beauty, and the funny thing is her voice has completely changed. She sounds very posh, and she definitely wasn't that well-spoken when we were at school," recalled one of her contemporaries from St. Andrew's Prep.

The first topic of discussion was the proposal. "It was very romantic," said Kate. "There's a true romantic in there." She admitted to being genuinely stunned when William asked her to marry him. "I thought he might have thought about it, but no, it was a total shock when it came and very exciting." William revealed that they had been talking about marriage for some time. "We've talked about today for a while . . . for at least a year, if not longer. It was just finding the right time. I had my military career and I really wanted to concentrate on my flying, and I couldn't have done this if I was still doing my training, so I've got that out of the way and Kate's in a good place in terms of work and where she wants to be, and we both just decided now was a really good time."

He also spoke movingly about why he had chosen his mother's ring. "It's very special to me. As Kate's very special to me now, it was right to put the two together," he explained. "It was my way of making sure my mother didn't miss out on today and the excitement and the fact that we are going to spend the rest of our lives together." They agreed that it was a "real relief" to finally be engaged, although Kate said it had not been an easy secret to keep: "We had quite an awkward situation because I knew that William had asked my father, but I didn't know if my mother knew. So I came back from Scotland, and my mother didn't make it clear to me whether she knew or not, so both of us were there sort of looking at each other."

William was remarkably candid about why he had waited eight years to propose. "I wanted to give her the chance to see in and back out if she needed to before it all got too much," he said. "I'm trying to learn from lessons done in the past and I just wanted to give her the chance to settle in and see what happens on the other side." They talked about their breakup in 2007, and Kate confessed it had been an unhappy time but insisted that she had come through it a stronger person. "You find out things about yourself that maybe you hadn't realized," she said.

She also spoke of her gratitude to William's father, who she said had welcomed her into the family early on. She described Charles as "very, very welcoming, very friendly." When Mr. Bradby asked Kate how it felt to be marrying into the most famous family in the world and her feelings about the late Princess of Wales, Kate stumbled for the first time. "Obviously, I would love to have met her," she said softly. William stepped in. "There's no pressure," he insisted. "No one is trying to fill my mother's shoes — what she did was fantastic. It's about making your own future and your own destiny, and Kate will do a very good job of that." They spoke about the importance of family and how they hoped to start their own in the future. "It's very important to me and I hope we will be able to have a happy family ourselves," Kate said. "We'll have to start thinking about that," William added.

With the nation glued to their televisions that evening, Kate paid a quiet visit to Westminster Abbey with Helen Asprey, William's trusted diary aide, who had been designated as one of the wedding planners. As Kate walked up the aisle, her footsteps echoing around the empty pews, she marveled at the scale and beauty of the abbey and the enormity of what lay ahead.

By the end of the month, the Palace announced that the wedding day — which was also to be a national holiday — would take place at Westminster Abbey on Friday, April 29, 2011. It was where William's mother's life had been celebrated at both her funeral and memorial service, and he thought it a fitting tribute to her. Both he and Kate loved the sacrarium, a raised platform at the abbey's high altar, which afforded them an intimate place to exchange their vows. In keeping with tradition, Dr. Rowan Williams, the Archbishop of Canterbury, was to marry them into the Church of England, of which William would one day be the head. Charles arranged for his good friend, the Bishop of London, Richard Chartres, to give the address. The Dean of Westminster, Dr. John Hall, was asked to conduct the service. The twin choirs of Westminster Abbey and Her Majesty's Chapel Royal, together with the London Chamber Orchestra, the trumpeters of the Household Cavalry, and the RAF Fanfare Team were appointed to fill the abbey with music.

While William returned to work, Kate decided to put her photography exhibition on hold so that she could fully focus on planning her wedding. Unlike other brides, Kate not only had a wedding to organize, she was also being intensively prepped on everything, from how to handle the media to constitutional matters. Sir David Manning, one of the Queen's most senior aides, had been tasked with ensuring she was properly briefed on state and foreign affairs, ceremonial matters, and crucially, the order of hierarchy when she was in the company of senior royals. A former British ambassador to the United States, Sir David taught Kate the protocol on receiving heads of state and foreign crowned heads, before whom she was expected to curtsy. When she attended the Queen's Christmas drinks party at Buckingham Palace that month for the very first time, Kate got the opportunity to put her training to use. She curtsied to Prince Charles and Camilla in the presence of the Queen, and she was also required to curtsy, or bob, to blood royals, including the Duke of York's daughters, Princesses Beatrice and Eugenie. It might have felt slightly strange because the young women occasionally socialized together, but it was the order of precedence.

Kate was happy to be spending her last Christmas as a single woman with her family; she knew once she was married, she would be expected at Sandringham every year. William was on duty at RAF Valley on Christmas Day, and as usual they were both together in Scotland for the New Year. Kate's twenty-ninth birthday was a typically low-key celebration, and instead of having a party, she and William spent her birthday weekend in North Yorkshire at the wedding of their friends Harry Aubrey-Fletcher and Louise Stourton. Not wanting to upstage the bride, Kate arrived separately from William through a side entrance with her protection officer in tow. She still found being shadowed a strange experience, and although she got along well with her protection officers, it felt unnatural having to tell someone where she was going and what she was doing every minute of the day. Possibly the strangest thing was having an armed guard with her when she went home to Bucklebury.

Kate divided her time between Anglesey and London, where she had regular meetings at Clarence House. She had taken the advice of some of her girlfriends who had found mood boards useful in the runup to their own weddings. Kate set about archiving cuttings from books and magazines and took the mood boards into the planning meetings. She wanted nature to feature strongly, and when she had the idea to bring maple trees into the abbey, Charles, who was picking up part of the bill together with the Queen and the Middletons, referred her to his florist, Shane Connolly. According to one senior aide, "William and Kate were told that anything they wanted was possible and Charles and the Queen made their full households available to them both." There was speculation in the press from the engagement day onward about everything to do with the wedding, from who was designing Kate's dress (a secret she was determined to keep until the wedding day) to how she would wear her hair. According to James Pryce, she decided on a demi-chignon in February and had considered flowers in her hair. "One of the ideas was to have lily of valley because it is beautiful, British, and seasonal, but then she decided she wanted to wear a tiara. She was very firm about what she wanted, and 'romantic' was the key word."

The Queen had suggested the couple carry out a brief tour of Great Britain ahead of the wedding and courtiers set to work preparing an itinerary to include Wales, Scotland, Ireland, and the north of England. Their first walkabout took place in Anglesey, and on a windy February morning, they launched a new lifeboat at Trearddur Bay, not far from RAF Valley. The next day they flew to St. Andrews University, as William had been asked to be the patron of the six hundredth anniversary appeal. Hundreds of wellwishers lined up to meet the couple, and as they talked to students, they recalled their own happy days in their university town. "It feels like coming home," said William, while Kate appeared to momentarily forget her etiquette and greeted the crowds with an endearing "Hi!" After visiting the university, they made a fleeting trip to Fife.

"I have to try and keep up with him," Kate joked as she shook hands with some of the crowd. Dressed in an eye-catching scarlet dress and jacket, her outfit by Italian designer Luisa Spagnoli was such a hit that it sold out online within hours, leading fashion writers to predict that Kate was set to be just as great a style icon as Diana.

When the couple visited Northern Ireland at the beginning of March, the "Kate effect," as it was now referred to in the newspapers, was evident once again after the Burberry trench coat she wore sold out within hours. Kate seemed overwhelmed with the reception she received, and as she gamely flipped a pancake to mark Shrove Tuesday, she felt moved to show her gratitude and addressed those who had waited to see them: "Thank you for giving me such a warm welcome." The crowds were just as warm in Lancashire, where not even torrential rain could dampen the spirits of the people who queued for hours for a glimpse of the couple. As hundreds of local people gathered behind the police barriers, cameras poised, waving Union Jacks, there was much talk of how slim Kate was in the flesh. It was reported in the press that she had dropped a dress size and had to have her engagement ring tightened. "Are you nervous?" one wellwisher asked as Kate accepted a bouquet of rain-drenched flowers. "Of course I am!" she responded.

The Palace considered the tour so successful that it was decided William and Kate should visit Canada and the United States after their wedding. This young and glamorous couple appeared to be breathing new life into the monarchy, and a national poll conducted then by the *Sunday Times* found that the majority of the public thought William would make a better king than Charles. Many said the heir should step aside so that William could take the throne upon the Queen's death.

Kate was having weekly update meetings at Clarence House, and by the end of March, most of the key decisions about the ceremony and the wedding reception had been made. Mr. Lowther-Pinkerton was in charge of the plans, but the couple made the final decision on everything. Kate had asked Charles to help her choose the music for the ceremony, and the pair spent hours listening to songs and hymns on Charles's iPod. Camilla treated Kate and Pippa to lunch so that they could discuss the forthcoming nuptials. A senior aide said that the duchess was eager to be a part of the preparations: "Camilla is very fond of Kate, and she wanted the chance to hear all about the plans and offer to help if she could in any way. It was a case of the family helping Kate as much as they could."

After much deliberation about the guest list, by March, the gilt-edged invitations, which were addressed from the Queen, were sent out. The comptroller of the Lord Chamberlain's office, Sir Andrew Ford, together with the Queen's private secretary, Sir Christopher Geidt, had drawn up a guest list, but William had balked when he saw it. "There was very much a subdued moment when I was handed a list with 777 names on — not one person I knew or Catherine knew," William told the British broadcaster Alan Titchmarsh. "I went to her [the Queen] and said, 'Listen, I've got this list, not one person I know — what do I do?' and she went, 'Get rid of it. Start from your friends and then we'll add those we need to in due course. It's your day.' "

Unlike Charles's wedding to Lady Diana Spencer, which was a state occasion, William as heir apparent was not obliged to invite the same number of dignitaries because he was not next in line to the throne. However, the heads of the Commonwealth and certain crowned heads had to be invited as a matter of protocol. Traditionally, recent royal weddings have followed a format: the ceremony is followed by a wedding breakfast before the newlyweds leave for a honeymoon at Balmoral, but William and Kate intended to do things differently. They wanted a dinner and party for their closest friends and family on the night of the wedding, so it was decided that canapés would be served at a champagne reception at the Palace for six hundred guests. The Queen agreed to give them Buckingham Palace for their wedding night so that the newlyweds could host a wedding party. "The Queen would have wanted to accommodate their wishes as much as possible," said Lady Elizabeth Anson. "They had been to lots of their friends' weddings, and they had a clear idea of what they wanted and the Queen understood that."

It wasn't the only break with tradition. William and Kate wanted a "historic but modest" wedding. Kate wanted to arrive at Westminster Abbey by car rather than in the state coach, and at the couple's request, and in keeping with their wishes to be relatively frugal, it was decided that extended members of the royal family and visiting royals were to be ferried from Buckingham Palace to the abbey in minibuses. They also wanted it to be a wedding for the people, so fifty of the couple's guests were drawn by lots from the charities they supported and invited to the ceremony in the abbey. They decided not to have a traditional wedding gift list and instead asked for donations to twenty-six charities that they handpicked, among them an antibullying organization, Beat Bullying, that Kate personally wanted to support. It was a cause close to her heart ever since her painful experiences as a teenager at Downe House. The charitable fund was hugely popular, and members of the public helped to raise over $1 million for the couple's chosen causes.

William and Kate had asked Pippa to be the maid of honor and Harry to be best man, and the two of them were in charge of planning the evening party. Meanwhile, Kate was busy meeting with florists, cake makers, and the clergy. As part of her marriage preparations, she was confirmed into the Church of England. Although she had been baptized at birth, the Middletons were not regular churchgoers and Kate had never been confirmed. William and Kate, as future King and Queen of Great Britain, would be the heads of the Church of England one day, so they were expected to attend church every Sunday. Religion is embedded in the royal family, members of which until recently were not allowed to marry Catholics in order to preserve the Church of England faith, which was established in the sixteenth century by King Henry VIII. Kate was baptized at St. James's Palace in a private ceremony in March, to which only her family and William were invited.

There were top-secret dress fittings and clandestine trips to Hampton Court Palace, where the lace for her bridal gown was being hand-stitched by a team of seamstresses. The Palace had hired Anthony Gordon Lennox, a voice coach who was helping to prepare Kate for the wedding day. He used breathing techniques to help her relax and taught her how to project her voice so that it would fill the abbey. One of the exercises she was required to do was record herself on video camera and watch the footage to see how she came across.

Wedding fever had not only gripped the nation, but the world. An advertisement for one mobile phone company featured a spoof of the wedding day, complete with royal look-alikes, which became a YouTube sensation. William and Kate apparently downloaded it, finding it "hilarious," according to their friends. Meanwhile, in America, countless documentaries were made about

Kate's rags-to-riches life, and her romance with William was deemed such a fairy tale that a feature-length movie was made about their university romance. The royal palaces in England and Scotland reported a record number of visitors. Westminster Abbey was busier than ever, with queues to get in, and thousands of street parties were being planned around the country for the wedding day itself. Official merchandise such as tea towels and commemorative bone china was hugely popular, festive bunting sold out, and Michael and Carole's website Party Pieces enjoyed weeks of bumper sales. The site had launched a "British Street Party" range of goods, which was selling well. It seemed every-one wanted to cash in on the wedding or anything to do with Kate. The see-through skirt that she wore in the St. Andrews fashion show where she famously caught William's eye was sold at auction for $118,000. The designer had vowed never to sell a "part of fashion history," but when a mystery bidder offered to pay in cash, she capitulated.

The official Royal Wedding website received thousands of hits every day. The engagement pictures, which had been shot by Diana's favorite photographer, Mario Testino, had been posted on the site, along with pictures from the Middleton family album of a three-year-old Kate rock climbing in the Lake District and visiting Petra in Jordan. The fact that Kate had spent her early childhood in the Middle East had only just become public knowledge.

Behind the scenes, Michael and Carole were in constant contact with the Palace. Historically, in-laws have always been kept at an arm's length, but in this case the Middletons were being allowed to contribute to the wedding, together with the Queen and Prince Charles. William had promised Michael and Carole they would always be included in their lives and his in-laws wanted to make a financial contribution. It was quite unprecedented. When Lady Diana Spencer and Sarah Ferguson married into the royal family, their families complained bitterly at being left out in the cold once their daughters married into royalty.

Carole and Michael were kept abreast of developments as the wedding took shape through a hotline to the St. James's Palace Press Office. Courtiers appreciated that, not coming from nobility, the Middletons might need some help navigating through all the rigmarole and protocol of a royal wedding. They were an ordinary family thrust into a most extraordinary situation, and there were a number of adjustments to be made to their lives within a relatively short space of time. The Middletons had already faced accusations in the press that their business was shamelessly cashing in on the royal wedding by stocking themed memorabilia. Carole called Mr. Lowther-Pinkerton for advice. When Britannia-themed scratchcards complete with crowns — which were deemed rather tacky and in poor taste by some sections of the media — went on sale on the site, aides suggested withdrawing the products, which were then discontinued online. Michael and Carole found themselves in a difficult position: they had a business to run and a team of staff to employ, and everyone else was making a pretty penny out of the royal wedding. Nonetheless, they had to be careful not to be seen as exploiting their daughter's position. There were practical elements to consider as well. Since the engagement, there had been a permanent media presence outside the family home, and there was global interest in the other Middleton siblings.

Although Kate benefited from round-the-clock royal protection, her family did not, and Michael and Carole discussed security matters with William's aides at the Palace, who suggested a London-based private security firm, Salamanca. Run by Heyrick Bond-Gunning, a former captain of the Grenadier Guards, the firm specializes in personal protection for the rich and famous and charges a daily rate of over $1,500. Michael and Carole considered it a wise investment. Although the Chelsea apartment that Pippa lived in was fitted out with a state-of-the-art security system from when Kate lived there, Pippa was still relatively exposed in London and was now regularly followed by the paparazzi. There were genuine fears that she might be the subject of a kidnapping plot, and Michael and Carole looked into upgrading her BMW sports car to a bombproof Audi like her sister's.

The invitations and the order of service for the ceremony were being taken care of by Buckingham Palace, but Michael and Carole had been invited to draw up their own guest list and the North Lantern in the abbey had been reserved for their family and friends. They were in constant communication with Mr. Lowther-Pinkerton and Helen Asprey, who explained that only the immediate family would be invited to the lunchtime reception at Buckingham Palace. It was a delicate matter; Carole and Michael had friends from all corners of the world coming to the wedding. Some were family, others were old friends who had moved as far away as Australia. A handful of people were also coming over from Mustique. Michael and Carole decided to invite guests to a hotel in Central London, so courtiers assisted them in booking the Goring Hotel, a stone's throw from Buckingham Palace. The establishment is popular with the royal family and was one of the Queen Mother's favorite places in London. Carole started planning a pre-wedding supper and post-wedding barbecue in the hotel's gardens, and Mr. Lowther-Pinkerton advised them that they would also need a coat of arms, a prerequisite for any royal bride.

As they did not come from aristocratic lineage, the Middletons didn't have a family crest. Lady Diana Spencer, Sarah Ferguson, and Sophie Rhys Jones all had family insignias when they married into the family, but the Middletons would need to register a petition for their own crest. Any individual in the United Kingdom can apply for such an insignia, but the College of Arms decides whether to accept the petition. Michael liaised closely with Garter Principal King of Arms and Senior Herald Thomas Woodcock from the College of Arms, and with Kate's input, they agreed to incorporate acorn sprigs within the design. Kate loved the notion that from tiny acorns great oaks grow, and the part of Berkshire where they lived was famous for its oak trees. The design, in blue, white, and red, to reflect the colors of the Union Jack, comprised three acorns, one to represent each of the Middleton children, and at the center was a gold chevron that represented Carole, the matriarch of the family, and acknowledged her maiden name, Goldsmith. There was a line down the middle of the crest — a play on the Middleton family name — and white chevrons to represent their love of mountains, skiing, and the great outdoors. The crest cost nearly $7,000, and according to Thomas Woodcock, the family was pleased with the final design, which they were all allowed to use from then on. "They had a very strong idea of what they wanted, particularly the acorns, which were Catherine's idea."

Carole and Kate were in daily contact, and when they were seen visiting fashion designer Bruce Oldfield's Knightsbridge store in Beauchamp Place, it was reported that the famous couturier, a favorite of the late Princess of Wales, had landed the coveted commission. Designers Daniella Helayel, who created Kate's engagement dress, Jenny Packham, Amanda Wakeley,

Sarah Burton, and Alice Temperley were also rumored to be in the running for the commission of the century, but Kate was determined that her wedding dress should remain a secret until the moment she walked into the abbey. She wanted it to be a surprise for William, and the only people who knew the identity of the designer were her mother and her sister. According to Kate's hairdresser, James Pryce, "Kate described the dress from the waist up and said that it had a V neckline with lace sleeves, but that was really all we knew."

With all the planning, shopping, and liaising, William and Kate rarely had a quiet moment together, and they were grateful for the peace and solitude they enjoyed in Anglesey. Just weeks before the wedding, the Queen asked William if he would travel to Christchurch in New Zealand, which had been badly hit by an earthquake that had claimed many lives. He was back in time for his stag weekend, which had been planned by Harry and William's closest friend, Thomas van Straubenzee. The weekend before the wedding, spent somewhat ironically at a twelfth-century former monastery in North Devon, was one long party. Harry had arranged a competitive program of water sports, pub crawls, and drinking games, and the group, which included Guy Pelly, Tom Inskip, and Hugh and Ed Van Cutsem, emerged from the weekend the worse for wear after drinking bottles of vintage port supplied from Charles's cellar. Kate was too busy planning the wedding to organize a hen night, so Pippa threw a small party for her closest girlfriends.

As April drew to a close, the pressure of planning a royal wedding had begun to show on Kate, whose clothes seemed to hang off her. Carole, who was on a strict protein-only diet in order to shed a few pounds ahead of the big day, made a point of reminding Kate to eat, calling her every evening to check whether she had had supper. Her dress designer was summoned to Clarence House to make the necessary adjustments, and in addition to the final dress fitting, there was one last run-through with her hairdresser.

There was a rehearsal of the actual ceremony at the abbey the day before the wedding as well as a dawn run-through of the wedding-day procession. William's regiment, the Household Cavalry, responsible for ceremonial occasions, had been preparing for weeks, making sure every uniform was spotless, buttons and boots were polished, and the manes of their horses — two of whom had been named William and Catherine — were brushed to perfection. While most of London was still sleeping, there was a practice of the processional route from Westminster Abbey to Buckingham Palace. The Queen's carriages were driven through a ghostly Central London, horses trotted along Westminster's Whitehall in the chilly morning, and soldiers performed their drills in front of their commanding officers. The countdown had begun, with time-honored British precision.

After a holiday to the Seychelles where they sealed their future with a secret pact to get married, the couple are pictured on a night out and look truly happy to be back together in October 2007. (© Copetti/ Photofab/Rex Features)

Kate and William are pictured at the Boodles Boxing Ball in June 2008 in aid of the Starlight Children's Foundation. Kate worked closely with the organization and also made top-secret visits to a children's hospice in Hampshire. (© Davidson/ O'Neill/Rex Features)

Finally, it's official! William and Kate announce they are to marry and pose for the world's media in the state apartments of St. James's Palace on November 16, 2010. (© Samir Hussein/WireImage/ Getty Images)

ABOVE LEFT: Kate carries out her first official engagement with Prince William before becoming a royal bride. The couple named a lifeboat in Anglesey in Wales where they have lived for the past three years. (© Phil Noble/AFP/Getty Images)

ABOVE RIGHT: Kate's last day as a commoner. She waves to the cameras on the eve of her wedding, flanked by her most trusted confidantes, her mum Carole and sister Pippa. (© dpa picture alliance/Alamy)

ABOVE: Not one kiss but two, William and Kate follow the royal tradition of kissing on the famous Buckingham Palace balcony, but it is all too much for little bridesmaid Grace Van Cutsem who is frightened by the cheering crowds. (© Leon Neal/AFP/Getty Images)

BELOW: The Middletons are now a part of the Royal Family. William promised Kate he would keep her beloved family close and he has kept to his word. (© AFP Photo/Hugo Burnand/Clarence House/Getty Images)

Like the late Princess Diana, Kate is kind, compassionate, and happy to breach royal protocol so that she can hug a seriously ill child who asks for a cuddle in Canada. (© AFP/Getty Images)

Kate shows she has the common touch as she poses for royal fans in Canada on the couple's very first overseas tour on behalf of Her Majesty the Queen in June 2011. (© UK Press/Getty Images)

The Queen has taken her new granddaughter-in-law under her wing. Kate was honored to join the Queen during her Diamond Jubilee tour of the UK in June 2012. (© Max Mumby/Indigo/Getty Images)

William, Kate, and Harry await the Olympic Torch. All three
were ambassadors for the 2012 Olympic Games and were
thrilled to be able to support their joint passion—sports. (©
Anwar Hussein/Getty Images)

William and Kate hug as Team
GB secures another gold medal.
(© Pascale Le Segretain/Getty
Images)

Kate puts on a headscarf and a brave face as she deals with her biggest crisis to date. She and William were in Malaysia when a French magazine published pictures of the Duchess sunbathing topless in the south of France in September 2012. (© Getty Images)

William and Kate make their tour of South East Asia and the Pacific in September 2012 look like a second honeymoon as they get into the spirit of Soloman Island life. (© Chris Jackson/Getty Images)

Kate shows she is still a deft hand at hockey when she opens a new sports pitch at her old school. Her athletic prowess put reporters off the pregnancy rumors circulating at the time. In fact, Kate was in the early stages of her pregnancy. (© Getty Images)

Kate makes her last public appearance at Trooping the Colour before the birth of baby Cambridge. She dressed head to toe in baby pink. (© Samir Hussein/Wire Image/Getty Images)

Now we are three—William and Kate present their newborn son to the world and pose for the media on the steps of St. Mary's hospital in Paddington. Prince George Alexander Louis of Cambridge was named two days after his birth. (© Ruaridh Connellan/Barcroft Media/Landov)

CHAPTER 11
MR. AND MRS. WALES

It was just after 6:00 A.M., and the morning sunshine streamed through the sash windows of the Royal Suite of the Goring Hotel, where Kate had spent her last night as a single woman. Outside, a lone road-sweeper brushed the street clean while Union Jack–themed bunting fluttered on the police barriers that ran the length of Beeston Place in Central London. Several photographers with long lenses and ladders were setting up their equipment on the pavement.

Hundreds of wellwishers had waited for hours the previous afternoon to greet Kate as she arrived at the hotel with her mother and sister from lunch with Camilla at Clarence House. There had been cries of "Good luck" and "Enjoy your big day," as cameras and smart phones were held high in the air for a final picture of Kate before she emerged the next morning as a royal bride.

The Queen had offered Kate a suite of rooms at Buckingham Palace on the eve of her wedding, but she had politely declined, preferring to be with her family. Her parents had organized a bridal dinner, and Kate was grateful for the chance to catch up with old family friends, some of whom she had not seen for several years. It had been a special evening, and Prince Harry, who had been dining with his brother and father at Clarence House, joined the party for a nightcap. Kate had retired to bed before 11:00 P.M., joking that she needed her beauty sleep, although she knew she would not be likely to sleep a wink. William, who like all grooms was not allowed to see his bride until the ceremony, had gone on an impromptu walkabout to meet the crowds outside Clarence House at 8:30 P.M. with his brother. The crowds had stayed, cheering the groom and singing "For he's a jolly good fellow" long into the night, and William had heard them from his bedroom window, sleep eluding him, too. "They were singing and cheering all night long, so the excitement of that, the nervousness of me, and everyone singing — I slept for about half an hour," he recalled.

Kate decided not to turn on the television. The news channels were devoting almost all their coverage to the wedding day, not a calming prospect for an already nervous bride. Neither was the prototype of Queen Victoria's wedding dress, which usually formed the centerpiece of the Royal Suite in a glass-fronted wardrobe next to the four-poster bed. The gown had been removed, and in its place Kate's wedding dress was hanging on a mannequin made exactly to fit her measurements. The layers of duchess satin and hand-embroidered lace were a work of art. Kate had worked closely with Sarah Burton, the head designer at Alexander McQueen, overseeing every stage of the creative process. The ivory satin bodice was slightly padded at the hips to accentuate Kate's waist and give the dress a Victorian feel, and hand-embroidered flowers had been stitched into the skirt. Sarah Burton had sneaked into the hotel for a final check the night before the wedding, wearing a hood over her head so that the waiting cameras could not get a clear shot of her.

Kate glanced at the day's itinerary. In less than half an hour, the hairdressers — eight of them — from the Richard Ward salon in Chelsea were due to arrive to start working on the bridal party. "It was strangely quiet as we drove through the city," remembered James Pryce. "We could see the police setting up the balustrades, and as we pulled up at the Goring Hotel, I saw that an awning had been erected over the entrance. The road was then closed off, and by that point the paparazzi were all in place. We started working on the aunts and uncles and the rest of the bridal party while Kate got ready."

Royal brides traditionally have flower girls, but Kate had wanted bridesmaids, and the couple had chosen four: William's cousin Lady Louise Windsor, the Earl and Countess of Wessex's seven-year-old daughter; William's three-year-old goddaughter, Grace Van Cutsem, the daughter of his friend Hugh Van Cutsem and Rose Astor; Eliza Lopes, Camilla's three-year-old granddaughter; and Margarita Armstrong-Jones, the Queen's nephew Viscount Linley's eight-year-old daughter. They were all placed under the charge of Pippa, the bride's maid of honor. They had also chosen two pageboys: William Lowther-Pinkerton, the ten-year-old son of William's private secretary; and Tom Pettifer, his former nanny Tiggy Legge-Bourke's eight-year-old son.

A suite had been designated for hair and makeup, and by 8:30 A.M., Kate was ready for Mr. Ward and Mr. Pryce to start work. Although Pippa and Carole had professional makeup artists, Kate preferred to do her own in the privacy of her dressing room. Her smoky-eye makeup was her trademark look, and she expertly applied her kohl pencil and shaped her brows. She was grateful to have a professional on hand to give her a touchup so that she looked flawless for the cameras, but Kate was determined to look like herself. Having been given the choice of three tiaras from the Queen's personal collection, she opted for the delicate and ornate "halo" tiara that had been commissioned by George VI in 1936 for the Queen Mother, who then passed it on to the Queen as an eighteenth birthday present.

The hairdressers worked through a checklist as they created the demi-chignon, half up, half down hairstyle. "I had a sheet with instructions on and ticked the list off one by one while James worked on the hair," said Richard Ward. According to James Pryce, the most complicated part was securing the tiara. "We backcombed the top to create a foundation for the tiara to sit around, then did a tiny plait in the middle and sewed the tiara on. Richard and I were both just chatting to her. Kate didn't want TVs on and we didn't talk about the wedding. This was about Kate being in her own space and we couldn't hear the noise from the street or anything." With her tiara in place, Kate went to another room to get into her dress. "It took about forty-five minutes," recalled James Pryce. "She was in her room, and I knocked on her door and went in. She was standing in her dress with Sarah and a few assistants working on her. I was like: 'Wow, you look amazing.' It was all too much to take in. Once I'd checked her hair over and made sure the tiara was secure, she left the room. I could hear the roar from the crowd as she left with her father."

William and Harry had left Clarence House shortly after 10:00 A.M. in a chauffeur-driven Bentley state limousine. Dressed in the bright scarlet uniform and cap of the Colonel of the Irish Guards, a title the Queen bestowed on William just before the wedding, the groom and his best man, who was dressed in his heavy ceremonial Blues and Royals uniform, looked resplendent.

There were cheers and shouts from the crowds who stood behind the police barriers. A major security operation had been taking place for weeks leading up to the wedding day; sewers and lampposts, traffic lights and public trash cans had been inspected, and manholes had been uncovered, leaving nothing to chance. The wedding day was a prime target for a terrorist attack; as well as the British royal family, there were fifty foreign heads of state attending and senior members of government, along with celebrities. The city had been on a constant terror threat alert since the London bombings in July 2005. There were also fears of republican demonstrations; the wedding was reported to be costing $30 million and the security bill alone, which would be met by the taxpayers, was close to $8 million. But as the royal brothers drove slowly down Horse Guards Parade that morning, the only chants from the flag-waving masses were celebratory.

Stepping out of the car, they turned to wave to the thousands of people who lined the streets. Entering Westminster Abbey, they were greeted by the Dean of Westminster, and as they walked up the aisle together to await the bride, forty minutes before she was due to arrive, it was impossible not to imagine how proud William and Harry's mother would have been. William seemed excited, though his habit of wiping his palms and clenching his jaw gave away his nerves. Sweat pads had been stitched into his heavy jacket to help him stay cool. At one point Harry made a quip, and William visibly relaxed and went to chat with his mother's side of the family, the Spencers, who had been given a front-row pew in the abbey. The church held many memories for the family, particularly William's soon-to-be-married uncle, Diana's brother Earl Spencer, who had delivered his now-famous and moving eulogy at the princess's funeral in the very same church.

It had been agreed that William and Harry would wait in the chapel of St. Edward the Confessor, which is separated from the high altar by a gilded screen and was where the abbey's marriage registers would be signed at the end of the wedding service. The chapel, which houses the shrine of St. Edward, is the burial site of medieval kings and queens. The great stone tombs would have been enough to send shivers down William's spine, but he was relieved to be away from the buzzing congregation and the TV screens that had been erected in the abbey so that everyone could see what was happening at the high altar.

The congregation had been gathering since 8:45 A.M., and every one of the guests had to go through rigorous security checks. As well as being scanned by metal detectors, they had been asked not to take photographs in the church and to arrive in plenty of time so that they could be seated before the VIPs arrived. Given that this was a royal wedding, there was a hierarchy among the guests, and celebrities were at the bottom of the pecking order.

Surprisingly, there was no seating plan in the nave, where most of the congregation was assigned pews. Among the sea of brightly colored outfits and designer hats were a number of familiar faces. David Beckham, who had worked with William on England's unsuccessful bid for the soccer World Cup, was proudly sporting his Order of the British Empire, and his heavily pregnant wife, Victoria Beckham, showcased a navy dress from her latest collection. The film director Guy Ritchie, who, the week before the wedding, had been revealed as a distant cousin of Kate's, arrived with his wife. Kate and William had also invited Joss Stone, whom they had gotten to know after she sang at the Diana memorial concert. Sir Elton John, who seemed to be struggling with the heat from the overhead lights, was accompanied by his husband. Tara Palmer-Tomkinson, an old family friend, caused a stir by dressing head to toe in electric blue. There was much pointing and waving, greeting and air kissing while everyone kept an eye on the great west door to see who would arrive next.

The Prime Minister and senior cabinet ministers had been instructed to take their pews ahead of the visiting heads of state and foreign royals, and they were seated in the stalls behind the choir. Whereas Prime Minister David Cameron was appropriately attired in his morning suit, his wife, Samantha, attracted some criticism from television commentators for choosing not to wear a hat. She was an anomaly, as most of the well-turned-out guests had heeded the formal dress code and opted for hats.

Certainly the visiting royals and the extended members of the British royal family did not disappoint in the hat department. They knew what was expected of a royal wedding, and as they piled out of the minibuses, which had escorted them from Buckingham Palace, there was an explosion of color, feathers, and netting. William's cousin Zara Phillips, who arrived with her fiancé, rugby player Mike Tindall, had opted for an oversized black hat that she struggled with as she stepped out of the rather unglamorous coach. Princess Beatrice, who was driven in a car with her sister, at the insistence of their father, Prince Andrew, had taken a risk with an extraordinary creation by milliner Philip Treacy, which was picked to pieces by the fashion brigade watching with eagle eyes and commenting live on the arrivals. With its bizarre and complex loops and tentacle-like flourishes, it was compared to an octopus and a giant pretzel.

The sight of kings and queens descending en masse from silver buses was something to behold, but they didn't appear to mind, and as they took their seats in the north and south stalls, they, together with crown princes and princesses, earls and countesses, sheiks and sultans of countries around the world, found themselves seated with many young guests. Over 1,000 of the 1,900-strong congregation were William and Kate's friends, and they had been seated in prime pews. These were friends from all aspects of their past and present, including childhood friends, school friends, university friends, and colleagues from work. There were girlfriends and boyfriends from their past, among them William's first love, Rose Farquhar; Arabella Musgrave and Jecca Craig, as well as Kate's ex-boyfriend from St. Andrews, Rupert Finch, and Harry Blakelock, the boy who had broken her heart when she was a schoolgirl. Kate had invited a significant contingent from Marlborough, including Emilia and Alice and their old headmaster, Edward Gould. Clearly fond of some of her former teachers, she had also included David Gee, her favorite mathematics teacher at St. Andrews Prep, as well as her former headmasters, Robert Acheson and Jeremy Snow, who were all surprised to be seated alongside royals, representatives of the church, and members of the cabinet.

The mother of the bride arrived with James shortly after the crowned heads of state and, as protocol required, before Charles and Camilla, and Queen Elizabeth II and Prince Philip. Dressed in a pale sky-blue Catherine Walker dress suit, Carole looked youthful and elegant as she smiled at some of the faces she recognized in the congregation. On the arm of her only son, she made her way to the high altar, followed at a discreet distance by the family's bodyguard, Bond-Gunning.

The Middletons' guests were seated in the north lantern and had clear views of the sacrarium, where the couple would exchange their vows. This was a wedding in which everyone was to be treated as equals, so seated immediately opposite the royal family were Michael's brothers, nieces, and nephews, along with some cousins and Carole's elderly cousin Jean. "I was the only

346

member of Carole's side of the family to be invited," said Mrs. Harrison. "It was one of the most special days of my life and quite an incredible experience to be sitting in the Abbey with so many people. I felt truly honored."

Carole and Michael's guest list included trusted and loyal friends who had touched their lives over the years. There were also more recent friends from Mustique, among them their yoga teacher, Gregory Allen, and his partner, Elizabeth Saint; the island's tennis coach, Richard Schaffer; and Basil Charles, the owner of Basil's Bar. Carole's brother, Gary, had a second-row seat with his eight-year-old daughter, Tallulah, and his ex-wife, Luan. Dressed in top hat and tails, he was the model of discretion and generously swapped seats with Camilla's daughter, Laura, so that she could have a better view of her daughter walking in the bridal procession. Carole and Michael had not forgotten the loyalty of the residents and shopkeepers in Bucklebury who had protected them from the media and respected their privacy during Kate and William's courtship. The local pub landlord along with the postman and the village butcher, Martin Fiddler, were all seated. "It was amazing to be invited. My wife and I have known Carole since she was a young single woman," said Mr. Fiddler. "We have seen her married and watched the children grow up, and to see Catherine walk up the aisle was so very special. We had a good position in the abbey, which made us feel even more touched. We had amazing views and could see everything. The earlier you got there, the better seats you got, because there wasn't a seating plan. Carole and Michael coped brilliantly with the pressure — they all did. Mike looked like the proudest man in the world walking up the aisle, and Carole looked stunning, and I remember thinking how composed she was. I imagine there were lots of nerves and possibly a stiff drink before the service."

Charles and Camilla, dressed in a pretty pale-blue dress, were the last members of the royal family to arrive, ahead of the Queen and Prince Philip. Pristine in his Royal Navy Number One dress outfit, Charles was greeted by the Dean of Westminster and made sure that everything was in place ahead of the bride's arrival.

The crowds roared their approval as the Queen and the Duke of Edinburgh pulled up at the abbey and a trumpet fanfare sounded. The Queen, who had just celebrated her eighty-fifth birthday, was dressed in a dazzling primrose-yellow dress that reflected the spirit of the nation and the unexpected spring sunshine. According to courtiers, she had been in a joyful mood for days. She is known to love weddings and was delighted that her grandson was now settling down with the woman he loved. The courtiers said she was "practically skipping with joy" before she departed the Palace.

To the rousing march from *The Birds* by Charles Hastings Parry, the Queen and the Duke of Edinburgh made their stately walk down the red carpet and up to the high altar, led by Charles and Camilla. It was quite a moment in history, Charles walking with the woman he had always loved, in the very same place where Diana's funeral had taken place. It was a scene that many, Charles included, believed might never happen. As Prince Philip walked alongside the Queen, it must have brought back memories of their own wedding day sixty-four years earlier in this, the most holy and sacred abbey in the kingdom. The congregation fell silent as the Queen took her place in the front pew.

At exactly 10:50 A.M., Kate and her father stepped out of the Goring Hotel. The awning over the threshold made it impossible to see the wedding dress in full. There

was a glimpse of lace and plenty of train —
6.5 feet, in fact — which had to be carefully
piled into the waiting Rolls Royce Phantom.
At one point, Michael seemed to be buried
in tulle, causing Kate to giggle. She wanted
some pictures of this special moment and
asked her friend Millie Pilkington, a professional photographer who has known the
family for years, to climb into the front seat
and take some photographs. As father and
daughter passed Buckingham Palace and
headed down the Mall to Horse Guards
Parade, they waved at the crowds, a sea of
red, white, and blue that stretched as far as
they could see. Michael took his daughter's
hand and turned to smile at her. The eyes
of the world were upon them, but in the
backseat of the glass-roofed Rolls Royce, it
was just Kate and her father sharing a very
special moment. Like any other proud
father, this was a moment of huge significance in his life, the first of his children's
weddings.

The car pulled up in front of the great
west door and Kate stepped out onto the
red carpet, her train unfolding like a flower
behind her. The collective cheer prompted a
smile from the radiant bride. Some of the
spectators had camped out for several nights
to secure their front-row positions, and this

was the moment they had been waiting for. In her glittering tiara and ivory-and-white satin gown, she looked every inch a princess. The train was regal, modest, and incredibly beautiful. The antique Chantilly and English lace bodice that was nipped in at the waist was exquisite, and the dipped neckline a touch daring, but entirely elegant. Commentators compared the gown to Grace Kelly's wedding dress, and only at that moment was it revealed by the Palace that the designer was Sarah Burton. The news was met with much excitement; Burton was one of Britain's most exciting designers at one of the country's most famous fashion houses, and it was seen as a poignant tribute to Alexander McQueen, who had committed suicide a year earlier. Kate had scored an ace; her dress was traditional yet contemporary, timeless but fashion-forward. Fashion editors commended the design as inspired and perfect.

Kate smiled at Pippa, who told her she looked beautiful. So did Pippa. Kate had wanted her younger sister to dress in white, and the fitted bias-cut gown, also designed by Sarah Burton, with its scooped neckline, suggestion of cleavage, and tease of buttons down the back to her bottom, was almost as sensational as Kate's wedding dress. It was typical of Kate's generosity and her self-confidence not only to dress her sister in white but also to want her to wear such a stunning gown. While Pippa tended to the train, Kate turned around to face the crowds. One day the British people would be her subjects. It was the same thought that had struck Diana, who had paused and waved to the nation, as was expected of royal brides, before she climbed the stairs of St. Paul's Cathedral. But while Diana had seemed full of trepidation, Kate, who was older and more experienced in her role as a royal consort, exuded an amazing sense of confidence and purpose. They were both royal brides, but Kate and Diana, for all the comparisons, were two very different women.

As Pippa made sure every pleat was in place, the little flower girls checked their floral headdresses and held on to their white-rose bouquets. The pages, grinning proudly, took their positions at the back of the bridal procession. Inside the abbey, Sarah Burton and James Pryce were on hand to make any final adjustments. Finally, the church bells that had been tolling since the bridegroom's arrival ceased, and the London Chamber Orchestra played the first chords of Charles Parry's "I Was Glad." The music filled the great church with the spirit of the occasion. "There was a collective gasp as Kate entered the abbey. I looked up and saw this beautiful silhouette — it was the most special moment," recalled James Pryce. "Watching her walk up the abbey was just magical. She glided and was breathtakingly beautiful." William kept his eyes fixed firmly on the altar, but Prince Harry couldn't resist turning around. "She's here. Just wait till you see her!" he said, grinning.

Walking slowly past the avenue of English maple trees and exquisite displays of her favorite lily of the valley, Kate breathed in the sweet scent, remembering to stay calm and focused on the moment. Arms linked with her father, they both kept their gazes fixed ahead as they walked the 318 feet to the high altar. This was Kate's final journey as a middle-class girl — she would leave the abbey a future Queen. When she reached the altar, William finally turned to face his bride. His eyes widened. "You look beautiful," he exclaimed. Sensing Michael's nervousness, he cracked a joke. "We're supposed to have just a small family affair," he whispered to his soon-to-be father-in-law.

With everyone in place, the organ ceased and the congregation fell silent as the service began. It was traditional and beautiful, in keeping with the Anglican faith, and punctuated with the couple's chosen hymns, including "Jerusalem," one of Princess Diana's favorites. There were nods of encouragement and grins of sheer pleasure between William and Kate, the gentle brushing of hands, and at one point a wink of encouragement.

William had opted not to wear a wedding ring, and as he presented Kate with hers — a simple band made from a piece of Welsh gold that the Queen had given them as an engagement present — he appeared to struggle to get it on, prompting nervous glances from the congregation and a reassuring smile from Kate. When she spoke, her voice was clear and audible. Nerves had gotten the better of Diana, who had muddled Charles's names, but Kate managed "William Arthur Philip Louis" in crystal-clear tones. As they exchanged their vows, their eyes locked. There at the high altar, it really was just the two of them. Amid all the preparations, pomp, and pageantry here, in the House of Kings where thirty-seven kings and queens had been invested since William the Conqueror was crowned on Christmas Day, the union of the future King and Queen of England was taking place. This was living history, and the wedding, which would be replayed many, many times over the years, was a reminder of the power of the monarchy and the love the country felt for its great and unique establishment. This was a landmark within the century — a marriage that would secure the thousand-year-old lineage of the House of Windsor and move it forward. History was being made, and the future of the monarchy seemed destined to succeed with William and Kate, a perfectly suited bride and groom, pledging their love and commitment to one another in the presence of God.

The vows were traditional, but Kate, the modern bride amid so much tradition, chose not to obey but to "love, comfort, honor, and keep." They had discussed their vows with the Archbishop of Canterbury, who counseled them in the months leading up to the wedding, and both William and Kate agreed they would prefer not to "obey," which somehow seemed so incompatible with the equality on which their relationship was founded. Upon the bride's "I will," there was a collective cheer up and down the country and around the world. Close to 2 billion people were watching the ceremony on television, and across the Atlantic many Americans had woken at dawn to witness the couple exchange their vows. On the other side of the world in Sydney, all-night parties were already in full swing to celebrate the royal union.

The couple's choice of lesson from Romans 12, delivered by Kate's brother, James, highlighted the virtues of self-sacrifice, modesty, honesty, and leadership. It was the only reading during the service, and James, who had suffered from dyslexia throughout his life, had learned the verses by heart. The Bishop of London gave a sermon in which he described marriage as a "hope in troubled times." He asked the congregation, and the rest of the world, to pray for the couple, adding, "It is good that people in every continent are able to share in these celebrations, because this is, as every wedding day should be, a day of hope." It was, he reminded them, the festival of St. Catherine of Siena, and touchingly, he spoke of the family that he hoped would bless the couple. He ended his address with a prayer the couple had written themselves in which they thanked God for their families and for "the love that we share and for the joy of our marriage." Once the Dean of Westminster had blessed the couple, the congregation burst into "God Save the Queen," and the bride and groom were led to the Chapel of St. Edward the Confessor to sign the register, away from the television cameras.

As William took his bride's hand to leave the abbey as man and wife, the London Chamber Orchestra played William Walton's magnificent "Crown Imperial." Kate, now a future Queen, curtsied deeply to the reigning monarch. "Amazing," Queen Elizabeth II declared of the wedding afterward, her single word summing up the mood of the nation.

Outside the great west door, the open-topped State Landau carriage stood gleaming in the April sunshine. As William and Kate stepped into the very same horse-drawn carriage that had taken Charles and Diana back to the Palace after their wedding nearly thirty years earlier, Kate turned to William, "Are you happy?" she asked. "Amazing, amazing," replied William. "I am so proud you're my wife," he replied, according to one of several lip-readers who had been tasked with relaying the asides that day. It was a touching moment that perfectly summed up why William adored her. Whereas he was used to all the fanfare, Kate was not, yet her instinct was to ask him if he was happy. He was always her first thought.

Thousands of servicemen and women lined the route back to Buckingham Palace. Soldiers, sailors, and airmen, among them some of William's colleagues from the RAF, each had a part to play, along with the ten-deep crowd, whose applause was a constant and tumultuous roar right up to the Palace gates. "It's mad, it's mad," William repeated to his bride as he looked out at the forest of upturned flags and past the temporary media village that had been constructed at Canada Gate for the thousands of journalists who were covering the event. The couple was genuinely touched by the public support in advance of the wedding, which they had described as "incredibly moving," and now, looking at the throngs of people lining the streets, they could only marvel at the loyalty and joy of the British people.

In front of the famous balcony that looks onto the gleaming Queen Victoria memorial, the crowds waited and waited, their cameras fixed on the very same spot where Prince Charles had kissed Diana. Years later, the Duke of York and Sarah Ferguson had followed suit, making the royal kiss something of a tradition.

When William led his bride out through the glass doors and onto the balcony at 1:25 P.M., the noise was deafening as the crowds clapped and cheered for what seemed like an eternity. "Kiss, kiss, kiss," they chanted. "Oh wow," said Kate, who appeared deeply moved by the spectacle. As the bridesmaids and pages, as well as the couple's families, followed onto the balcony, the roar grew into a crescendo. Carole and Michael stood next to Charles and Camilla and waved, not quite believing the sight before them. Pippa said something that made the Duke of Edinburgh smile, while Harry chatted with James. The Queen stood with her hands behind her back, surveying her subjects and beaming broadly. William and Kate waved. They knew what the crowd was cheering for, and finally, William turned to kiss Kate. It was more of a peck than a kiss, and the crowd cheered for more. William grinned. "Let's give them another one. I love you," he said as a Lancaster, a Spitfire, and a Hurricane thundered overhead. This time the kiss was longer and the crowd louder, so much so that little Grace Van Cutsem cupped her hands to her ears as she looked down rather grumpily. The Queen took this as a cue to leave and was followed by her family. William and Kate were the last to leave, Kate glancing over her shoulder to bid the crowd one final wave good-bye.

Inside, the 650 guests who had been

invited to the champagne reception were served canapés. "Many of the guests were on the other side of the Palace and couldn't actually see what was happening on the balcony, so they watched on televisions," recalled Lady Elizabeth Anson. William and Kate spent close to an hour greeting their guests, some of whom they had never met before. Along with the ceremony, this was the formal part of the day and the newly-weds were required to meet the heads of the Commonwealth and the visiting royal families. After the cutting of the cake — a traditional two-tiered fruitcake adorned with English roses, Scottish thistles, Welsh daffodils, and the Irish shamrock, made by the British cake maker Fiona Cairns — Charles gave a short speech in the Picture Gallery, against the backdrop of one of the world's greatest collection of Old Masters. He welcomed his daughter-in-law into the family, telling guests, "We are lucky to have her." He also reminisced about William's childhood, saying, "It feels like only yester-day I was building houses out of chairs in the living room for William. On one occa-sion I bought a pedal car for him so he could drive around the garden. I told him he could drive around the old cedar tree, but he must not bump into the cedar tree.

William drove round once, twice, and then crashed into the cedar tree. Well, that was the end of the pedal car." Unable to resist poking fun at his elder son, he also cracked a joke about William's thinning hairline. William, who took to the stage briefly to thank everyone for coming, retaliated with a joke about his father's expanding waistline. There was much merriment and laughter, and a toast to the bride and groom's happiness.

Carole and Michael mingled easily with the guests and seemed impressively relaxed with their new in-laws. The Queen had invited them for lunch at Windsor Castle the week before the wedding so that there would be no awkwardness on the big day, and according to courtiers, the date had been a resounding success.

Touchingly, William introduced Kate as "Mrs. Wales" when he addressed the wedding party, even though the couple was now officially the Duke and Duchess of Cambridge, titles bestowed on them by the Queen that morning as a wedding gift. "Prince William had changed into a more comfortable military coat, and he was laughing. It was rather wonderful; they had managed to have what felt like a family wedding in a most extraordinary setting," recalled Lady Elizabeth Anson. "Prince Charles's speech was very warm and loving and very funny. The reception was remarkably relaxed and really felt like a family affair."

By 3:30 P.M., guests were asked to make their way to the garden to wave the couple off. William had asked his father if he could borrow his treasured blue Aston Martin Volante, Charles's twenty-first birthday present from the Queen, to drive down the Mall to Clarence House. The car had been polished for the occasion, and much to William and Kate's surprise Harry had it decked out with "L" plates, a ju5t wed registration plate, and "W-and-C"–themed balloons. For good measure, a Sea King helicopter swooped down from the sky to escort them home. For the prince, there was something symbolic about driving his wife home, even if in the excitement of it all, he had forgotten to release the emergency brake.

Back at the Palace, the couple couldn't wait to run through the events of the day together. Careful not to crush her bridal gown, Kate changed into a fluffy terry cloth robe and they jumped like excited children onto the bed. They had recorded the televised ceremony and couldn't wait to watch it on playback. Harry joined them, and the three of them sat watching together. Kate was still wearing the Queen's priceless tiara. "It was lovely to see them so relaxed and happy. You could see how excited and in love they were," said James Pryce, who arrived at the Palace to arrange Kate's hair for the evening. "Kate was still wearing her tiara in the evening. We took it out and blow dried her hair."

Sarah Burton had created a second dress for Kate for the evening reception, a strapless floor-length ivory satin gown with a diamante sash. Teamed a white angora wool bolero to ward off the evening chill, Kate looked every inch a fairy-tale princess. This was the part of the day they were most looking forward to — a sit-down dinner with three hundred of their friends and family and a party that would go on until dawn. The Queen and Prince Philip had already left the Palace by the time the couple's guests arrived. William's cousins Zara and Peter Phillips, Princesses Beatrice and Eugenie, and Earl Spencer's daughters, Kitty, Amelia, and Eliza, were among the first to be driven into the courtyard at 7:00 P.M. They were greeted by bagpipers in the candlelit courtyard and taken through to the champagne reception. Carole and Michael, who had gone back to the Goring

Hotel to see their guests after the wedding reception, had changed into their party clothes, as had Pippa, who had caused quite a sensation in her figure-hugging bridesmaid gown. Unbeknownst to her, she was now a global superstar — her name was trending on Twitter, and by the end of the day, Facebook groups dedicated to her derriere had thousands of followers. People wanted to know all about Kate's younger sister and how close she was to Prince Harry. The cameras had picked up on them leaving the abbey arm-in-arm and later, sharing asides on the Palace balcony. In fact, Pippa's date for the wedding day was her boyfriend of nearly a year, a handsome former Etonian and city financier, Alex Loudon, who had quietly become an intimate addition to the Middleton fold.

After vintage rose champagne from the Palace cellars, dinner was served at 8:00 P.M. At Kate's request, the room had been lit by hundreds of candles and every table set with nineteenth-century solid gold plates and cutlery dating back to the reign of King George III. The couple had named the tables, which were adorned with white roses, after some of their favorite places, among them St. Andrews; Lewa Downs; Rhoscolyn, one of their favorite villages in

Anglesey; and Tetbury, the Gloucestershire village near Highgrove. They had spent hours on the seating plans and deliberately mixed up their friends and family so that everyone could get to know each other. The supper menu, created by one of William and Kate's favorite chefs, Anton Mosimann, comprised organically sourced crab from Wales, lamb from Highgrove, and a trio of miniature trifle, chocolate fondant, and homemade ice cream. Charles had helped to select the white Mersault burgundy and Pomerol claret. Shortly after 9:30 P.M., once coffee and petits fours had been served, Harry, who was acting as master of ceremonies, switched roles to deliver a hilarious best-man's speech. Adorning a fez, he recounted how he and William played soldiers as little boys, a game that always ended with him being beaten up by his older brother. There were jokes about William's bald patch and his long-standing inability to keep up with Harry during drinking games. Referring to the newlyweds as the "dude and the duchess," he said, "William didn't have a romantic bone in his body before he met Kate." A great mimic, Harry impersonated his brother, calling Kate "baby" to much laughter, but the mood changed when he spoke movingly of his love for his sister-in-law and how lucky his brother was to have found a woman who loved him unconditionally. Chelsy, who was back together with Harry and was sitting at the next table, looked momentarily downcast, while Kate brushed away a tear or two. There were more tears when William stood up and described Kate as his "rock" and said how much his mother would have loved her. There were tears of laughter as Michael recalled the unforgettable moment when William landed his Chinook in the back garden. "I knew things were getting serious when I found a helicopter in my garden. I thought, *Gosh, he must like my daughter.* I did wonder how William was ever going to top this if they ever got engaged. I just thought, *What will he do?* You can't get much better than that, and we are certainly not used to princes landing helicopters in the garden!" He credited his "beautiful daughter" for her nerve and steadiness as they walked down the aisle and thanked the royal family for welcoming his family so warmly.

There was more laughter when William's two best school friends, Thomas van Straubenzee and James Meade, delivered a witty sketch about the prince, including references to his wild partying and the drunken occasion during which he wore a ladies' thong. There were jokes about the fact that Kate beat William "at everything — especially sports." Then, when the speeches came to an end, Harry announced that all the guests were to make their way to the Throne Room for the surprise that he and Pippa had been planning for weeks. It was perhaps just as well that the Queen and the Duke of Edinburgh were not there. The priceless chandeliers had been covered up and in their place were strobe lights, glitter balls, and a giant dance floor, which dominated the 120-foot long room. The dais, where the thrones usually had pride of place, had been replaced by a disco booth and a cocktail bar. Pippa had arranged for the room to be scented with Kate's favorite candles and for bowls of Haribo candies to be placed on the surrounding tables. The bar served a variety of drinks, including Boujis-inspired Crack Baby cocktails, a blend of champagne, vodka, passion fruit, and Chambord raspberry liqueur. William and Kate had been involved with the music and had asked the British singer Ellie Goulding to perform her chart-topping song "Starry Eyed" as their first dance. "It was an amazing honor to be asked. The atmosphere was incredible and it is a night I will never forget," Miss Goulding said afterward. She sang a number of covers, and Charles and Camilla took to the dance floor to her version of Elton John's "Your Song." Later on, a DJ took over, and Carole requested one of her favorite songs, the 1986 Jermaine Stewart song "We Don't Have to Take Our Clothes Off," as she and Michael bowed out of the party, leaving William and Kate to enjoy the rest of the night with their friends. The dancing continued until 2:30 A.M., when guests were invited to the gardens for a firework display. Catherine wheels had been pinned to the trees, and the twenty-second-long burst of red and white sparks could be seen from over the Palace walls, although the crowds had long since dispersed. When the final rocket had soared, William and Kate were driven across the courtyard in an open-topped RAF-personalized Fiat 500 to the Belgian Suite, where they were to spend their wedding night.

Back in the Throne Room, Harry declared it was time "for some serious partying," and the decks were turned up for one final tune. Merry from the Crack Baby cocktails, Harry suddenly launched himself into the crowd. "Harry literally stage dived — it was a great finale," one reveler remembered. It was certainly a party none of the guests would ever forget.

Shortly before 11:00 A.M. the next morning, William and Kate emerged from Buckingham Palace and strolled, hand-in-hand, across the lawn for their first photo session as husband and wife. The sun was bright overhead, and the couple, looking remarkably fresh-faced, announced they were heading off for "a private weekend." The Queen, who was in residence at Sandringham, had made Windsor Castle available to them so that they could enjoy some time alone before heading home to Anglesey, where William was due to resume work. "I am glad the weather held off. We had a great day," Kate said as she and William made their way across the courtyard to their waiting helicopter.

Going home to Anglesey at the end of what was surely the best weekend of their lives must have been something of an anticlimax, but as she pushed a cart around the parking lot of the local supermarket just days after the magnificent ceremony, Kate was glowing. Dressed in leggings and a sweater, her hair flowing in the breeze, Mrs. Wales, as William had affectionately called her on their wedding day, looked like the happiest girl in the world.

Eleven days after their wedding, William and Kate left for their honeymoon, leaving the country as unobtrusively as they were able. William had planned the two-week-long vacation down to the finest detail, but he had kept the destination secret from Kate. "By going back to work before leaving for their honeymoon, they were able to escape," said a friend of the couple. "It was a deliberate decoy."

Kate had been told to pack for the sun, and it was only when they arrived at the airport that William told her they were flying to North Island in the Seychelles. It was a romantic gesture; the Seychelles was where they had made their secret pact to marry when they stayed in Desroches, and now, four years later, they were returning as husband and wife. They flew by private jet to Mahé, the largest island in the archipelago, and then took a helicopter to North Island, a four-mile-long private island shaded by coconut groves and surrounded by cliffs. The exclusive North Island Lodge had been booked immediately after their wedding, and William had waited for one of the luxury wooden bungalows to become available. The sensational rooms looked out onto the crystal clear Indian Ocean and had private gardens, an outside deck where they enjoyed morning yoga sessions, their own plunge pool, and a spectacular open-air bathroom with a sunken bath that was filled with frangipani flowers each night by their private butler. Back in England, William had gone to great lengths to keep the honeymoon a secret, so he was upset when the island's owner told a Hamburg newspaper: "Yes, we rented the island to the British royal family. Prince William and his Kate are spending their honeymoon there." The news traveled around the world, and William, who was keeping a close eye on events back at home, where his grandmother was carrying out an historic trip to Ireland, knew that they would most likely be photographed now that the secret was out.

Determined not to let the whereabouts of their honeymoon location spoil the holiday, William arranged champagne picnics on the beach and a sunset cruise so that they could tour the island. During the days, they relaxed on the beach, working on their tans while admiring the island's turtles. At their villa there was a butler on call for them day and night, and a private chef who cooked whatever they wanted. William had sent a list of their favorite foods ahead of their arrival, including Philadelphia cream cheese, quail eggs, Granny Smith apples, and rather surprisingly, brussels sprouts. The latter immediately prompted rumors that Kate was trying to get pregnant. Sprouts are rich in folic acid, which is recommended for women who are trying to conceive.

When the couple returned to England at the end of May, it was back to reality with a bump. The President of the United States and the First Lady were in London for a state visit, and the Queen asked William and Kate to come to Buckingham Palace to meet with them just days after they touched down on British soil. It was their first official duty as newlyweds, and the Obamas, who had not been invited to the royal wedding, were eager to meet the Duke and Duchess of Cambridge. William charmed the President, while Kate and Michelle Obama "instantly hit it off" during the twenty-minute meeting. It was a canny public relations move on the Queen's part — William and Kate were set to visit the United States the following month, and the fact that the Obamas had been dazzled was an auspicious start.

CHAPTER 12
A TOUR OF DUTY

The celebrity crowd gathered on the sundeck and watched the Jaguar pull up. There was a collective gasp as Kate stepped onto the red carpet, stunning in a floor-length rose-pink sequined organza gown. As William escorted his wife past the banks of photographers, the flashes popped against the dusky night sky. They led the way into the cocktail reception, pausing before moving inside to admire the high divers displaying their acrobatic prowess at a deepwater pool.

The evening, to celebrate the tenth anniversary of one of their foundation's chosen charities, Absolute Return for Kids, was the couple's first engagement since their wedding. Every one of the wealthy guests wanted an audience with the newlyweds and had paid $7,600 for the privilege. Inside, cameras were banned, but it didn't stop the well-heeled throng from taking pictures on their mobile phones. "Where is your husband?" one guest asked when he was introduced to Kate. "We always get split up at these kind of things," she explained, but she didn't seem to mind and was just as starstruck by the celebrities she was introduced to as they were by her. She was particularly pleased to be seated at the same table as British actor Colin Firth, whose performance in *The King's Speech* she had so admired. After supper, William addressed the guests and announced that he and Kate were committed to helping "young people who really need it." There was much applause and several wolf whistles, and William joked that he couldn't wait to tell his grandmother about the amazing night and the divers in tight Speedos.

In truth, it was most likely not the topic of conversation when the couple joined the Queen that weekend for the Trooping the Colour. The parade — an annual procession by the Queen's troops on Horse Guards Parade next to Buckingham Palace to celebrate the sovereign's birthday — marked the Queen's eighty-fifth birthday and was a rather nerve-racking occasion for both William and Kate. William was to ride on horseback in the event for the very first time, alongside Prince Charles, the Duke of

Kent, and Princess Anne, to give the royal salute to his grandmother while Kate was to accompany the Duchess of Cornwall in the carriage procession. It was the first public outing for the couple since their wedding, and a record number of people were packed into the Mall to see them. William and Kate joined the family for the traditional balcony appearance, and Kate, who had chosen a cream dress and jacket by Alexander McQueen for the occasion, seemed comfortable and relaxed as she chatted with Camilla and Sophie Wessex, Prince Edward's wife.

Kate had spent the past few weeks in meetings with Sir David Manning, the Palace adviser who had helped the couple prepare before of the wedding, and Jamie Lowther-Pinkerton, both of whom would be accompanying them on their forthcoming tour of Canada and California. She had never been to the United States or Canada, and William had forewarned her that the tour would be immense fun but also hard work. For all the pomp and ceremony, palatial stays, lavish receptions, and unveiling of plaques, they would be working twelve-hour days and there would be little downtime. Sir David had spent weeks educating Kate on Canada's constitution, while she brushed up on her basic school-level French for their visit to Quebec and read up on Canada's history. In keeping with their no-frills lifestyle, the couple had agreed to travel light, and their entourage consisted of only seven staff. This was considered very modest by Palace standards; the Prince of Wales and the Duchess of Cornwall usually traveled with an entourage of at least a dozen, including a doctor, an equerry, valets, and even an artist. "We've kept it as tight as we possibly can," explained Mr. Lowther-Pinkerton, who had planned the eleven-day trip in conjunction with the Queen's private office, the Foreign Office, and the Canadian government, which was picking up the bill. In her only nod to vanity, Kate had asked her hairdresser, James Pryce, to join her. She had elected not to have ladies-in-waiting after their wedding; like William, she did not like to be fussed over, but it did mean that there was no one to travel with her, assist with her wardrobe, and collect bouquets while they were on touring.

At the Palace, there was some debate over whether Kate would need a personal dresser. Camilla insisted she would need someone to help her press and arrange her dresses in advance, but Kate was adamant that she could cope. She had asked her mother to help her shop for clothes that were elegant and practical, and Carole had sought the services of a local boutique in Berkshire. The royal wardrobe was no small matter; Kate would require at least forty outfits. There would be days when she would require as many as three changes. She usually shopped at High Street stores like Reiss and L.K. Bennett, but for this it was important that she have a working wardrobe of designer clothing. Sarah Burton had already created a number of outfits for the tour, as had two other British designers, Alice Temperley and Jenny Packham. Their timeless red-carpet dresses were exactly the sort of look Kate loved, and the Prince of Wales had generously paid for them.

Kate scored an immediate hit with the Canadian public as she descended the steps of their private plane in Ottawa in a navy lace dress designed by Montreal-born Erdem Moralioglu. Arriving for the Canada Day celebrations, William and Kate were taken to Parliament Hill by horse-drawn carriage. They were accompanied by the Governor General and an escort of red-coated Mounties and bearskin-clad Canadian Grenadier Guardsmen. Greeting them was an estimated crowd of 300,000 wellwishers, waving their red-and-white flags and cheering loudly. It was hot, and the strength of the sun caused Kate's makeup to melt, but as she took her place on the stage, she didn't let her smile slip. "We love you, Kate," the crowd chanted. Some of the young women in the crowds were wearing fascinators, a tribute, they said, to their new style icon, whose own bright-red headpiece incorporated a maple leaf, the country's national emblem.

William had been concerned about how Kate would cope with the punishing agenda and the huge media interest — more than 1,400 journalists were covering the tour — but she proved herself to be resilient and professional. She didn't seem to tire of meeting new people and happily shook hundreds of hands every day. Unlike the Queen, she chose not to wear gloves, and when it came to planting a tree at the Governor General's office in Ottawa, she shoveled away with gusto in four-inch stilettos. The image of Kate, spade in hand, brought back memories of Diana, who had planted an oak tree in the very same spot twenty-eight years before, on William's first birthday. Diana and Charles had brought their son on the tour with them, and as William admired the now-towering oak they had planted, he appeared overcome with emotion. Like the oak, he had grown over the years, but his mother, who had nurtured him from the day he was born, was no longer around to watch him thrive. It meant everything to him that he was here with the woman he loved the day after what would have been his mother's fiftieth birthday. Kate had paid her own tribute to the mother-in-law she would never know by wearing a dress designed by Diana's favorite designer, Catherine Walker.

There were several planned meetings with dignitaries and statesmen, but in order for the tour to be as relaxed as possible, the couple asked not to have too many official lineups, and to be addressed by their first names. William had made sure the tour incorporated some of Kate's interests, and when they attended a cooking class in Montreal, she couldn't wait to change into her chef's whites to prepare an Îles de la Madeleine lobster. When they traveled overnight from Montreal to Quebec City down the St. Lawrence River aboard HMCS *Montreal,* she joked that sleeping in a bunk had not been very comfortable but she didn't once complain. And she was delighted to be visiting Prince Edward Island, the picturesque setting of one of her favorite books, *Anne of*

Green Gables. There, the royal couple took part in a dragon boat race across Dalvay Lake, and while Kate took the helm with her crew, William rowed in his, beating Kate's team by a whisker. They were so competitive, William revealed, that they had never actually finished a game of tennis or Scrabble, but as he helped her out of the boat, he hugged her warmly.

When the Prince gave a demonstration of how to land a Canadian military Sea King on the water — a skill known as "water birding" — Kate clapped and cheered, taking pictures on her camera so they could have their own album from the trip. They looked very much a team; William had a habit of guiding his wife by the small of her back. He was on hand to assist when there were wardrobe malfunctions, helpfully zipping up her fleece on one chilly occasion and standing behind her when a frilly yellow dress she was wearing fluttered up in the wind, threatening to reveal her underwear. There were lingering gazes and jokes for the crowds.

When they headed to the Northwest Territories halfway through the tour, William arranged for them to have a night off on remote Eagle Island, also known as Honeymoon Island, to which they paddled in a canoe. They were the only visitors, and for once even their bodyguards didn't join them. A meal of local delicacies, including caribou and cranberries, had been prepared ahead of their arrival, and they watched the midnight sunset together. They had, royal observers noted, achieved the impossible and made an official visit look like a second honeymoon.

They were treading in famous footsteps: the Queen had visited Canada the year before, and although the republican debate bubbled constantly below the surface, the popularity of the royal visits was living proof that the majority of Canadians still wanted the Queen as their head of state. When William and Kate traveled to Calgary to open the annual rodeo, they were greeted like rock stars. Decked out in white Smithbilt cowboy hats, jeans, and cowboy boots, they looked like fresh-faced celebrities. Kate's grandfather, Peter, had trained as an RAF pilot in Alberta during World War II, so she had been particularly anxious to visit.

At the end of the tour, as they boarded the steps of the Canadian Air Force jet bound for Los Angeles, they were waved off by Prime Minster Stephen Harper. "We haven't seen a love-in like that since the first visit of the Beatles," he told them with a smile. "Everywhere you went, you left a trail of utterly charmed Canadians in your wake."

A similar "love-in" greeted them in Los Angeles. At a charity polo match in Santa Barbara, wealthy guests paid up to $4,000 to lunch with the royal couple. Their appeal was universal, and at a British Academy of Film and Television Arts dinner in downtown LA to celebrate upcoming British talent in the film industry, they dazzled and charmed some of the town's most influential people. They chatted with Tom Hanks and Jennifer Lopez, shook hands with film director Quentin Tarantino, and enjoyed their time with movie producer Harvey Weinstein and the actress Nicole Kidman. "Will and Kate Conquer America" was the headline on a commemorative issue of *People* magazine, which crowned them America's new king and queen.

Back at home, aides briefed the Palace that the tour had been a resounding success. Kate, who was only eleven weeks into her royal tenure, had proved a flawless and priceless ambassador for Great Britain. The Queen wrote to William and Kate to congratulate them, while the British press labeled "Team Cambridge" a triumphant success. When Charles and Diana had visited Canada after their wedding, Diana had been the real star, eclipsing her husband and, in doing so, badly wounding his ego and denting his pride. Kate and William had been equals, and when the crowd chanted for Kate, William had proudly ushered her in their direction. There was no jealousy on his part — instead, he was delighted that Kate was such a natural.

The press decided the moniker "Waity Katie" no longer applied, rechristening her "Stately Kate." The transition in the young prince was also noted. When William had visited Canada as a shy teenager, he had hated being the center of attention, and even as a student prince, he had resented the media attention to his life. With Kate at his side, he seemed content, more accommodating of the cameras and ready to embrace his destiny.

Back in Anglesey, William and Kate eased back into married life. William had instructed his aides to keep their diaries clear of official engagements, as he was desperate to get back in the cockpit. Kate had let slip during one walkabout in Canada that she worried every time her husband went off on a rescue mission, but she accepted that it was part of his job and her role as an army wife was to support her husband. Although she loved the peace and quiet of their life in Anglesey, she was sometimes lonely when William was on shift and was often left without enough to do.

Fortunately there was a new project to occupy her: William and Kate had been given a new London home at Kensington Palace by the Queen. The two-bedroom house, known as Nottingham Cottage, which was situated within the Palace compound, was billed as a "starter home" so that they could move out of Clarence House and have their own London base.

They had been to visit Kensington Palace at the start of the year before their wedding, when the Queen had offered them a number of options, including suites at St. James's Palace and Buckingham Palace as a London residence. Both William and Kate loved KP, as Diana used to refer to the royal residence. William had suggested living in Apartments 8 and 9, his childhood home, which evoked many happy memories of learning to ride his bike in the courtyard, but according to a friend, Kate had found the idea "creepy" and far preferred the late Princess Margaret's Apartment 1A, which was being used as office space and the headquarters for the Prince of Wales's drawing school. The three-story property, with its forty rooms and walled garden, would, she suggested, make a fabulous London family home. It was in need of extensive renovation, and so it was agreed that the couple would live at Nottingham Cottage until the renovation was complete, with plans to move in sometime in 2013.

Situated next to Wren House, the former residence of the Queen's cousin, the Duke of Kent, Nottingham Cottage has a pretty front garden. Kate had revealed in Canada when she planted the ceremonial tree that she is an avid gardener, and as well as planting some bulbs, she also started on a small refurbishment and had the house painted. With the help of British interior designer Kelly Hoppen, who helped her choose fabric swatches and soft furnishings, Kate soon made the house their home. With just two bedrooms, a living room, a very small dining room, and a kitchen, it was small but delightful. It suited them well, and on weekends, when they were in London to catch up with family and friends, Kate would have her hairdresser or beautician come to the house: "It was more private and relaxed. She would be having treatments, while William was making tea and toast in the kitchen. It was all very relaxed," recalled one regular visitor.

Most of their time was spent in Anglesey, where their lives were simple and low key. While William was working, Kate began looking into the charities and organizations that she was interested in working with, and she started researching on the Internet. Hundreds of organizations had written to the Palace, desperate to have her patronage, and she was eager to find out more about some of them. Until now, she had only worked with Starlight and intended to develop her philanthropic role. She also took great pleasure in overseeing the running of their Anglesey home. They had a house cleaner but no other staff. It was William's job to put the trash out, with Kate in charge of keeping the pantry stocked and cooking meals. She had started making jam and was seen stocking up on canning jars at the local hardware shop. She also loved hill walking in the countryside and continued to take photographs of the coastline and the dramatic mountains. In the evenings, she cooked, and they loved staying in and watching a selection of DVDs, such as *The Killing*, in marathon sessions. Sometimes they ordered pizza for delivery, and they often drank at the nearby White Eagle pub. Occasionally they went to the cinema, sneaking in unrecognized in baseball caps with a large bucket of popcorn to share. It was the ordinariness that William thrived on, and they loved the fact that they were never spied on. "People around here have taken them to their hearts. You won't catch anyone tweeting gossip about them as they go about their day-to-day business," said Jack Abbott, chairman of the local Treard-dur Bay lifeboat station, part of the Royal National Lifeboat Institution, which the couple had visited earlier that year.

William wanted to make the most of this newly wedded bliss, confiding to friends that he was living on "borrowed time." He knew that at some point, he would be expected to take on more royal duties and that they would have to move back to London. That June, his grandfather, Prince Philip, had turned ninety and announced that he planned to scale back his official engagements. He had suffered a number of bouts of ill health and acknowledged it was time to slow down. "I reckon I've done my bit," he said with characteristic understate-ment. The Queen was in full agreement, and William knew that alongside his father and Harry, whom the Queen called her "substi-tutes," he would be expected to do more. The Queen had given William her blessing for the couple to enjoy two years of married life in Anglesey without the pressure of full-time royal duties. It meant that William could complete a full tour of duty with the RAF while Kate settled into royal life at her own pace. Back in 1947, the Queen had enjoyed two carefree years in Malta after her wedding while Philip was serving with the Royal Navy, and they were some of the happiest times of her life. Granting the couple some time out of the limelight was her way of helping Kate with the transition. There was also the matter of starting a family, something both William and Kate were eager to do.

Traditionally, royal brides conceive within months of getting married. The Queen was pregnant with Charles three months after her wedding, and Diana became pregnant two months after her wedding day. William and Kate had been married for three months and were in no hurry. Secretly, they hoped it would happen relatively quickly in the peace and solitude of their Welsh home. Kate had confided to her best friends that she was "desperate" to become a mother, and the press were on constant "baby-bump" watch. This royal bride, however, appeared to be getting thinner. When the couple attended William's cousin Zara Philips's wedding in Scotland at the end of

July, Kate appeared to have lost even more weight since her wedding, prompting some concern among her family and friends, and her weight loss was noted by the ever-watchful media.

Like many brides, Kate had dropped a dress size ahead of her big day, but she had not put any of the weight back on since. During their trip to Canada and the States, she looked exceptionally thin, even when standing next to some of Hollywood's famously slender stars. Her busy travel itinerary on tour had meant they sometimes skipped meals, and Kate often nibbled on muesli bars to keep her energy levels up. She was reported to have dropped down to a UK dress size six, also known as "size zero" in America, where, among celebrities, it was something of a trend. Kate had always had a healthy, athletic figure, but these days she was a slip of her former self. Diana had developed an eating disorder within the first year of her marriage, such was the stress of her new role, and courtiers were anxious to make sure Kate stayed healthy and well. Her aides insisted her slim frame was due to her exercise regimen and healthy eating. When she was hailed as a role model for skinny women on a number of controversial pro-anorexia websites, however, she was upset and determined to distance herself from the controversial sites. She took her position seriously and wanted to be a healthy role model for her many admirers. She also knew that if she wanted to get pregnant, she ought to put on a few pounds.

The summer of 2011 afforded William and Kate some time to relax, so at the end of August, they traveled to Scotland to spend the bank holiday at Balmoral. The Queen was delighted to hear that Kate had spent some of her time drawing up a short list of charities she wanted to work with. Together with Jamie Lowther-Pinkerton and Rebecca Deacon, another of Prince William's eleven-strong team of aides who had been assigned to assisting the duchess, Kate had been quietly visiting a number of charities and organizations. She had read up on the ones she was interested in. It was important to her, as it was to William, that she not be just an ornament; they both wanted to be actively involved with their charities, and Kate wanted to represent causes she was genuinely passionate about. One charity that caught her eye was The Art Room, a small British charity based in Oxford that uses art as therapy to help disadvantaged youngsters. Its director, Juli Beattie, had written to the Palace asking if

Kate would consider working with them, and she was delighted when the duchess visited an inner-city school in Islington in North London to see the charity's work firsthand. Juli remembered, "Initially, her private secretaries came to visit The Art Room at the Robert Blair School, and then she came so that she could meet the children and see firsthand what The Art Room did. She was pleased to see that we were faithful to our mission statement and the work that we do with the children. She was genuinely interested in how we use art as therapy. We were delighted when she offered to become our royal patron."

Kate was also eager to work with children's hospices, and having already seen firsthand how children benefited from the care available at Naomi House, she found out more about the East Anglia's Children's Hospices organization and made a private visit to the charity's hospice in Milton in Cambridge. According to the charity's chief executive, Graham Butland, "We got a call from St. James's Palace saying the duchess was keen to see our work. They asked if she could visit our hospice in Cambridge so that she could come and see the children and meet some of the staff. We were told it had to be absolutely private and confidential and there could be no press. She drove herself to the hospice and spent an hour meeting the children. It was apparent from the beginning that she had a genuine interest in our work. She met some severely handicapped children, and she was fantastic with them." Addiction, particularly in young people, was another area to which Kate wanted to lend her support, and she had researched the work of the small British charity Action on Addiction. The charity's chief executive, Nick Barton, remembered, "We didn't actually write to the Palace to request the duchess's patronage because we didn't think we would have a chance. We were stunned when her people came to us and said she was interested in our charity. When I went to meet Catherine, she told me she had spent a lot of time researching the problems young people face, and she said the subject of addiction seemed to be a big issue. That's how she found us. We are eternally grateful that she did."

Kate also wanted to work with either a gallery or a museum. In September 2011, she visited the National Portrait Gallery in Central London. According to the director, Sandy Nairn, she spent the day learning about how the gallery operated and how major exhibitions were staged: "I got a call saying she was exploring and researching the charities she was interested in, and we were asked if we were happy for her to come and research and see us behind the scenes. She came at the end of the month and spent most of the day with us, which was great. She was interested in finding out how we organized exhibitions, and we showed her what a working day was like. At the end of the day, she came into the galleries and into the public spaces to see the work."

These visits were kept out of the media. The Palace wanted to give Kate time to think about the charities before making an announcement in the new year. The public had barely seen the royal couple since their return from Canada, and their official engagements were deliberately few and far between. In Diana's first year of being a royal wife, she carried out hundreds of official duties, but since her wedding, Kate had undertaken fewer than fifty. There were unkind references to her in the press about her being "the Duchess of Dolittle," but she ignored the taunts and instead focused on making the right choices about the organizations she was investigating. She had decided she would only take on a handful of causes to begin with so she could be closely involved rather than spreading herself too thin. In September, William and Kate visited The Royal Marsden's new cancer treatment center in Surrey and hosted a reception for their joint charitable foundation at St. James's Palace. Then in October, while William was busy working shifts, Kate stood in for the Prince of Wales at a charity dinner at Clarence House, which was deemed to be a great success. The following month, she and William flew to Copenhagen for their very first joint humanitarian mission, a visit to a UNICEF relief depot where food supplies for the famine-stricken east coast of Africa were being packed. It was a part of the world they both loved and knew well, so when the Crown Prince and Princess of Denmark, who had been at their wedding, invited them to join them to pack aid relief for hungry families, they made themselves available. Kate caused a flurry of speculation that she might be pregnant after she repeatedly patted her tummy, which was hidden beneath an oversized coat during the trip to Copenhagen, and declined to try some peanut butter while she and William packed aid supplies.

The matter of a royal bump was a much-discussed topic and was even the subject of new legislation in the Houses of Parliament, where the rules of succession were in the process of being revised. Prime Minister David Cameron had proposed a change to the antiquated succession laws at the biannual meeting of Commonwealth heads in Perth in October, and the revision had been universally approved, although it still needed to be passed in the Houses of Parliament and made law by the Commonwealth realms. Essentially, the new law would mean that if the couple's firstborn was a girl, she would become Queen regardless of any male heirs born afterward. Previous governments had tried to implement the change of law, but the proposed amendments — which also prohibit any heir to the throne from marrying a Catholic — had never been passed. Now there was a real reason for change, and with the backing of the government, the Queen, and the Commonwealth, it looked set to happen, and William and Kate were the catalyst. "Put simply, if the Duke and Duchess of Cambridge were to have a little girl, that girl would one day be Queen," said Mr. Cameron. The revision would also mean that the law preventing members of the royal family from marrying Catholics, in order to preserve the Church of England, would be scrapped. There was every chance that Kate could be writing royal history once again.

As 2011 came to a close, Kate prepared for her first Christmas at Sandringham, flitting between excitement and panic. Although she was more comfortable now in the presence of royals, the festive period would be a challenging new situation. Camilla and Sophie, the Countess of Wessex, had volunteered themselves as mentors to Kate and were extremely useful in advising her on how to behave, how to dress, and what she should and should not do at court. Sophie, especially, was able to relate to Kate; although she came from a noble lineage, she was a career girl before she married Prince Edward, and like Kate, she was a modern royal bride. She and Edward had courted for six years before their wedding in 1999. It had given Sophie, a public relations expert, an opportunity to adapt to royal life. During that time, the Queen had taken an immediate liking to her new daughter-in-law and asked her to assist Kate. The Queen by now had gotten to know her granddaughter-in-law better. They had carried out their first engagement together that summer when they viewed Kate's wedding dress on display at Buckingham Palace following the royal wedding. The Queen had declared the exhibit "horrible" because of the eerie way the dress was modeled on a suspended mannequin, but Kate had taken no offense. The two women had met privately on a number of other occasions, and anticipating that Christmas might be an intimidating experience for the newest member of her family, the Queen had asked her private office to update a court manual known as the Order of Precedence in the Royal Household.

The book, essentially a guide for new recruits on how to behave in the presence of the royal family, was most useful to Kate, even if it was rather confusing. It had last been updated when Camilla married into the family, and it offered detailed instructions on who Kate was expected to curtsy to, both in private and public, when she was with William, and when she was alone. It gave advice on the royal pecking order, and who should be the first and last to arrive at events such as Trooping the Colour and Royal Ascot. Kate knew from her training with David Manning that she was always required to curtsy to the Queen, the Duke of Edinburgh, the Prince of Wales, and Camilla, whether or not she was with William. According to the court rule book, when Kate was not with William, she was still expected to curtsy to blood Princesses Beatrice and Eugenie, Princess Anne, and the Queen's elderly cousin, Princess Alexandra. Somewhat uncomfortably, Sophie Wessex and less senior members of the family were now expected to curtsy to Kate, who, as William's wife and a future Queen, was further up the order of precedence. Although it may seem rather archaic, according to courtiers, the order of precedence is important so that the Queen is not overwhelmed by her family when it comes to greeting them all at once, and to ensure there is no confusion at public engagements.

There was advice on what to expect at Sandringham; the family is instructed to arrive according to precedence on Christmas Eve and the Crown equerry issues a timetable detailing who should arrive when. The least senior members of the family — cousins and extended family members — are expected first, whereas Prince Charles, as heir, is the last to arrive shortly before lunchtime. The Queen and the Duke of Edinburgh always travel by train from King's Cross to King's Lynn. Although a private family occasion, Christmas is a formal affair at Sandringham, and Kate was told that she had to have up to five outfit changes a day. She was advised to pack full-length evening gowns and jewels for dinner. At home, the Middletons opened stockings in their pajamas, but there would be no lounging around at Sandringham, where one was expected to be properly attired for breakfast, lunch, tea, and dinner. Every family member was assigned either a butler or a maid, whom they were expected to tip at the end of the stay. Kate had been looking forward to shooting but was told that in the presence of the Queen, a lady does not take a gun, so instead she would have to stay with the beaters, whose job is to flush the birds from the thicket into the direction of the guns. Each evening, there would be a cocktail party before dinner, which would be served at 8:15 P.M. sharp. According to Lady Elizabeth Anson, "In the morning you are dressed for breakfast, then you change for shooting. You come back to the house and change for tea at about 5:30 P.M. into a wool dress or a suit with a skirt. In the really old days there were tea gowns, which were like long velvet dressing gowns. . . . Then you come down for drinks, still in your tea dress. It is before this that the Queen takes a bath and does her face, so her change for dinner is usually quick — the point is not to get caught out and think you have lots of time to change before dinner. The Duchess of Cornwall and the Countess of Wessex were there to give Kate advice, and she wouldn't have had to worry about pressing her clothes. She would have had a maid who would have laid her clothes out and chosen her dress for the night."

Kate had put much thought into both her clothes and presents for her first Windsor-family Christmas, deciding that her jars of homemade preserves would be perfect gifts. Joke presents always went down well, and she reportedly bought Prince Harry a "grow your own girlfriend" kit. William had explained that the family exchanged only small offerings and the Queen was always the first to open gifts, which were lined up on a trestle table in the Red Drawing Room and opened on Christmas Eve rather than Christmas Day, which the Queen believes should be an entirely religious day. Diana had embarrassed herself when, at her first family Christmas, she handed out expensive gifts, such as cashmere sweaters, which were considered ostentatious.

Kate was in church on Christmas morning along with the rest of the family, where prayers were said for the Duke of Edinburgh, who had been taken ill on the night before Christmas Eve and airlifted to a hospital after suffering chest pains. A crowd of nearly 3,000 people gathered outside St. Mary Magdalene Church on the Sandringham estate, numbers that had not been seen for many years. Certainly, the gathering of glamorous young royals made it an attractive and colorful spectacle. Kate had opted for a plum hat by milliner Jane Corbett and a coat in the same color. Princess Beatrice, who had caused a sensation at the royal wedding with her choice of garish headware, had opted for a subtle black pillbox, while newlywed Zara Phillips showed that she could keep up with Kate in the fashion stakes with an eye-catching ruched designer hat. Flanked by William and Harry, Kate wished the crowds a Merry Christmas before they headed back to the main house for a lunch of traditional turkey, cold meats, and all the trimmings, served on silver salvers. It was all very different from the relaxed Christmases at home with her father dressing up and James pulling out the Christmas puzzle. This year, Kate watched the Queen's speech with the monarch.

It must have been a surreal close to a formidable year. An ordinary girl from a very normal family, Kate was now seen as the rising star of the royal family. It was a daunting but exciting prospect. There was a part of her that deeply missed being with her own family. She was particularly sad not to be with her sister, who was heartbroken after having recently split up with her boyfriend, Alex Loudon. The former Etonian had ended the year-and-half-long romance, and Pippa's new celebrity status was rumored to be at the root of the split. She had become a global superstar following the royal wedding, and offers for interviews, modeling contracts, and book deals had come flooding in. Pippa edited an online magazine for Party Pieces and still worked part-time for an events company in London, and now she was working on her first book, having signed a six-figure publishing book deal just before Christmas. She graced magazine covers and was sent free designer clothes and handbags. But there was a downside to her new fame. Like her sister, Pippa couldn't buy a coffee or go shopping without being photographed. For Alex, who came from a very private aristocratic family, it was too much. Kate felt a measure of responsibility, as she knew that everyone in her family was in a vulnerable position now that she had become Her Royal Highness, the Duchess of Cambridge.

For Michael and Carole, it had been a slightly easier transition. They were able to live in relative peace at their home in Bucklebury, protected by the local community. "We tend to know when Catherine's in the village, because we see the protection officers and they often come in for a cup of tea," said Martin Fiddler. "It's lovely that William and Catherine still come here. We often see them and the family walking — we give them a wave and let them get on with their lives." William had kept his promise that they would not be left out in the cold, and earlier that same year, Kate's parents had been invited to Royal Ascot at the personal invitation of the Queen. They enjoyed lunch at Windsor Castle and arrived at the world-famous racecourse in the royal procession by horse-drawn carriage. Watching from the comfort of the Royal Box, they happily chatted with Princess Beatrice and Princess Anne and, as avid horse-racing fans and part owners of a racehorse named Sohraab, they spoke knowledgeably about the sport that the Queen has always loved. It meant a lot to Kate that so much effort was being made to include her family.

In January 2012, she chose to celebrate her thirtieth birthday at the family home, where Pippa and Carole had organized a special supper. William had already given Kate her present, a delightful black cocker spaniel from a litter of pups belonging to James's dog, Ella. Kate named him Lupo, the Italian word for wolf. The Middletons are wildlife enthusiasts and are friends with a local villager who runs a wolf protection charity in Berkshire.

It was deemed the perfect opportunity to announce she would be taking on working roles with the National Portrait Gallery, The Art Room, East Anglia's Children's Hospices, and Action on Addiction. She had also decided to work with the Scout Association. As a former Brownie and someone who loves camping and the outdoors, she was said to be particularly excited about this commitment. According to the Palace, she wanted to be actively involved and would spend the coming weeks visiting her chosen causes. The fact that her diary was so busy was a blessing. William was leaving for the Falklands for a six-week-long tour of duty at the start of February, and Kate, who had been dreading the time apart, moved from Anglesey to Nottingham Cottage.

She was understandably nervous about going solo, in particular about giving her first public speech. Until now, she had always had William to guide and support her. Her first visit to the National Portrait Gallery to view an exhibition of Lucian Freud's work in early February was a gentle introduction to her new life as a working royal. She used to visit the gallery as a student and being involved with its work was a dream come true. As she mingled with guests and commented on the exhibition, she seemed to be enjoying herself. As well as promoting the arts in London, Kate hoped to heighten the gallery's profile. The gallery had never had a patron before, and according to the director, Sandy Nairn, Kate's affiliation gave it a real platform. "The duchess opens us up to a wide range of people, some who might not know who we are. She is such a recognized public figure both in this country and abroad, having her as a patron is a very positive thing for us."

Compared to Diana's first public engagement, when she trembled with nerves as she switched on the Christmas lights on Regent Street, Kate was poised and composed. She had followed William's advice to be herself, though she was apparently teased by her family for her new "plummy" voice when she gave her first public speech at a hospice in Ipswich. Her frequent pauses and emphasis on certain words suggested she was still receiving voice coaching, but her passion for her causes was not something that had to be learned. "She had about 150 people standing watching her in the room, and several millions a camera lens away. It was a huge test for her," said Graham Butland, the chief executive of East Anglia's Children's Hospice who worked with Kate on her speech. "I think she was nervous, but she did really well. When she stepped off the platform, there was a genuine sigh of relief. I think she has grown a lot in confidence, and what she has achieved is amazing. She has raised the profile of children's palliative care around the world." When she visited a children's hospital in Liverpool on Valentine's Day on February 14, Kate was visibly moved when a sick four-year-old hugged her, and when later in the day she visited a rehabilitation center, she made a point of chatting to some of the people who had waited hours to see her. Some of them had brought red roses and handmade Valentines. She told one young fan that William had remembered to send her a card and flowers. She wasn't afraid to get her hands dirty, and when she visited The Art Room's headquarters in Oxford, she donned an apron so that she could join an art class. It was impossible not to draw comparisons with Diana, who had loved helping children.

Kate had little time to miss William while he was away. In March, she joined the Queen and Camilla for the opening of the Diamond Jubilee Tea Salon at Fortnum &

Mason in London's Piccadilly. The invitation from the Queen was quite deliberate and sent a clear message: here were three generations and potentially two future Queens, and this was history in the making. As they admired a crown-shaped cake and sipped tea, the three women appeared to get along well.

That same month, the Queen invited Kate to Leicester for the start of her Diamond Jubilee tour of the United Kingdom. It had been decided that the Queen and the Duke of Edinburgh, whose health was still a concern, would travel around the country while the immediate family would tour the Commonwealth realms. The Jubilee celebrations, to commemorate the Queen's sixty years on the throne, were deemed hugely important, and trips to the Commonwealth countries and realms had all been planned as part of the celebrations. Prince Harry was to visit Brazil, Belize, Jamaica, and the Bahamas, while Prince Edward and Sophie Wessex headed to the Caribbean. Prince Andrew would visit India, while Princess Anne toured Mozambique and Zambia. Charles and Camilla were to carry out the lion's share of the tour and in the coming months would visit Scandinavia, Canada, Australia, New Zealand, and Papua New

Guinea. Kate and William had been asked to travel to Asia and the South Pacific in September.

With another overseas tour to carry out, the Diamond Jubilee celebrations in June, and the London 2012 Olympics that summer, in which Kate, William, and Harry would be representing Team Great Britain as ambassadors, Kate had a lot on her plate and confided to one courtier that she knew she had "a lot to learn." The Queen had made it clear she was there to help, and taking Kate to Leicester was her way of showing her the ropes. She could have invited any one of her grandchildren to join her for the first day of her historic tour, but she had asked Kate. William had benefited from years of mentoring from his grandmother; Kate's tutelage was to be a crash course. As they walked through the city in the sunshine, the crowds cheered and waved Union Jacks. Kate was careful to follow the Queen's lead, falling in line behind her and watching and learning from her every move. The Queen and her advisers were shrewd enough to see that Kate had "star" quality. In her daringly above-the-knee skirt and towering stilettos, which she had selected herself for the day, she added a sprinkling of glamour, while the Queen and the Duke of Edinburgh brought majesty, history, and familiarity.

The start of June marked a weekend of celebrations for the Diamond Jubilee — and Britain was ready to celebrate. Street parties had been planned around the country as the nation celebrated a double national holiday. On Sunday, June 3, there was a spectacular river pageant down the River Thames. A concert outside Buckingham Palace had been organized with some of the biggest performers in the world taking to the stage on that Monday, and finally, on Tuesday, which marked the close of the celebrations, there was to be a service of thanksgiving at St. Paul's Cathedral.

There had been some resistance about the cost of the celebrations, given that Britain was already footing an $18-billion bill for the summer Olympics. But the $15-million river pageant was being funded through private sponsorship, and the greatest boat trip the country had ever seen was a resounding success, despite the driving rain. Millions of spectators packed the banks of the river and the bridges above to watch the flotilla of 1,000 boats sail from Wandsworth to Tower Bridge.

The Queen and the royal family sailed downriver aboard the *Spirit of Chartwell,* a specially commissioned barge, and for five hours they stood in the freezing wind and rain, waving to the spectators.

In true British spirit, no one was going to let the rain put a dampener on the occasion, but the horrendous weather did take its toll on the Duke of Edinburgh, who was admitted to a central London hospital on Monday with a bladder infection. His absence was felt at the pop concert at Buckingham Palace, where 500,000 people cheered loudly at Charles's request in order that his father might be able to hear from his room at the King Edward VII private hospital. A spectacular fireworks display brought the evening to a climax, and William and Kate, who had been dancing in the Royal Box with the rest of the family, continued the party at a VIP reception for the artists and performers at the Palace afterward. It had been a wonderful night.

Tuesday marked the final day of celebrations, with a service of thanksgiving at St. Paul's, followed by a lunch at Westminster Hall and then a carriage procession to Buckingham Palace, all of it culminating in a royal aircraft display. The Duke of Edinburgh was still hospitalized, so during the service Charles sat next to his mother, who cut a lonely figure and looked lost without her husband. Later that afternoon, as the carriage procession made its way to the Palace, the crowds, easily as many as had watched William and Kate marry in the spring, filled every patch of red on the Mall from Admiralty Arch to the Queen Victoria Memorial. The sky was pregnant with rain, but it held off while the eighty-six-year-old monarch arrived home in the State Landau carriage. It was quite a moment; sitting next to her was Camilla. Once an outsider who was blamed for the breakup of the Wales's marriage, the Duchess of Cornwall was now given pride of place next to the Queen. There was an excited buzz among the flag-bearing crowds, cheering for their monarch from the street. When she emerged on the famous balcony, there was a thunderous roar, after which the crowd burst into the national anthem before the heavens opened. It was a pared-down House of Windsor standing on the balcony as the RAF jets soared overhead and a rifle salute marked the end of the four-day-long celebrations. At the center, the Queen was flanked by her "substitutes," the Prince of Wales and Prince William. Then there was Harry, "the spare," and Camilla and Kate. At the Queen's Golden Jubilee in 2002, all of her children and grandchildren had joined her on the balcony, but now the Queen wanted to send out a new message and a vision for the future. The monarchy was now a smaller, tighter entity. This royal lineup was deeply symbolic — it was about dynasty, a unified royal family, and succession. This was the future. The only hope now was that the Duke and Duchess of Cambridge would announce a royal pregnancy before the year was out to complete a most triumphant Diamond Jubilee.

Right now the royals were riding the crest of a wave. The family had seen its popularity soar around the world since William and Kate's wedding, which had seemed impossible after the tragedy of the death of Diana, the acrimonious divorces, and scandals that were better forgotten. At the core of this different perception were William and Kate, who symbolized a new hope. In just over a year of being in the public eye, Kate had proved to be a sparkling asset, and it was impossible to imagine the royal family without her. With the Duke and Duchess of Cambridge at the forefront, the future of the British monarchy looked brighter than it had in decades.

CHAPTER 13
A VERY IMPORTANT
ANNOUNCEMENT

Still riding high following the success of the Diamond Jubilee celebrations, Kate was excited to be closely involved with the 2012 Olympic Games at the end of the summer. Both she and William believed it was a way of uniting the nation, and with the eyes of the world once again on the capital, they were eager to do their part to promote Great Britain. Kate was fortunate enough to join the British women's hockey team for a practice match, proving she was still deft at the game by scoring a goal. She and William traveled to Dorset to watch the British sailing team and were in the stands cheering on his cousin Zara Phillips as she secured the silver medal in the Equestrian Eventing final. Hugging each other as they watched Chris Hoy pedal to victory, William and Kate reflected the overriding excitement of the nation as another member of Team Great Britain added a medal to the tally.

It had been an idyllic summer for Kate, with plenty to celebrate. William had turned thirty at the end of June, marking the milestone birthday with a small party with their friends. The prince's coming of age was seen by the media as a pivotal moment, and there was much speculation about what he planned to do with his future. His tour of duty with the RAF was due to end in the spring of 2013, fueling questions about whether he would quit the RAF in order to take on more royal engagements. There was talk among senior courtiers that William would have to start taking on more public engagements to relieve the pressure on the Queen and the increasingly frail Duke of Edinburgh. One source commented, "William has been told he has to decide whether he wants to be a pilot or a prince." There was also the question at the back of everybody's mind as to when Kate and William might start a family. In consideration of all this, William was given an extended deadline until after Christmas to make up his mind about his RAF career.

Kate, meanwhile, was settling into her new role as a working royal. By the end of the jubilant summer of 2012, she had carried out a handful of engagements. Wanting to bring a personal touch to her charities, she had invited a number of children from The Art Room to Kensington Palace to watch an exclusive screening of *The Lion, the Witch and the Wardrobe.* She also hosted a barbecue for The Scout Association on a beach close to her home in Anglesey, during which she helped the children gut fish and catch crabs. Her very first garden party at Buckingham Palace was, unsurprisingly, one of the most popular of the season. In fact, the only thing that overshadowed an otherwise fulfilling summer was the publication in *Woman's Day* of photographs of her and William on their honeymoon in the Seychelles. Although it was fifteen months after their holiday, the pictures of the couple swimming in the sea and walking on the beach were still deemed newsworthy by the Australian magazine. The British newspapers had made a deal with the Palace to leave the couple alone during their honeymoon and consequently refused to publish the images, but William and Kate were disappointed that not everyone had respected their wishes.

When they flew to the South of France at the end of August, they both fervently hoped they would be left alone by the world's press. It felt entirely possible — the Queen's nephew Lord Linley, the son of William's aunt, the late Princess Margaret, had lent William and Kate his beautiful hunting lodge, the Château d'Autet, in the Luberon region in Provence, where they were promised total peace and privacy. Set on 640 acres of countryside and surrounded by fields of lavender, the terra cotta–tiled house was exquisite. They spent their days reading, relaxing on the sun terrace, and swimming in the pool. Secure in the knowledge that the area had been swept by their security team, Kate felt confident enough to slip off her bikini top as she sunbathed by the pool one afternoon. Toned from vigorous sessions in the gym, she was confident in her body and wanted to look her very best. Sunbathing topless was not something she usually did. When Pippa had once sunbathed topless in Ibiza, she was photographed by a paparazzo and Kate learned a valuable lesson. But here, at a family member's holiday home on private land, she believed she was safe.

Kate had recently stopped drinking alcohol and, taking advice from her friends who had had babies, was eating plenty of lean protein and dark-green vegetables, rich in folic acid. At thirty, the age at which she had always hoped to have a child, it seemed that Kate was preparing herself. It was reported in the press that she had consulted a fertility expert in order to ensure that she would have no problems getting pregnant, but the Palace refused to comment on the story.

Once their holiday was over, William and Kate began to concentrate on their royal tour of Asia and the South Pacific. On September 10, 2012, the couple boarded a Singapore Airlines flight to Shanghai International Airport, where they were greeted by ecstatic crowds. The British High Commissioner to the Republic of Singapore, Antony Phillipson, was in charge of accompanying William and Kate on their engagements, and he described them as "global superstars." When they visited the Singapore Botanic Gardens to name an orchid in their honor, hundreds of people waited for hours to see them, and throughout their stay in the city, wellwishers camped outside the Raffles Hotel in the city center where William and Kate were staying.

Despite the intense heat, Kate displayed an abundance of energy and enthusiasm, her warm smile putting people at ease. In Kuala Lumpur, she delivered her debut overseas speech at the Hospis Malaysia with confidence, the audience moved by the heartfelt emotion of her words. Kate had been eager to use this occasion to direct the spotlight on the work of hospices, as she knew that with her profile, she could raise awareness globally.

It was while they were in Malaysia that a French magazine, *Closer,* made an audacious decision to publish a paparazzo's pictures of Kate sunbathing topless in the South of France. William and Kate had had no idea they had been photographed by a long lens, and because of the time differences, by the time they woke on the other side of the world, the magazine was already being sold on newsstands in France, the pictures a global sensation. Briefed over breakfast by their private secretary, Jamie Lowther-Pinkerton, they were furious, finding the publication of such personal images devastating and the timing deeply embarrassing. The tour had been going so well, and to be thrust into the headlines in such a humiliating manner was extremely stressful.

Nevertheless, William and Kate continued with a visit to the Assyakirin Mosque, the largest in the country. In keeping with religious protocol, Kate covered up in a pale gray dress and wore a headscarf. Jamie

Lowther-Pinkerton had advised them that the best policy was to smile and carry on with their work, and as they made their way to their next appointment — a visit to a public park to watch a cultural show — Kate smiled as she shook hands and accepted bouquets from wellwishers. It was only at the end of the day, according to aides on the tour, that they finally got to see the pictures and the salacious headline: "Oh my God! The photos that will go around the world."

Aides in London were in talks with lawyers in Paris in a bid to get an injunction so that the pictures could not be reproduced, while the Palace announced it planned to take legal action against the photographer and the magazine at the behest of the couple. Back in Britain, newspaper editors unanimously agreed they would not publish the pictures, but this news in itself was a front-page story broadcast around the world. Later that afternoon, within minutes of leaving a tea party at the British High Commission, William instructed his aides to issue a statement condemning the magazine and the photographer that read, "Their Royal Highnesses have been hugely saddened to learn that a French publication and a photographer have invaded their privacy in such a grotesque and totally unjustifiable manner. The incident is reminiscent of the worst excesses of the press and paparazzi during the life of Diana, Princess of Wales, and all the more upsetting to the Duke and Duchess for being so." Back in England, Prime Minister David Cameron denounced the magazine: "We echo the anger and sadness of the Palace. They are entitled to their privacy."

The thorny ethics of privacy and the royal family were always a concern, but unfortunately for Kate and William, it was at this moment hugely topical. Several weeks earlier in August, Prince Harry had found himself in hot water after being photographed naked, cavorting with a young woman while playing a game of strip billiards with a group of friends. The image was leaked to the American gossip website TMZ, and within hours of being posted, the photograph had gone global, despite attempts by St. James's Palace to have it removed. The *Sun* later published the picture on its front page, despite a request not to do so from St. James's Palace via the Press Complaints Commission. Kate's situation, however, was perceived differently; people took a less judgmental line — she hadn't been doing anything controversial —

and one aide summed the mood up well: "Their Royal Highnesses had every expectation of privacy in the remote house. It is unthinkable that anyone should take such photographs, let alone publish them."

Back in the Far East, Kate remained dignified throughout this episode, a combination of her calm personality and well-honed media training. Arriving in Borneo, they were both determined to enjoy their visit to the Danum Valley Field Centre in Sabah, as they had been looking forward to seeing endangered orangutans in the rain forest there, and by the time they visited the Solomon Islands, they looked truly happy and relaxed, making it appear more like a honeymoon than a working tour.

Returning home a few days later, William and Kate wanted to get back to normal. While the prince reported for work at RAF Valley, Kate stayed in London so she could visit their new apartment at Kensington Palace. The extensive refurbishment of Apartment 1A was well underway. It involved complete rewiring of the seventeenth-century palace, an overhaul of the antiquated plumbing, and the removal of asbestos from the property. Kate was closely involved with the redesign, cutting ideas out of home magazines for mood boards like those she had used for her wedding. Although the British taxpayer was picking up the bill for the renovation work, William and Kate were paying for interior redecoration, and Kate busied herself selecting fabrics, wallpapers, and paint colors.

As well as William and Kate's London apartment, which was to be their principal family home, the Queen had gifted them Amner Hall on the Sandringham Estate in Norfolk. As a child, William had spent many happy weekends at the late Georgian property, which had once been the home of the Van Cutsem family. Plans were being submitted to the local council for some additional building work to make the property more private and secure, and much to Kate's relief, the house would be available to her parents at Christmas, now that she was expected to be at Sandringham for the holidays.

Meanwhile, Michael and Carole were also house hunting. Party Pieces, whose staff now comprised thirty full-time team members, was reported to be making profits worth millions of dollars. They had made an offer on a beautiful Grade 2–listed Georgian house called The Manor, half a mile from Oak Acre in Bucklebury. Situated off a quiet and secluded country lane, it afforded privacy and space, with wonderful views over the surrounding fields and the picturesque Pang Valley. The eighteen-acre property had a swimming pool, a tennis court, seven bedrooms, a library, an elegant drawing room, and an impressive entrance hall decorated with hand-painted silk wallpaper. There were also a number of outbuildings on the property that could be used by William and Kate's security team when they visited.

Carole and Michael seemed to have relaxed into their role as royal in-laws, but Pippa was still going through a period of adjustment. Although she had been placed in *Time* magazine as one of the one hundred most influential people in the world and was concentrating on her career as a professional party planner, she faced a backlash in the media, accused of cashing in on her royal association when she signed a six-figure book deal to write her first book on the art of entertaining. And when she was photographed in Paris with a male friend who brandished a fake gun at a photographer following their car, Pippa found herself having to navigate out of a media storm without the sophisticated palace PR machine to assist her. She was making more headlines, at times, than her sister.

Still, Kate was not short of column inches, and speculation was growing over when she and William might start a family. Since the autumn, she and William had been busy opening exhibitions and traveling around the country on official engagements. In November, they visited Cambridge, their namesake, for the very first time to open a support center for the homeless. When William was presented with a tiny sleepsuit bearing the words "Daddy's little co-pilot," he appeared delighted and said, "I'll keep that," prompting a frenzy on Twitter that Kate might be expecting. However, when she readily accepted an invitation to open a new sports field at her old school, St. Andrews Prep, and joined an impromptu game of hockey in a pair of high-heeled boots, she put royal watchers off the scent that she might be pregnant and instead the media reported on her attractive new bangs. The truth, however, was that Kate was nearly two months' pregnant. Only William, her mother, and Pippa knew, eight weeks being far too early to make an official announcement.

Kate and William had decided they would make the announcement at Christmas after the baby's first scan, but Kate was overwhelmed by severe morning sickness. Initially, she was not alarmed, having read up on the early stages of pregnancy, but when the sickness did not abate after a weekend of being violently ill, William called the royal physician. It was early December, and the Prince had been away shooting in Hampshire. When Kate called to tell him she was feeling even worse, William drove to Bucklebury. On Monday, she still showed no signs of improvement, so the royal doctor advised her to go to King Edward VII's Hospital in central London. There, Kate was diagnosed with hyperemesis gravidarum — acute morning sickness — a serious condition that risks depriving the mother and baby of essential nutrients.

Worried about his wife and unborn baby's health, William had to deal with the likelihood that Kate's condition and hospitalization might be leaked to the press or, worse still, go global on Twitter. After speaking with Jamie Lowther-Pinkerton, it was agreed that St. James's Palace would issue a statement confirming the pregnancy, announcing that Kate had been admitted to the hospital. As he had ahead of news of their engagement, William called his grandmother and father to tell them of Kate's condition and forewarn them that her pregnancy was about to be made public. William also e-mailed Harry, who was then serving in Afghanistan.

While Kate was put on a rehydration drip and bed rest, the news was announced via a press statement and Twitter, both of which led to the couple's official website crashing. Within moments, there was a frenzy of excitement around the world, where twenty-four-hour news channels and newspapers dedicated their broadcasts to the conception of a new third-in-line to the throne. On Twitter, the news started trending within minutes, with celebrities and politicians exclaiming their joy and sending the couple their best wishes. A cause for national celebration, David Cameron was among the first to publicly extend his congratulations to the couple, together with the Archbishop of Canterbury, who had married them. Across the Atlantic, President Obama and his wife issued a statement saying that it was "welcome news." But the excitement was, of course, muted, the concern about Kate's health and the early stages of pregnancy at the forefront of people's minds. Although the Palace had refused to comment on how many weeks pregnant she was, they said that she would remain in the hospital "for several days and will require a period of rest thereafter."

In the press, there was speculation about when the couple might have conceived, the due date, and whether, because of the acute morning sickness, they might be expecting twins. There was much commentary over the implications should the couple's first-born be a daughter, because revisions to the Succession to the Crown Act were being passed through Parliament during the current session. The Queen, who was sympathetic to Kate's condition, having suffered from morning sickness herself, was aware that the proposed changes to the laws of succession were of paramount importance. Then there was also the matter of a title and the proposed amendments to ancient legislation drafted by King George V in 1917 that stipulated that the HRH title should be restricted to the children of the sovereign, the children of the sovereign's sons, and the eldest son of the Prince of Wales's eldest son, meaning that if William and Kate were to have a daughter, she would not have an HRH title.

Column inches were devoted to who might be asked to be godparents, with Pippa and Harry being named as favorites. Prince Charles spoke of his delight at the prospect of becoming a grandfather, telling reporters: "I'm thrilled — marvelous. It's a very nice thought to become a grandfather in my old age, if I can say so." Michael and Carole visited Kate in the hospital but declined to comment to the press, and three days later, Kate was discharged. William, who had been at his wife's side every day, accompanied her down the hospital steps. Sensibly wrapped up against the winter chill in a coat and scarf and holding a pretty bouquet of yellow flowers, Kate looked tired but happy. As she walked to her waiting car, she smiled at the cameramen and waiting crowds. "I'm feeling much better, thank you," she said.

Accompanied by a police escort, the couple headed straight home to Kensington Palace so that Kate could rest. She was advised to stay in London rather than head back to their home in Anglesey so that she could be readmitted to the hospital quickly if she suddenly became ill again. A team of doctors, including the Queen's surgeon gynecologist, Alan Farthing, and his predecessor, Marcus Setchell, were on call twenty-four hours a day to take care of her. She was under strict orders to rest and keep hydrated. Her aides canceled all immediate engagements, hoping that the media interest would die down now that Kate was out of the hospital.

This might have been the end of this

unfortunate beginning to Kate's pregnancy, but a tragedy was around the corner. During Kate's admission, a pair of Australian DJs had made a prank call to the King Edward VII's Hospital, impersonating the Queen and Prince Charles and asking to be put through to Kate. It was the middle of the night in the United Kingdom, and despite their unconvincing accents, they were transferred by a nurse manning the switchboard to the ward where Kate was being treated and given an up-to-date medical briefing on Kate's condition by the attending nurse. The presenters Mel Greig and Michael Christian, who worked for Sydney's 2DayFM breakfast show, broadcast the call live and described it as "the easiest prank call we've ever made."

When news of the hoax call broke, there was outrage. William was said to have been livid, while the chief executive of the hospital, which has treated members of the royal family for decades, described it as a "foolish prank," launching an immediate investigation into the hospital's phone security. But then things took a serious turn, and just days after the hoax call, Jacintha Saldanha, the nurse who had transferred the DJs' phone call to Kate's ward, was found hanged in her nurses' accommodation. According to her family, the forty-six-year-old mother of two had taken her own life because she was so ashamed of what she had inadvertently done. Kate was at Kensington Palace when she received the news, and according to her aides, she was devastated, as was William. What should have been the happiest announcement of their lives had been overshadowed most terribly by a pointless death.

Kate was told to try to remain calm for the sake of her unborn baby. The Palace refused to comment, but privately she was said to be "badly shaken." When William returned to work at RAF Valley, Carole and Pippa moved into the Palace until she was given the all clear by her doctors to go to Bucklebury, where she continued to make a good recovery. As this was only days before Christmas 2012, it was agreed that it would be more relaxing for Kate to remain with her family in Oak Acre. Naturally, William wanted to be with Kate, and for the first time he was excused from being at Sandringham.

After quietly celebrating her thirty-first birthday at home, Kate and William decided to join the Middletons for their annual trip to Mustique. This year, Pippa's new boyfriend, stockbroker Nico Jackson, was joining them, but the relaxing holiday was overshadowed when Kate and William were photographed walking on one of the island's beaches. Once again, the British papers agreed not to publish the images, but *Chi,* an Italian gossip magazine, splashed on its cover the images of Kate showing her small bump off in a bikini, much to the couple's wrath. They were still reeling from the topless pictures and "disappointed," according to Palace aides, that once again their privacy had been invaded at a deeply personal time in their lives. Returning home, Kate was unwittingly at the center of a controversy involving a lecture given by the award-winning novelist Hilary Mantel, in which she appeared to criticize the duchess. The media widely reported the author's comparison of Kate to a "machine-made princess" and a "shop window mannequin" with a "plastic smile," and though Hilary Mantel insisted her comments had been taken out of context, Kate rose above the distorted media coverage, smiling for the cameras as she left Hope House, an all-women's shelter that she supported.

Now that she was feeling better, she was determined to fit in as many engagements as she could before retiring from public life to prepare for the birth. In March, she braved the snow to join a scout volunteer training day in Windermere in the Lake District. There was an even greater surge of goodwill toward the couple now that a baby was on the way. During a walkabout at a St. Patrick's Day parade in Aldershot in Hampshire, Guardsman Lee Wheeler asked her, "Do you know if it's a girl or boy?" to which she replied, "Not yet. I'd like to have a boy and William would like a girl. That's always the way." When Kate, William, and the Prince of Wales opened a new outdoor center for young people at Dumfries House, Kate let slip to one staff member that the baby was due in mid-July, then adding, "Although babies have their own agenda." The couple's press officers refused to confirm the exact date, and Kate showed no signs of slowing down.

At every engagement she attended, Kate seemed to glow. Her skin was radiant, her trademark hair was even glossier and thicker than usual, and she continued to thrill the fashion brigade by stepping out in gravity-defying designer heels. She was quizzed constantly about how she was feeling and whether she was nervous about the imminent arrival, but she didn't seem to tire of the attention. It was reported that the couple had bought a pale-blue baby carriage, and British bookmakers took bets on what the couple would call their firstborn, with Elizabeth, Alexandra, and Charlotte being the most popular girls' names and George, James, and Alexander the favorites for a boy.

Like the royal wedding, it was a great opportunity for the memorabilia market, and manufacturers around the country were keen to cash in on the eagerly anticipated arrival. In true British style, there was a surge of royal-themed baby goods, from HRH embossed sleepsuits to crown-crested potties. Even the gift shops at the royal palaces stocked up on baby-themed memorabilia.

Meanwhile, Kate had not one but three nurseries to furnish. As well as Kensington Palace, where the nursery occupies most of the top floor, the couple had a designated baby room at Michael and Carole's house and at their new Norfolk home. They were still not sure whether they would be remaining in Anglesey long term, but provisions were made in their Welsh home for the baby. Intriguingly, there were reports in the British newspapers that Kate planned to move back home with her parents once William's two-week paternity leave was up. This was met with a degree of surprise by courtiers at the Palace, who had expected Kate and the newborn heir, as was traditional, to stay in royal residence. Although Diana had pushed the boundaries of royal protocol when William was born by opting to give birth in a hospital rather than a palace, this was a first. Kate had also decided against hiring a nanny and a maternity nurse, instead choosing to have her mother on hand to help her in the early weeks of motherhood. She told friends she hoped to have a natural birth, and she started to get familiar with breathing techniques to assist her in labor. Like her own mother, she planned to breastfeed. When she was photographed shopping for baby clothes and a Moses basket in Kensington with Carole, it was evident just how closely involved with the baby preparations Carole was. There was even some speculation in the tabloid press that Kate wanted her mother in the delivery room.

William was open to the idea of Kate moving back home after the birth, even if it did pose something of a problem for the protection officers and courtiers who were said to be concerned about the plan. The idea had its advantages, as the couple had been told that their apartment in Kensington Palace would not be ready in time for the birth because the discovery of asbestos had delayed the renovation schedule. They were still living at Nottingham Cottage with its two small bedrooms, so the more spacious prospect of her family home was appealing.

The couple had decided that the baby would be born at the private Lindo Wing of St. Mary's Hospital, a National Health facility where the royal family's gynecologist Alan Farthing is based and where both William and Harry were born. Such was the importance of the impending birth that Marcus Setchell, the Queen's surgeon gynecologist, postponed his retirement so that he could help deliver the baby. Once Kate had carried out her final engagement — the Trooping the Colour at Buckingham Palace on June 15 — it was time for her to bow out of the limelight and figure out her birth plan. On the advice of friends, she consulted London-based antenatal expert Christine Hill. Rather than go to a session attended by other expectant mothers, Kate booked two private appointments so that she and William would have some idea of what to expect. Together they mastered breathing techniques that help with pain management during labor, and Christine Hill, who described Kate as a "delightful girl," advised her to relax as much as possible.

It was a hot summer and Kate retreated to her new family home as often as she could, grateful for the use of the swimming pool. Although she joked that excitement over Andy Murray's sensational win at Wimbledon might bring on an early labor, she pretty much took things easy as instructed. While her family joined the royals for the Coronation Festival to celebrate the sixtieth anniversary of the Queen's anniversary at Buckingham Palace in July, Kate stayed at home and put her feet up.

It had been reported in the British press that Kate was due to give birth on July 13, so since the end of June, the media had been assembling outside the Lindo Wing. Photographers equipped with extra-long ladders secured their positions with black duct tape, even paying members of the public to keep their place overnight. Broadcasters from around the world followed suit, and within days the entire pavement was crammed with journalists and reporters, all anxious to be the first to report the news of the birth. It was one of the hottest summers in England on record, and as the mercury soared into the high nineties, the ongoing story known as the "Great Kate Wait" in the media dominated the news headlines. The merest hint of activity fueled a frenzy that Kate had gone into labor. When a helicopter landed at Kensington Palace or a police car swept through Bucklebury, the cameras were ready to roll, and news desks around the world were on red alert. False rumors that the duchess had gone into labor sent the Twitter-sphere into a meltdown on more than one occasion. The couple, however, stayed remarkably calm, and while Kate spent the weekend of her reported due date with her family in Bucklebury, William, who was still working shifts at RAF Valley, played a charity polo match at Cirencester in Gloucestershire, a helicopter on standby just in case.

By the following weekend, there was still no announcement from the Palace. It wasn't just the hot and flustered media throng that was growing impatient. Charles and Camilla continued their engagements around the country and admitted to wellwishers that they were "waiting for the telephone to ring," while the Queen told one little girl during a walkabout at Lake Windermere in Cumbria that she hoped the royal baby would "hurry up" because she was planning to go to Balmoral for her annual vacation.

It was in the early hours of Monday, July

22, that Kate finally went into labor and the couple was driven into the hospital through one of the back entrances, cleverly giving the assembled press pack camped at the front of the hospital the slip. At 7:30 A.M., the Palace Press Office issued a statement confirming that Kate was "in the early stages of labor" and that things were "progressing normally," news that was broken to the world via the rolling news networks and broadcast on every radio station. The "Great Kate Wait" was nearly over.

THE LITTLE PRINCE

His Royal Highness Prince George Alexander Louis of Cambridge entered the world at 4:24 P.M. on Monday, July 22, weighing an impressive eight pounds, six ounces. With a wisp of dark hair and a perfectly proportioned little nose, he sported a "good set of lungs," according to his proud father. Kate had endured a nine-hour labor on the hottest day of the year, and William had been at her side throughout.

Not only was she faced with the overwhelming prospect of giving birth for the first time, but Kate was also carrying the weight of expectation of an enthralled nation and a worldwide audience of millions tuned in via television and radio. Outside the hospital and at Buckingham Palace huge crowds gathered, together with representatives from the world's media. This was, after all, the birth of a future sovereign — and the first Prince of Cambridge — in nearly two hundred years. Waiting for the arrival of a new heir to the throne is a royal tradition. When the Queen was born in 1926, thousands congregated outside 17 Bruton Street in Mayfair, eager for a glimpse of the new princess, and similarly, the crowds amassed in thousands when the Prince of Wales was born in 1948, the birth made public by a live announcement on the BBC.

Finally, after endless speculation and a wait that had become a global phenomenon, Kate was rewarded with the son she had longed for, a beautiful baby boy who shared the same Cancer astrological sign as his father and Diana, the grandmother he would never meet. Tucked away in a private suite on the third floor of the hospital, it must have been a deeply emotional and special time for the couple as they held their baby for the first time. Not wanting the moment to pass too quickly, they decided to keep the arrival a secret for several hours, telling only their immediate family members. Protocol dictated that William call his grandmother on a specially encrypted phone upon the birth. Then there were calls to Kate's parents in Bucklebury, her sister and brother, Prince Charles and Camilla, and Prince Harry, all of whom were relieved and elated in equal measure.

A minute before Big Ben struck 8:30 P.M. and dusk fell upon London, the couple gave their aides permission to issue a statement via e-mail and Twitter, announcing the birth. It was a last-minute change of plan. Traditionally, the notice of birth — a bulletin bearing the news of the baby's sex, weight, and time of birth and signed by the royal medical team — is taken from the hospital to Buckingham Palace, where it is posted on an easel in the forecourt. But not for the first time, William and Kate decided they wanted to do things differently and that it would be "simpler and easier" to announce the news via e-mail and social media. The Clarence House tweet read: "Her Royal Highness the Duchess of Cambridge was safely delivered of a son at 4:24 P.M." The news sent Twitter into overdrive as 487 million people tweeted messages of congratulations.

The global media organizations broadcast the announcement simultaneously. When they did, an echo of cheers around the city could be heard from St. Mary's in Paddington to Buckingham Palace, where thousands had gathered to see the notice of birth. This document had by now been dispatched by an aide and driven to Buckingham Palace, where the Queen, having returned from Windsor Castle, was now in residence. The bulletin, posted at 8:48 P.M., read, "Her Royal Highness the Duchess of Cambridge was safely delivered of a son at 4:24 P.M. today. Her Royal Highness and her child are both doing well."

"It's a boy!" the crowds cheered loudly as they jumped into the fountains beneath the Queen Victoria Memorial. The Mall had finally cooled down after the blistering heat of the day. Many people remained in situ for hours, singing and celebrating and soaking up the atmosphere long after the lights at the Palace had gone out. Down the road, the fountains at Trafalgar Square were illuminated with blue lights to herald the arrival of the baby prince, along with Tower Bridge, while the lights of the BT Telecom Tower, one of the tallest landmarks in the city, lit up to beam the news "It's a boy" to the capital. William and Kate issued a simple statement, saying, "We could not be happier," and the Queen exclaimed that she and Prince Philip, who was at Sandringham recovering from abdominal surgery, were "delighted." The Prince of Wales issued a statement that he was "enormously proud and happy" to become a grandfather for the first time. Speaking outside 10 Downing Street, David Cameron said, "It is wonderful news. I am sure that right across the country and right across the Commonwealth, people will be celebrating." They were. Indeed, messages flooded in from around the world, President Obama wishing the couple much happiness: "Michelle and I are so pleased to congratulate the Duke and Duchess of Cambridge on the joyous occasion of the birth of their first child." In Canada, the Governor General tweeted, "Wonderful news," while in Australia and New Zealand, they were waking up to the happy news.

Dr. Setchell, who had emerged from the hospital after the birth to tell the waiting media the baby was "beautiful," had advised Kate to stay in the hospital overnight. William ordered takeout pizzas and slept at his wife's side, next to their son. They had not yet decided what to call their firstborn, despite having drawn up a short list of their favorite boys' and girls' names. Kate had affectionately referred to her bump as "grape" while she was pregnant, and there was a flurry of betting on the baby's name ahead of the birth.

The next morning, their first as parents, must surely have been surreal. Outside on the street, the rolling news stations were reporting every hour on the story, and at Buckingham Palace, a media village had been erected at Canada Gate on the Mall in order to broadcast every development of the breaking story. The front pages of the morning newspapers all carried the news of the baby prince, with the tabloid newspaper the *Sun* changing its masthead for the occasion to "The Son." A forty-one-gun salute was fired in Green Park by the King's Troop Royal Horse Artillery at the same time as a sixty-two-gun salute at the Tower of London.

Shortly after lunchtime, following a visit from Dr. Setchell, Carole and Michael arrived to visit their daughter and first grandchild. They waved to the crowds before hurrying up to Kate's room on the third floor. When they emerged, an hour later, they were beaming. Carole, in a pretty summer frock, approached the press pack and addressed them for the very first time. Asked how her first grandchild was, she lit up and revealed she had enjoyed a first cuddle: "Marvelous, thank you very much, absolutely wonderful." She said the new parents were "both doing really well and we are so thrilled."

Prince Charles and Camilla were on their way to London, having carried out engagements in the north of England, and arrived soon afterward. When Charles emerged, twenty minutes later, his smile said it all, and upon being asked about the baby, he playfully pointed his finger and told newscasters: "You'll see in a minute."

The wait felt like hours, the hush of anticipation silencing the press corps, whose cameras were trained on the hospital's double glass-paneled doors. Behind them, William and Kate made a last-minute check to ensure that the baby heir, whom Kate had swaddled in a shawl, was settled and happy. It was 7:00 P.M. in the evening and the as-yet-to-be-named Prince of Cambridge was about to make his first public appearance on the very same steps where, thirty-one years, one month, and one day before, Charles and Diana had presented William to a jubilant nation.

On the pavement, packed together like sardines, the crowd stood behind police barriers. Some had camped overnight to secure their position. A handful of them had also been there to watch Charles and Diana make the same short journey all those years ago. The doors of the Lindo Wing finally swung open, and the family emerged to a riot of flashes, celebratory cheers, and calls of congratulations. As Kate negotiated her way down the stone steps in her wedge sandals, not once taking her eyes off her precious baby, it was impossible not to think of the woman in whose footsteps she was following. On her left hand she wore Diana's engagement ring, its sapphire and diamonds sparkling in the early evening light, and she had chosen a baby-blue-and-white polka dot dress similar to the patterned dress Diana had worn when she left the very same hospital with William. Possibly it was her way of paying a personal tribute to Diana, who would have been thrilled to be a grandmother. With a winning smile and her wide, warm eyes, she absorbed the incredible spectacle before her. As if on cue, baby Cambridge stretched his tiny fingers in front of his crumpled face as though he were giving the world a wave.

Then it was William's turn, and taking great care, he leaned into his wife, his arms held out in front of him to receive the swaddled baby. He looked down at his son with a look of joy and disbelief. Camera phones were held high in the air to capture the amazing scene, while TV reporters paused for breath to enjoy the moment. They had been allowed to ask a few questions of the couple, and when asked how she was feeling, Kate looked close to tears of joy: "It's very emotional and such a special time. I think any parent will probably know what this feeling feels like." She added proudly that William had "done the first nappy already," and when asked what they planned to call the baby prince, William revealed, "We're still working on a name so we will have that as soon as we can." After observing, "He's a big boy, he's quite heavy," he joked that the baby had his wife's looks, "Thankfully, and way more hair than me." After the brief press conference, it was time to head home, and, addressing his wife as "Poppet," William accompanied Kate back into the hospital. When they reemerged, William, with shirt sleeves rolled up, was carrying his son in a baby seat, which he expertly clipped into the waiting Range Rover, while Kate sat in the back next to the baby, stroking his little fingers. Once again, the shutters of hundreds of cameras clattered noisily, filling the evening sky with lightning-like flashes as William broke with tradition, just as he had on his wedding day, and climbed into the driver's seat. As he took the wheel and glanced in the rearview mirror at his wife, he smiled. This was what it was all about, the three of them and the wonderful future that lay ahead of them. As they swept through the wrought-iron gates to Kensington Palace, this was just the beginning.

EPILOGUE

The birth of Prince George of Cambridge, now the third in line to the throne, heralds a new future for the monarchy. Together, William and Kate have secured the lineage of succession, a fourth living generation of the House of Windsor. They are also writing the future history of the monarchy. Kate has proved to be a priceless ambassador for the royal family, and now she has fulfilled the ultimate role by producing an heir. Not since the births of Princes William and Harry has there been such strong interest in the arrival of a royal baby, and though, in the end, their first child wasn't the little girl to rewrite royal history, the arrival of the baby prince destined to become King George VII is a historic occasion.

As they make the seismic transition to parenthood, William and Kate face the same steep learning curve of any new mother and father. In addition, however, they have a greater challenge — how to raise their baby as "ordinary" within the goldfish bowl of royalty. There are, of course, dangers of becoming too "normal" and informal, the risk of tarnishing the tradition of this unique institution, but one imagines that under the Queen's tutelage and the guidance of William's enlightened father, the couple will strike the right balance.

The greatest obstacle to the Cambridge family is undoubtedly the thorny issue of privacy, for there is an unprecedented interest in Kate and William — and now Prince George — which will only magnify as the years pass. Just as William's life has been chronicled, so too will his son's. There will be a fascination in everything — his first tooth and first steps, his early years in the nursery, his first day at school, and far beyond. Living at Kensington Palace in London, the family is likely to have a more public life than the relatively quiet life William and Kate led pre-baby in Anglesey. The couple is fiercely protective of their private lives but Prince George has been born into a digital age where smart phones are ubiquitous and daily life is charted on social networking sites. Fortunately, both William and Kate are sufficiently media savvy and no doubt have been looking to secure an agreement with the British media that grants restricted access to their lives and their son in return for peace and privacy the rest of the time.

As they showed on their wedding day, William and Kate have their own way of doing things, and this will pave the way for the future. Once they are in residence in Apartment 1a in Kensington Palace, the wheels of change will be set in motion. The couple's team of courtiers and press aides has already relocated to Kensington Palace, where a new court has been established. Prince Harry will be living next door, but the couple will have to make do without their trusted private secretary, Jamie Lowther-Pinkerton, who is retiring, marking the end of an era.

Over the years, Prince Charles has privately campaigned for a slimmed-down monarchy, and now William and Kate are at the forefront of this new streamlined House of Windsor. The royal family signifies tradition, stability, and continuity in an age of flux and media proliferation, but it must also continue to modernize in order to survive. Its future is under scrutiny not just here in Great Britain, where Scotland will next year vote on a referendum to become independent, but within the Commonwealth. Indeed, elsewhere in the world monarchies have collapsed, perceived as costly and anachronistic. The royal family's historic right to reign is no longer a given; its existence must be justified, together with its cost to the taxpayer. It is largely because of the Queen, who has ensured the gradual evolution of the royal family, that the British monarchy is still a much-loved institution, as was evident from her Diamond Jubilee celebrations. William and Kate have the power and potential to cement the monarchy's future. They are respected the world over and have helped ensure that the royal family will continue on as one of Great Britain's most coveted assets.

With the Duke of Edinburgh's cutting back on royal duties and the Queen's recent decision to scale back her overseas travel, William and Kate will be expected to carry out more official engagements than ever before. The two-year grace period the Queen granted the couple from full-time royal duties after their wedding is over, and they must now accept a future of royal service. There is talk of an overseas trip in 2014, possibly to Australia and New Zealand, and if this happens, it seems inevitable that they will take Prince George with them, just as Diana and Charles took the nine-month-old William when they, too, visited the Southern Hemisphere as new parents in 1983.

There is, according to well-placed sources, some pressure on William to give up his career as a Search and Rescue Force pilot, in order to fulfill his obligations to Queen and country. He now has a life-changing decision to make. So far, William has resisted the pressure, determined to forge a career independent of his birthright. But now he is a father, and there is a genuine need for him to join his own father as a shadow king alongside Queen Elizabeth II.

Although they plan to do things their way, William and Kate appreciate that they must also respect tradition. Later this year, their baby — potentially a future head of the Church of England — will be christened by the Archbishop of Canterbury. Unlike past royal generations, however, he will go to a local nursery rather than be educated by governesses and will go to school, like his father. Before then, there will likely be stroller walks in Kensington Park Gardens and trips to the nearby shops, which Diana so enjoyed making with her sons. Of course, there will be holidays at Balmoral in Scotland and Christmases at Sandringham, but Prince George will probably spend just as

much time with his grandparents in Bucklebury as he will in royal residences. William
promised Kate's parents before they were
married that they would always be a part of
their lives, and he has been true to his word.
The Middletons have been more warmly
embraced than any other in-laws.

There is little doubt that Kate has brought
much-needed vibrancy and a freshness to
the House of Windsor. She has charisma
and the ability to connect with people from
all walks of life. Prince George of Cambridge has been born into wealth and
heritage. He has a loving and dedicated
father who has a clear vision of what the
monarchy should represent, and a thor-
oughly modern mother who has embraced
her new role as a member of the royal family, while injecting her own unique brand of
warmth.

If William and Kate strike a balance
between informality and royal tradition,
Prince George will have the very best of
both worlds — a life of royal privilege,
coupled with the same loving and ordinary
family upbringing that Kate enjoyed and
William always wanted. That will surely be
a winning combination in his future role as
King of the United Kingdom.

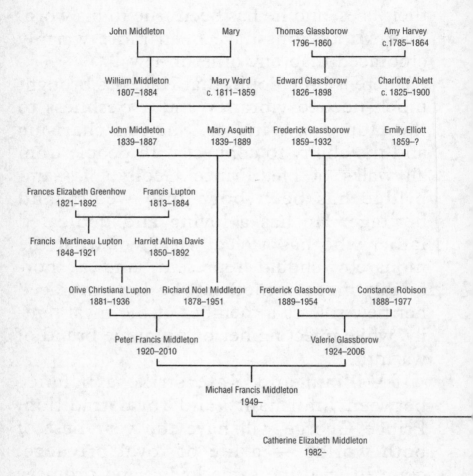

John Middleton — Mary

Thomas Glassborow
1796–1860 — Amy Harvey
c.1785–1864

William Middleton
1807–1884 — Mary Ward
c. 1811–1859

Edward Glassborow
1826–1898 — Charlotte Ablett
c. 1825–1900

John Middleton
1839–1887 — Mary Asquith
1839–1889

Frederick Glassborow
1859–1932 — Emily Elliott
1859–?

Frances Elizabeth Greenhow
1821–1892 — Francis Lupton
1813–1884

Francis Martineau Lupton
1848–1921 — Harriet Albina Davis
1850–1892

Olive Christiana Lupton
1881–1936 — Richard Noel Middleton
1878–1951

Frederick Glassborow
1889–1954 — Constance Robison
1888–1977

Peter Francis Middleton
1920–2010 — Valerie Glassborow
1924–2006

Michael Francis Middleton
1949–

Catherine Elizabeth Middleton
1982–

KATE MIDDLETON'S
FAMILY TREE

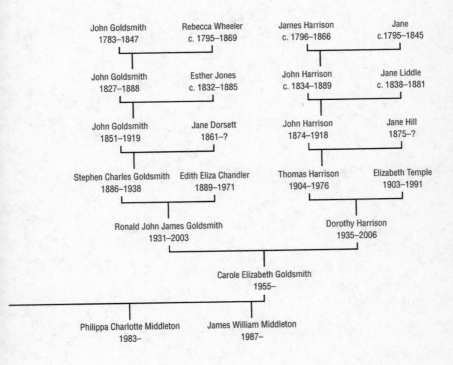

John Goldsmith
1783–1847

Rebecca Wheeler
c. 1795–1869

James Harrison
c. 1796–1866

Jane
c.1795–1845

John Goldsmith
1827–1888

Esther Jones
c. 1832–1885

John Harrison
c. 1834–1889

Jane Liddle
c. 1838–1881

John Goldsmith
1851–1919

Jane Dorsett
1861–?

John Harrison
1874–1918

Jane Hill
1875–?

Stephen Charles Goldsmith
1886–1938

Edith Eliza Chandler
1889–1971

Thomas Harrison
1904–1976

Elizabeth Temple
1903–1991

Ronald John James Goldsmith
1931–2003

Dorothy Harrison
1935–2006

Carole Elizabeth Goldsmith
1955–

Philippa Charlotte Middleton
1983–

James William Middleton
1987–

BIBLIOGRAPHY

Bradford, Sarah. *Queen Elizabeth II: Her Life in Our Times.* Viking, 2011.

Clench, James. *William and Kate: A Royal Love Story.* HarperCollins, 2010.

Debrett's. *A Modern Marriage: A Royal Celebration.* Simon and Schuster UK, 2011.

Jobson, Robert. *William and Kate: The Love Story: A Celebration of the Wedding of the Century.* John Blake, 2011.

Joseph, Claudia. *Kate: The Making of a Princess.* William Morrow Paperbacks, 2011.

Junor, Penny. *Prince William: Born to Be King.* Hodder and Stoughton, 2012.

Middleton, Pippa. *Celebrate: A Year of Festivities for Families and Friends.* Viking Adult, 2012.

Morton, Andrew. *Diana: Her True Story.* Simon and Schuster, 1992.

———. *William and Catherine: Their Lives,*

Their Wedding. Michael O'Mara Books, 2011.

Nicholl, Katie. *William and Harry: Behind the Palace Walls.* Weinstein Books, 2010.

———. *The Making of a Royal Romance.* Weinstein Books, 2011.

Seward, Ingrid. *Royal Entertaining and Style.* M Press, 2010.

Smith, Sally Beddell. *Elizabeth the Queen: The Life of a Modern Monarch.* Random House, 2012.

Smith, Sean. *Kate.* Simon and Schuster UK, 2012.

ACKNOWLEDGMENTS

First, I would like to thank Harvey Weinstein for being the inspiration behind this book and convincing me that I could write it in record time, having recently become a mother myself. I am also indebted to my wonderful editor, Gillian Sterne, who has been there for me every step of the way and helped me meet a punishing deadline. Thanks also to my family, especially my amazing husband, for always being so supportive of me, and my mother for always being there. Thanks also to my hardworking and talented researcher, Helena Pearce, who is as kind as she is fast. The team at Perseus and Weinstein Books is second to none, and I would like to specially thank David Steinberger for his vision, and Amanda Murray, Georgina Brown, Kathleen Schmidt, Christine Marra, and the entire publishing and PR team at Weinstein Books, both in the United States and the United Kingdom.

Thanks also to my agents, John Ferriter and Jonathan Shalit, and to my picture researcher, Melanie Haselden, who helped me secure some exclusive images of Kate — no easy feat. I must also thank the Press Office at St. James's Palace, which so kindly assisted me with some of my research, in particular Paddy Harverson, Ed Perkins, and Nick Loughran.

I have many people to thank for their insight, personal anecdotes, and agreeing to talk to me. Many have asked to remain confidential, and I have, of course, respected their wishes. You know who you are and that I am indebted to you always. Others have agreed to be named, and I would like to thank the following people for their trust and contribution:

Robert Acheson
Andrew Alexander
Denise Allford
Kevin Allford
Lady Elizabeth Anson
Nick Barton
Fiona Beacroft
Juli Beattie
Sir Chay Blyth
Jim Boyd
George Brown

Graham Butland
Sophie Butler
Michael Choong
Laura Collins
Jon Copp
Claudine de Montule
Richard Dennen
Isobel Eeley
Martin Fiddler
Joan Gall
Edward Gould
Jean Harrison
Joyce Harrison
Graham Hornsey
Paul Horsford
Professor Peter Humfrey
Brian Lang
Suha Phillip Ma'ayeh
Emily Maddick
Alex Martin
Helen McArdle
Charlie Moretti
Alistair Morrison
Sandy Nairn
Alan Needham
Ann Patching
Elizabeth Saint
Andrew Sands
Emma Sayle
Niall Scott

June Scutter
Jasper Selwyn
Dudley Singleton
Al Smith
Malcolm Sutherland
Neil Swan
Cal Tomlinson
Robin Vincent-Smith
Laura Warshauer

ABOUT THE AUTHOR

Katie Nicholl is the Royal Editor and Diary Editor for the *Mail* on Sunday and a contributing editor to *Vanity Fair*. In addition to her work in print, Katie has developed a successful broadcasting career as a contributor to Sky News and the BBC, and works extensively in America. She serves as Special Royal News Correspondent for ABC's *Good Morning America* and appears regularly on prime time TV shows including *Entertainment Tonight, Piers Morgan Tonight, The View,* and *The Lorraine Kelly Show.* Also the author of royal biographies *William and Harry* and *The Making of a Royal Romance,* she is a widely recognized authority on royal affairs. Visit her website at www.katie nicholl.com.

CG 5/14
SGR 7/14
Blen 9/14

BRAD 7/16
TER 9/16
CG 5/7
Blen 8/17
BAN 11/17
fair 3/18
SGR 8/18
HAR 10/18

Pls add MM/YY	
ASK	GCC
AL	GGR
AMR	HAR
AWK	LCC
BAN	LEG
BG	MT
BLEN 1-19	MSJ
BRAD 4/19	SFC
BRI	SO 2/21
CG	SVAD
CHL	TER
CLARE	VGH
FAIR	WR
GP	YOU